NORTH CAROLINA LAND GRANTS IN TENNESSEE, 1778–1791

Compiled by Goldene Fillers Burgner

Southern Historical Press, Inc.
Greenville, South Carolina

Copyright 1981
By: The Rev. Silas Emmett Lucas, Jr.

All rights reserved. No part of this publication may be reproduced, stored in a retrieval system, transmitted in any form, posted on to the web in any form or by any means without the prior written permission of the publisher.

Please direct all correspondence and orders to:

www.southernhistoricalpress.com
or
SOUTHERN HISTORICAL PRESS, Inc.
PO BOX 1267
375 West Broad Street
Greenville, SC   29601
southernhistoricalpress@gmail.com

ISBN #0-89308-205-8

Printed in the United States of America

LAND GRANTS

An estimate of the lands granted by the State of North Carolina within the Western Territory ceded by the said State to the United States of America.

Washington County 1778

	NAME	ACRES	LOCATION
1.	John Wallace	240	On the North Fork of Doe River including a crab orchard.
2.	David Reese	90	On both sides of Doe River on the side of a mountain.
3.	William Sharp	400	On the West Fork of Indian Creek, waters of Holston River.
4.	David Reese	320	On the waters of Lick Creek including a poplar valley.
5.	Samuel Harris	400	On North Lick Branch, waters of Lick Creek.
6.	David Reese	400	On the head of a branch the great falls of Lick Creek.
7.	Charles Robinson	640	On the south side of Holston on Sinking Branch - Brantleys Camp.
8.	William Sharpe	400	On Doe River including the great Crab Orchard.
9.	John Wallace	400	On a branch near the Great Nobb Licks of Lick Creek.
10.	Samuel Harris	240	On the North Fork of Doe River joining William Sharpe.

Washington County 1782

	NAME	ACRES	LOCATION
11.	Richard Caswell	400	On the head of a branch of Boones Creek.
12.	Richard Caswell	600	On the head branches of Lick Creek.
13.	Richard Caswell	640	On the waters of Big Limestone.
14.	Richard Caswell	640	Including the head spring of Big Limestone.
15.	Richard Caswell	640	Including the Big Pond Spring that runs
16.	Richard Caswell	640	On the head of Walnut Valley waters of Lick Creek.
17.	William Caswell	400	On both sides of Boones Creek above William Youngs.
18.	William Caswell	300	On the east bank of Big Limestone joining the Bald Knob.
19.	John Nowlin	400	On the north side of Watauga River joining Augustine Shoat.

20.	Andrew English	31½	On waters of Lick Creek joining his manor plantation.
21.	Drury Morris	199	Including a big spring of the Cedar Fork of Lick Creek.
22.	Thomas Talbot	200	On both sides of Gap Creek.
23.	William Runnels	104	On Roane Creek joining John Hoskings.
24.	James Coward	360	On South Fork of Boones Creek.
25.	Elias Hawkins	100	On southside of Roans Creek.
26.	William Griffin	104	On the South side of Roane Creek joining Edward Switains?.
27.	William Patterson	400	On Long Cain Brake of Watauga River.
28.	Michael Massengale	150	On the head of Hecory Creek.
29.	Charles Hays	400	Including Aaron Burlesons old Improvement.
30.	James Hickerson (Richerson)	99	On Little Sinking Creek waters of Watauga River.
31.	James Delaney	100	On Holleys Creek of Nolichucky River.
32.	Jonathan Tipton	150	On North Fork of Cherokee Creek.
33.	Uriah Hunt	300	On both sides of Boones Creek joining Joseph Duncan.
34.	Nathaniel Davis	199	On Lick Creek below Benjamin Pyburns.
35.	James Wheeler	97	Joining John Stewarts land in Jarrots Branch.
36.	William Odell	440	On the waters of Big Limestone and waters of Lick Creek.
37.	William Murphy	150	On both sides of Cherokee Creek.
38.	James English	100	On the waters of Limestone Creek.
39.	Dutton Lain	150	On the waters of Lick Creek Aruntons Mill Shoal Creek.
40.	Godfrey Carder	500	On north side of Watauga River at the mouth of Sugar Creek.
41.	Robert Allison	150	On north side of Watauga River called the black spring.
42.	James Martain	106	Joining John Trimble Stories and Andersons lines.
43.	William Richey	200	On waters of Lick Creek known by Punching Camp.
44.	William Richey	300	On a branch of Limestone on both sides of said creek.
45.	Daniel Dunham	200	On an east branch of Lick Creek.

46.	James English	200	On the Limestone Fork of Lick Creek.
47.	James English	200	On the Limestone Fork of Lick Creek.
48.	John Howard	99	On Sinking Creek of Lick Creek including Howards improvement.
49.	Alexander Campbell	224	On the east side of Big Limestone Creek.
50.	John McMahan	540	On the top of Indian Ridge on Knob Creek.
51.	Thomas Houghton	522	On the waters of Watauga and Doe Rivers.
52.	Alexander Croat	340	On the side of a knobb on Holston River.
53.	Daniel Henderson	250	On a small creek called Bean Creek.
54.	Alexander Campbell	100	On both sides of great Limestone Creek.
55.	David Stewart	292	On a branch of Big Limestone Creek.
56.	Jacob Mires	300	On Big Limestone Creek joining to Batt Woods.
57.	Henry Goacher	190	On the south side of Holston River.

Washington County 1783

58.	Andrew English	250	On the Sinking Fork of Limestone Fork of Lick Creek.
59.	Joseph Fowler	150	On the south side of Lick Creek joining Browns lines.
60.	Ambrose Hogges	200	On both sides of Cherokee Creek.
61.	James Grimes	200	On the waters of Sinking Creek.
62.	John B. McMahan	100	Joining his fathers south and east lines and John Gilliland's lines.
63.	Lanty Armstrong	300	On the waters of Big Limestone.
64.	Robert Wilson	239	On the head of Horse Camp Creek.
65.	Abednego Enmon	200	On the east branch of Big Limestone Creek.
66.	Samuel Flanaken	200	On a creek on the north side of Nolachucky River.
67.	James English	200	On a ridge on the side of a creek.
68.	Nathan Davis	200	On the head of the east branch of Lick Creek.
69.	Alexander Campbell	207	On the waters of Little Limestone Creek.

70.	Robert Campbell	400	On a branch on the east side of Big Limestone Creek.
71.	Jones Little	320	On the waters of Bush Creek joining William Ward's line.
72.	Dutton Lain	100	On the waters of Lick Creek joining his own land.
73.	Thomas Stewart	148½	Including a spring on the north fork of Big Limestone fork creek.
74.	William Berry	200	On the mill fork of Big Limestone and waters of Sinking Creek.
75.	James English	100	On both sides of Lick Creek on the side of a mountain.
76.	Thomas Hardeman	100	Joining Jesse and William Beans lines.
77.	James English	140	On the waters of Lick Creek in Cain Bottom.
78.	Baptist McNabb	600	On the west side of Buffaloe Creek a branch of Watauga.
79.	James Grimes	369	On a branch of Little Limestone Creek.
80.	Joseph Brown	439	On the north side of Nolachucky joining William Moores line.
81.	Edmund Williams	640	On the south side of Buffalo Creek joining Bentons lines.
82.	Joseph Bullar	200	On Little Limestone Creek joining Richard Humphreys lines.
83.	Thomas Baker	100	On the north side of Nolachucky River.
84.	Samuel Tate	455	On both sides of Watauga at the mouth of Elks Creek.
85.	Uriah Hunt	119	On the waters of Boone Creek and Watauga River.
86.	Vauch Dillingham	149	On a branch of Horse Creek including the Turnip Patch Improvement.
87.	Adam Sherrill	400	On both sides of Onion Branch an east branch of Little Limestone.
88.	John Holbrook	300	Including a mill seat and cain bottom on Long Fork of Lick Creek.
89.	Michael Highder	262	On an east branch of Buffalo Creek.

Washington County 1782

90.	Abednego Inman	200	On the north side of Big Limestone on Carracks Creek.
91.	Martin Webb	100	Joining said Webbs and Jacob Smiths line.

92.	William Sharpe	140	On both sides of Gap Creek.
93.	Nicholas Fain	400	On a branch of Little Limestone joining said Fain's line.
94.	Nathan Gragg	400	In the fork of Holston and Watauga Rivers.
95.	John Rice	177	On the south side of Holston River foot of Bays Mountain.
96.	Samuel Henry	150	On both sides of Dry Creek joining Edmund Williams.
97.	Robert Irwin	50	On the waters of Great Limestone Creek.
98.	David Campbell	143	On the east side of Mevry Branch north side a Knobb.
99.	Michael Smith Peter	374	On both sides of Stoney Creek.
100.	Joshua Houghton	352	On the north side of Watauga joining Jacob Chamberlin.
101.	Thomas Stuart	148½	On the waters of Lick Creek.
102.	John Carter	640	On the waters of Watauga River adjoining Emanuel Carter.
103.	Thomas Gillespie	83	On the south side of Nolachucky River.
104.	George Gillespie	394	On the north side of Nolachucky River.
105.	James Stuart	285	On the south side of Nolachucky River.
106.	James Moore	300	On Little Sinking Creek joining William Mados line.
107.	Drury Morris	97	On cedar creek waters of Lick Creek including the Horse Stamp.
108.	Benjamin Gist	400	On the waters of Lick Creek including a cain brake.
109.	Abraham Bradley	640	On the head of Cedar Creek.
110.	Nicholas Fain	200	On a branch of Little Limestone.
111.	John Honeycutt	296	On the south side of Holston River in the fork of two branches.
112.	Peter McNamee	570	On Shipman's Fork a branch of Big Limestone.
113.	Joseph Bullar	640	On the north side of Nolachucky at the mouth of Little Limestone.
114.	William McNabb	507	On a branch of Sinking Creek joining David Jobes lines.
115.	James Denton	403	On Sinking Creek joining David Jobes lines.
116.	Jesse Walton	437	On the southside of Nolachucky River joining Samuel Williams.

No.	Name	Acres	Location
117.	John Hoskens	510	On both sides of Roane Creek.
118.	John B. McMahan	300	On the head spring of Knobb Creek.
119.	James Wheeler	200	On the Clear Fork of Horse Creek.
120.	Adam Wilson	200	On the waters of Lick Creek known by the name of Fains Improvement.
121.	John Webb	550½	On the south side of Indian Creek.
122.	John Honeycutt	90	On the south side of Holston River.
123.	Hosea Rose	299	On the south fork of Cherokee Creek.
124.	Peter Plemon	200	On a south branch of Lick Creek.
125.	Thomas Mitchell	200	On an east branch of Big Limestone Creek.
126.	David McCord	250	On the waters of Big Limestone Creek.
127.	James W. Harris	199	On the north fork of Beech Creek and waters of Holston River.
128.	John Richey	491	On the Horse Pasture Branch.
129.	John Waddle	270	On Horse Creek the southside of Nolachucky River.
130.	John McCarrell	400	On Sinking Creek and waters of Nolachucky River.
131.	Joseph Harden	200	On the Roaring Fork of Lick Creek.
132.	William Hues	200	On Aulston Choles Branch.
133.	Gideon Morris	198	On a branch of Lick Creek including his improvement.
134.	John Pickens	250	On Big Limestone Creek joining John Robertsons lines.
135.	Jonathan Holley	100	Joining Scrubby Pane on Holleys Creek.
136.	James Willson	100	On Mill Fork of Big Limestone.
137.	Isaac Tommas	291	On the southside of Watauga River joining Buzzard Hill.
138.	William Murphy	94	On the north side of Nolachucky River.
139.	John McAdon	200	On both sides of Bullards Creek.
140.	Andrew Taylor	31	Joining Michael Hyde land and Christopher Cunningham's lines.
141.	Samuel Williams	384	On the west side of a branch on southside Nolachucky River.
142.	James Delany	100	On Cedar Branch.
143.	Phillip Shelly	100	On the Beaver Dam branch on the north side of Watauga River.

No.	Name	Acres	Location
144.	William Murphy	94	On the top of a barren hill and northside of Nolachucky River.
145.	William White	136	On the Fall Branch of Horse Creek.
146.	Samuel Sherril	312	On the South Side of Nolachucky joining John Waddle.
147.	William Randels	200	On the north side Nolachucky River on Sinking Creek.
148.	Abram Kuykendale	200	On the waters of Great Limestone.
149.	James Reddy (Roddy)	275	On the south side of Watauga joining Carruthers Cabin.
150.	Jeremiah Jack	320	On the southside of Nolachucky opposite the Old Station.
151.	Samuel Curry	181	On the southside of Holston River joining W. Lestons lines.
152.	John Hues	200	On a branch of Buffalo Creek.
153.	Daniel Keith	200	On the waters of Big Limestone Creek.
154.	Edward Swetain	100	On Mill Branch on the south side of Roane Creek.
155.	Abram Kuykendale	200	On the waters of Great Limestone southside Carrucks Creek.
156.	John Whealer	99	On the Clear Fork of Horse Creek.
157.	Simon Bundy	50	On the draft of Gap Creek near a sink hole.
158.	Samuel Henry	200	On Buffalo Creek joining Baptist McNabb's lines.
159.	William Watson	300	On Sinking Creek joining Joseph Denton's lines.
160.	Martha Sherril	100	On the south side of Nolachucky River.
161.	Edward King	640	On the north side of Watauga near the head of Lick Creek.
162.	John Blair McMahan	300	On the head spring of West Fork of Nob Creek.
163.	Garret Vinzant	200	On the Sinking Fork of Lick Creek.
164.	Robert Lusk	50	On the draft of Buffalo Creek.
165.	Drury Gooden	337	On the north side of Watauga including the manor place.
166.	Matthew Talbot	526	On the head of Brush Creek.
167.	John Mosely	49½	On a branch of Cedar Creek east side of Buffalo Ridge.
168.	John King	200	On both sides of Stoney Creek.
169.	William Murphy	400	On Lick Creek.
170.	Charles Duncan	190	On the South Fork of Horse Creek.

171.	Andrew Taylor	450	On both sides of Buffalo Creek.
172.	Joseph Bullar	150	On Sinking Creek joining McCartney's Mountain.
173.	Henry Earnest	45	On the north side of Nolachucky River.
174.	Josiah Hambleton	180	On both sides of Little Limestone.
175.	Charles Allison	400	On a miery branch - waters of Big Limestone.
176.	John Pemberton	300	On Fall Creek on the north side of Holston River.
177.	George Russell	99	On the waters of Boone Creek joining John McMahan.
178.	Robert Ellison	290	On the South Fork of Big Limestone.
179.	James Wray	123	On both sides of Cherokee Creek joining William Murphys.
180.	William Murphy	300	On both sides of Lick Creek.
181.	Amos Bird	300	On the north side Nolachucky joining Philip Adams.
182.	Joshua Houghton	640	On the southside of Watauga River.
183.	Samuel Culberson	400	On Indian Creek near a branch of Rock Creek.
184.	Andrew Martain	200	On both forks of Cedar Creek branch on Big Limestone.
185.	Thomas Jonaken	300	Joining Matthew Talbot's survey on Brush Creek.
186.	George Gray	488	On Cedar Creek of Holston River.
187.	William McBride	500	On Mill Creek on the waters of Nolachucky.
188.	John Laine	399	On Cedar Creek joining his former survey.
189.	Mesheck Hale	340	On the north side of Watauga River.
190.	Robert Campbell	600	On Little Sinking Creek.
191.	Thomas Brown	200	On the west fork of Morrison Mill Creek.
192.	Caleb Hunter	93	On the waters of Mill Creek - waters of Big Limestone.
193.	Robert Wilson	150	On the Cedar Fork of Big Limestone.
194.	Andrew English	50	On the waters of Lick Creek.
195.	David Hughes	600	On both sides of Little Limestone Creek.
196.	Samuel Jobes	513	On Kendricks Creek.
197.	Charles Roberson	257	On an east branch of Sinking Creek.

198.	William Stockton	300	On Dunham's Fork of Lick Creek.
199.	John Holley	300	On the north side of Nolachucky at the mouth of Holley's Creek.
200.	Thomas Johnstone	150	On the waters of Lick Creek.
201.	Andrew English	92	On the south side of Lick Creek.
202.	Charles Gentry	250	On a branch of Big Limestone Creek.
203.	Jonathan Tipton	566	On both sides of Cherokee Creek.
204.	Bartholomew Woods	558½	On the waters of Big Limestone Creek.
205.	Christopher Taylor	205	On the east side of Little Limestone.
206.	Titer Neave	300	On the south side of Watauga River.
207.	Robert Blackburn	224	On the south side of Little Limestone Creek.
208.	James Stinson	100	On an east branch of Little Limestone Creek.
209.	Isaac Bullar	200	On the north side of Nolachucky below mouth of Sinking Creek.
210.	George Russell	591	Joining Joseph Duncan's and Peter Neale's lines.
211.	Shadrach Morris	598	On the waters of Lick Creek.
212.	Martin Didwell	100	On Indian Creek.
213.	John Richey	310	On both sides of Big Limestone Creek.
214.	James Moore	300	On Little Limestone including Fowlers improvement.
215.	John Kuykendale	150	On the waters of Great Limestone Creek.
216.	Abram Kuykendale	100	On the waters of Great Limestone Creek.
217.	Robert Sevier	200	On the North Fork of Cherokee Creek.
218.	Christopher Cunningham	150	On the dry fork of Horse Creek.
219.	George Taylor	200	On Frank Holley Creek waters of Nolachucky.
220.	Samuel Harris	203	On the north side of Watauga called Boones Cain Brake.
221.	Robert Irvine	55	On the waters of Big Limestone.
222.	Edmund Williams	400	On the south side of Buffalo Creek.
223.	Matthew Talbot	500	On the north side of Watauga the mouth of Gap Creek.

No.	Name	Acres	Location
224.	Shadrick Morris	299	On a branch of Lick Creek joining Bonds old claim.
225.	John Tirey	100	On Cherokee Creek on the waters of Nolachucky.
226.	John Torbitt	150	Joining William Franks and Allisons lines.
227.	Thomas Tolbert	116	On the draft of Watauga River.
228.	Matthew Tolbutt	640	On the mouth of Buffalo Creek and waters of Watauga.
229.	Thomas Hardeman	190	On Boones Creek.
230.	Joseph Hardin	50	On the Roaring Fork of Lick Creek.
231.	Thomas Hardeman	35	On Boones Creek joining Bradley Gambills lines.
232.	John Waddle	179	On the south side of Nolachucky River.
233.	James Patterson	290	On a branch on the southside of Holston river.
234.	Andrew Reed	150	On Cove Creek the waters of Nolachucky River.
235.	William Russell	50	On Boones Creek joining Capt. George Russell's lines.
236.	Robert Been	440	On a branch of Lick Creek.
237.	Joseph Martin	299	On Sinking Creek the waters of Nolachucky River.
238.	Jacob Womack	262	On the west side of Fains Branch.
239.	Jesse Hoskins	146	On the east side of Roanes Creek.
240.	Adam Wilson Junr.	100	On Cedar Creek the waters of Big Limestone.
241.	Edmund Williams	500	On the south side Buffalo Creek.
242.	Alexander McFarlin	300	On the north side of Sinking Creek above the head of a big spring.
243.	James Grimes	355	On the Onion Branch.
244.	John Shelby	640	On the north side Watauga opposite the Tumbling Shoals.
245.	James English	100	On the waters of Lick Creek.
246.	Joseph Young	100	On the east side of Nolachucky on the east side of Buffalo Mountain.
247.	Leonard Adcock	130	On Limestone Fork of Lick Creek.
248.	Daniel Keith	99	On southside the Nobbs on the waters of Limestone.
249.	James Ray	199	On a branch of Cherokee Creek.

250.	Moses Brock	150	On the Middle Branch - waters of Cherokee Creek.
251.	Charles Harrington	300	On Dunhams Fork on both sides the Indian Path.
252.	James Harris	200	On both sides the north fork - waters of Holston.
253.	Samuel Henry	570	On the west side of Buffalo Creek.
254.	James Charter	130	On Little Limestone Creek.
255.	Charles Gentry	250	On an east branch of Big Limestone.
256.	Richard White	465	On both sides of Rones Creek.
257.	Aaron Burleson	200	On the waters of Lick Creek.
258.	John Bullar	400	On Grimes Branch on Little Limestone Creek.
259.	Robert Wilson	150	On the head of the Cedar Branch west side of Big Limestone.
260.	Robert Wilson	400	On the head Rones Creek and Little Limestone.
261.	William Dale	100	On the head waters of Boones Creek.
262.	Leonard Adcock	100	On the east branch of Lick Creek - waters of Horse Creek.
263.	Isaac Wilson	350	On the north side of Nolachucky below the mouth of Limestone.
264.	George Gillespie	211	On Sedar Branch of Big Limestone.
265.	James Harris	100	On the North Fork of Beech Creek waters of Holston.
266.	Samuel Culberson	450	On the waters of Indian Creek.
267.	Thomas Bales	640	On the north side of Long Fork of Lick Creek.
268.	Aaron Lewis	140	On the south fork of Cherokee Creek.
269.	Francis Hughs	99	On the waters of Sinking Creek.
270.	William Berry	200	On the headwaters of Mill Fork and Sinking Creek.
271.	John Chesolony	90	Joining the foot of Indian Ridge.
272.	Andrew English	300	On the Christian War Path.
273.	William Bell	239	On Big Limestone including the spring of Shipmans Fork.
274.	William Damron	120	On Little Doe River.
275.	Ruben Humphrey	150	On the north side of Nolachucky River.
276.	Henry Lyle	123	On Joes Pasture on the east side of Doe River.

#	Name	Acres	Location
277.	David Perry	222	On the north side of Big Limestone.
278.	Francis Allison	100	Joining John Allison Senr's. lines.
279.	Thomas Fletcher	100	On the Horse Ford on the waters of Holston River.
280.	Samuel Jobe	200	Joining said Jobe's first survey.
281.	George Gillespie	300	On the north side of Nolachucky River.
282.	John Lyle	640	On Little Limestone.
283.	Martin Didwell	400	On the northeast side Indian Creek.
284.	John Holley	250	On the west fork of Holleys Branch.
285.	William Ellison	195	On the Cedar Branch northside of Big Limestone.
286.	Leonard Adcock	100	On the west branch of Limestone fork of Lick Creek.
287.	David McCord	200	On the east side of Big Limestone Creek.
288.	John Joughton Junr.	200	On the north side of Watauga.
289.	James Taligham	90	On the north side Nolachucky River.
290.	Alexander Morrow	300	On the head of Big Limestone Creek.
291.	Nicholas Haile	640	On Sinking Creek.
292.	Stephen Easley	613	On Horse Creek joining Robersons Lines.
293.	Abednego Enman	200	On a branch of Big Limestone.
294.	Nicholas Haile	300	On Sinking Creek.
295.	William Trimble	475	On both sides of Little Limestone Creek.
296.	Thomas Jonakin	640	On Cedar Creek.
297.	James Stuart	397	On the waters of Boone Creek.
298.		300	On both sides of Hendrakes Creek.
299.	Richard Cocks	199	Joining James Allison and John Laine's lines.
300.	Moses Cavill	200	On Sinking Creek.
301.	William Murphy	130	On both sides Cherokee Creek.
302.	Evans Huetherly	200	On Little Doe River waters of Watauga.
303.	Ebenezer Byrum	200	On a small branch of Little Limestone Creek.
304.	Evan Shelby	640	On both sides Buffalo Creek.

No.	Name	Acres	Location
305.	John Waldrups	247	On Jarrott's Branch.
306.	William Nelson	220	Joining Hymphrey Gibson and Browns lines.
307.	Adam Wilson	640	On a branch of Big Limestone Creek.
308.	James Pearce	100	On the waters of Little Limestone Creek.
309.	Robert Irvine	100	On the waters of Great Limestone and north side of a ridge.
310.	William Campbell	100	On the north side of Sinking Creek.
311.	Joseph Goodwin	100	On both sides of Sinking Creek.
312.	David Hues	200	On Coopers Creek.
313.	James McCord	200	On Dunhams Fork of the waters of Great Limestone.
314.	Thomas Brown	200	On the west fork of Mill Creek.
315.	David Nance	400	On Cain Brake Branch - waters of Buffalo Creek.
316.	Joseph Penson	120	On Cherokee Creek.
317.	Joseph Mertain	150	On Cedar Fork branch of Big Limestone.
318.	William Hues	189	Joining to John Stuart and John Torbitts lines.
319.	Joseph Young	637	On Brush Creek southside of Watauga.
320.	William Richey	600	On the waters of Big Limestone Creek.
321.	Martin Webb	400	On Greasy Cove on Nolachucky.
322.	Edmund Roberts	300	On the Cedar Branch on waters of Big Limestone.
323.	John Patterson	200	On the head of Cedar Branch of Big Limestone.
324.	George Gray	399	On Cedar Creek on the waters of Holston River.
325.	Charles Barksdale	320	On the north side of Watauga at the mouth of Buffalow.
326.	John Potter	320	On both sides of Rones Creek.
327.	John Robenson	200	On a branch of Big Limestone.
328.	Shadrach Morris	200	On Morris Spring Branch waters of Sinking Creek.
329.	Robert Stephenson	45	On Lick Fork of Lick Creek.
330.	Evans Heatherly	200	On Little Doe River the waters of Watauga.
331.	Robert Rodgers	200	On the waters of Cherokee Creek.

No.	Name	Acres	Location
332.	Cornelius Bowman	100	On the lower side of Roan Creek and waters of Watauga.
333.	John Rice	74	On south side of Holston River.
334.	Daniel Kanady	394	On the head of Mill Creek of Lick Creek.
335.	Joseph Wilson	300	On Mill Creek Branch of Big Limestone.
336.	John Faine	100	On a branch of Cherokee Creek.
337.	Robert Allison	200	On Middle Creek south side of Nolachucky.
338.	Evans Heatherly	92	On Little Doe River.
339.	James McAdams	400	On Cherokee Creek.
340.	Robert Bailey	100	On the waters of Cherokee Creek.
341.	Charles Cunningham	590	On both sides of Buffalo Creek.
342.	Thomas Samples	100	On the east side of Big Limestone Creek.
343.	Robert Blackburn	200	On Horse Camp Creek waters of Lick Creek.
344.	Matthew Perrimore	500	On the Cow Pasture branch.
345.	William Wills	50	On Dry Creek joining Henrys line.
346.	Samuel Lyle	50	On the waters of Lick Creek.
347.	Baptist McNabb	112	On the waters of Buffaloe Creek.
348.	Samuel McFeeters	99	On Boldings Creek at the mud suck.
349.	John Williams	200	On the head spring branch above Sinking Creek.
350.	John Richey	190	On the Lick Fork of Lick Creek.
351.	Joseph Harden	200	On a branch of Roaring Fork of Lick Creek.
352.	William Beasley	115	On the waters of Lick Creek.
353.	John Honeycutt	300	On Dry Creek the waters of Holston.
354.	John Honeycutt	163	On the south side of Holston River.
355.	Alston Honeycutt	100	On the south side of Holston River above the Richland Creek.
356.	John Honeycutt	250	On the south side of Holston River above the Richland Creek.
357.	Alston Honeycutt	175	On the south side of Holston River on Spring Branch.
358.	Charles Hayes	200	On both sides Lick Creek the mouth of Raccoon Branch.
359.	Thomas Williams	10	On the gap of a mountain joining Arenton and Lyles Branch.
360.	Jonathan Bird	200	On Penson Branch.

361.	Isaac Johnston	100	On the waters of Lick Creek including Cain Break.
362.	Daniel Rawlings	200	On Plumb Creek and westside of Lick Creek.
363.	Andrew Reed	100	On the Cedar Fork of Lick Creek.
364.	Nathaniel Tracy	150	On a branch of Lick Creek.
365.	Thomas Randolph	200	On a branch of Big Limestone.
366.	Henry Massengill	220	On a high bluff on Watauga River.
367.	Patrick Carr	200	On the head of Sinking Creek the waters of Holston.
368.	William Semmons	200	On the head spring Mitchells Branch waters of Big Limestone.
369.	James Willson	300	On Camp Creek.
370.	Daniel Harrison	200	On Big Limestone Creek.
371.	James McCord	100	On the north side of his former survey.
372.	John Smyth	100	On Horse Creek.
373.	John English	100	On Little Limestone waters of Nolachucky.
374.	William Ritchey	150	On the west side of Lick Creek near the War Path.
375.	William Berry	25	On the waters of Mill Fork of Big Limestone.
376.	Daniel Reed	100	On the waters of Big Limestone.
377.	John Dunham	300	On the waters of Horse Creek.

Washington County 1783

378.	John Scott	135	On the north side of Watauga.
379.	David Robeson	100	On the waters of Big Limestone.
380.	Samuel Handley	200	On a branch of Sinking Creek the waters of Holston.
381.	John Bashine	173	On Onion Branch on Little Limestone Creek.
382.	Robert Willson	20	On Sinking Creek.
383.	James Stinson	147	On a branch of Little Limestone Creek.
384.	Asahel Rawlings	200	On Cain Creek on each side of the warpath.
385.	John McMahan	300	Joining Cobbs and Joseph Youngs lines.
386.	Francis Hues	300	On Camp Creek.
387.	James McCord	150	On the north side of the south fork of Big Limestone.

No.	Name	Acres	Location
388.	Andrew Reed	300	On the falling fork of Horse Creek.
389.	George Russell	100	On Cedar Branch.
390.	Andrew Thompson	100	On the waters of Big Limestone.
391.	Aaron Burleson Junr.	100	On Penson Creek.
392.	Isaac Odle	300	On a branch of Lick Creek.
393.	William Whitterdes	148	On a branch of Lick Creek.
394.	?		
395.	Daniel Kanady	120	Joining Leroy Taylor's line.
396.	John Hamilton	500	On the Mill Fork of Big Limestone.
397.	Daniel Kanady	340	On Camp Creek north side of Lick Creek.
398.	William Bigham	600	On the south side of Nolachucky River.
399.	John English	625	On the waters of Limestone Fork of Lick Creek.
400.	Samuel Fain	640	On the west side of Knobb Creek.
401.	John Pickens	200	On the waters of Lick Creek below the Walnut Valley.
402.	Daniel Harrison	?	On the waters of Big Limestone joining Blackleys lines.
403.	Isaac Johnston	100	Joining his other tract on the waters of Lick Creek.
404.	Joshua Houghton	524	On the south side Watauga.
405.	John Smith	100	On Little Limestone waters of Nolachucky.
406.	William Richey	55	On Big Limestone Creek.
407.	Samuel Trotter	100	On the east side of a branch above Big Limestone.
408.	William Berry	150	On the head of Sinking Creek.
409.	John Blair	150	On the waters of Big Limestone opposite Perrys Spring.
410.	David McCord	100	On a branch of Big Limestone joining his own land.
411.	James Wilson	249	On the Mill Fork of Big Limestone.
412.	Bradley Gambell	200	On the waters of Boon's Creek.
413.	John Adams	100	On the southside of Great Limestone Creek.
414.	Joseph Wilson	140	On the east side of a glade joining McBrides lines.
415.	Matthew Parramore	200	On the north fork of Lick Creek joining Indian Camp.

416.	Henry Massengill	100	On the waters of Watauga River.
417.	Thomas Brannon	50	On the Mill Fork - waters of Big Limestone.
418.	John Scott	1010	On the north side of Watauga.
419.	Aron Rawlings	200	On the southside of Carrick Branch waters of Lick Creek.
420.	James Pickens	42	Joining Chedd Morris survey.
421.	Caleb Hunter	166	On the waters of Big Limestone.
422.	Adam Wilson Junr.	200	On Cedar Branch waters of Big Limestone.
423.	Thomas Brandon	150	On the head waters of Mill Fork of Big Limestone.
424.	Curtis Williams	90	On the waters of
425.	Joseph Guest	100	On Dunhams Creek.
426.	James Hollis	450	On the waters of Holston River and Cedar Creek.
427.	William Hutton	200	On Little Limestone Creek.
428.	Joseph Tipton	172	On Sinking Creek.
429.	Emannuel ey?	200	On a branch of Lick Creek.
430.	John McLaughlin	200	On the north side of Big Limestone.
431.	Nathaniel Rawlings	300	On the waters of Lick Creek including a large lick.
432.	James Pickens	275	On the waters of Lick Creek joining his own survey.
433.	David Campbell	200	On the reedy fork of Sinking Creek.
434.	Michael Rawlings	200	On the waters of Cain Creek.
435.	Bartholomew Woods Senr.	200	On the waters of Little Nolachucky River.
436.	William Richey	200	On the west side of Lick Creek near the War Road.
437.	John Rawlings	200	On the waters of Lick Creek and includes the Clay land?.
438.	Robert Blackley	100	On the waters of Big Limestone.
439.	Robert Wilson	40	On Sinking Creek.
440.	Thomas Williams	200	On the first fork above the Bluff Creek.
441.	John McMahan	150	Joining on John Blear and Cobbs lines.
442.	John Kennedy, Samuel Kennedy & William Thomas	399	Joining Daniel Kennedy's survey.

443.	Matthew Parramore	200	On the Lick Fork of Lick Creek including the Double Licks.
444.	John Crawford	639	On the Cedar Fork of Horse Creek.
445.	Asahel Rawlings	640	On both sides of Lick Creek including Woods Camp.
446.	James Pickens	100	On the water of Lick Creek.
447.	Henry Cross	100	On the Cedar Fork of Lick Creek.
448.	Asahel Rawlings	268	On the north side Nolachucky River.
449.	Nathaniel Rawlings	200	On the south fork of Cain Creek.
450.	Robert McNutt	50	On the waters of Big Limestone.
451.	Robert Davis	50	Joining John Gillaland and James Wilson's lines.
452.	Joseph Wilson	100	On the east side of Mill Creek.
453.	Thomas Earley	200	On a branch of Buffalo Creek.
454.	Joseph Kerchendale	100	On the roaring fork of Lick Creek.
455.	Adam Wilson	100	Joining his own survey.
456.	John Wright	100	On the waters of Browns Creek.
457.	William Ritchey	299	On the Sinking Fork of Lick Creek.
458.	William Parks	450	On the waters of Stony Creek.
459.	William Dickson	100	On the waters of Nolachucky River.
460.	John McAdoo	95	On the Dry Valley.
461.	Samuel Trotter	100	On a branch of Mill Creek.
462.	John Allison Senr.	200	On the north side of Watauga River.
463.	David Campbell	200	On the head of Stoney's Creek.
464.	Joseph Wilson	100	On the waters of Mill Creek.
465.	John McNabb	300	On Nolachucky and French Broad Rivers.
466.	Daniel Kanady	438	On the waters of Big Limestone.
467.	Robert Box	100	On both sides Camp Creek.
468.	James McCord	?	On the east end of his former survey.
469.	Andrew Bunton	450	On the Holley Fork of Holston River.
470.	James Randolph	302	On a branch of Big Limestone Creek.
471.	William Berry	150	On the head of Sinking Creek.
472.	David Robison	400	On Dunham Fork - waters of Big Limestone.

473.	John Delaney	400	On the waters of Sinking Creek.
474.	Moses Moore	431	On Mill Fork Branch, waters of Big Limestone.
475.	Henry McLaughlin	100	On Mill Fork Branch, waters of Big Limestone.
476.	John Pickens	100	On the waters of Lick Creek.
477.	Robert Blackley	100	On the waters of Big Limestone.
478.	James Mitchell	300	On the west fork of Big Limestone.
479.	William Gudger	99	On Indian Creek and Grassy Cove.
480.	Aaron Lewis	200	Including a Cedar Spring joining his own survey.
481.	Thomas Brannon	100	On the waters of Roaring Fork of Lick Creek.
482.	James McBee	100	On or near the Flat Branch of Horse Creek.
483.	Aaron Lewis	100	On both sides the Limestone Fork of Lick Creek.
484.	Aaron Lewis	100	On the east side of his Cedar Creek survey.
485.	James Wilson Junr.	200	On the west side of Limestone including Wilson's Spring.
486.	Aaron Lewis	200	On the north side of the Limestone Fork of Lick Creek.
487.	Christopher Branch	200	On an east branch of Limestone.
488.	John McMackin	200	Joining the Indian Ridge and William Coxes land.
489.	Joseph Duncan	320	On the south branch of Boones Creek.
490.	William Barren	100	On the head of the Meadow a fork of Limestone Creek.
491.	Christopher Brank	100	On the waters of Little Limestone.
492.	James Taylor	640	On the south side of Watauga River.
493.	Thomas Evans	100	Lying between Martin Webb and John Webbs tracts.
494.	Pharoah Cobb	200	On the waters of Cedar Branch joining William Cobbs.
495.	Matthias Broils and Con Woolhight (Wilhoit)	200	On the south side of Nolachucky River.
496.	John Sevier	640	On the waters of Nolachucky including several islands.
497.	Samuel Wood	494	On a branch of Cherokee Creek.
498.	Asahel Rawlings	121	On the waters of Lick Creek.
499.	Joseph Barrons Senr.	50	On the falling rock waters of Sinking Creek.

No.	Name	Acres	Description
500.	Henry Reynolds	300	On the waters of Lick Creek joining McMurtrey's lines.
501.	John Russell	45	Joining his 400 acre survey and Dunhams line.
502.	Henry Massingale	400	On the waters of Watauga River.
503.	James Blythe	198	On the waters of Hendrick's Creek.
504.	William Hues	50	Joining Shotes, Scotts and his own lines.
505.	James Barrow	100	On the falling rock of the Sinking Creek.
506.	Thomas Mitchell	60	On the waters of Big Limestone.
507.	Henry Massingale	200	On the waters of Watauga.
508.	Thomas Johnson	200	On Lick Creek joining Shadrach Moores and Tyes lines.
509.	Robert Young Senr.	640	On the waters of Brush Creek.
510.	James Mitchell	200	On the south side of the North Fork of Big Limestone.
511.	George Barclay	100	On a branch of Big Limestone.
512.	Alexander Chambers	62	Joining Joshua Green's, Samuel Weavers and George Barclays lines.
513.	George Barclay	100	On a branch of Cherokee Creek.
514.	Humphrey Logan	200	On the south of Rock Creek.
515.	Aaron Lewis	100	On both sides of Lick Creek joining English's survey.
516.	David Mattock	150	On the waters of Doe River.
517.	John Hannah	150	On Little Limestone joining William Cunningham land.
518.	Christopher Chook	130	On the north fork of Sinking Creek.
519.	Charles Duncan	400	On the waters of Nobbs Creek.
520.	William Horner	200	On the waters of Sinking Creek.
521.	William Thornton	?	On the waters of Cherokee Creek.
522.	Alexander McQuin	50	On the waters of Big Limestone joining Campbell's land.
523.	John Howsar	200	On the branch of Lick Creek.
524.	Elijah Owen	200	On Sinking Creek including a big spring.
525.	James Bell	200	On Cherokee Creek at the Touch Me Not Gap.
526.	Jesse Been	500	On the Reedy Branch joining the Indian line.
527.	Samuel Bayles	300	Joining Thomas Brummeck's and William Meeks lines.

528.	David Huffman	146	On Cherokee Creek joining Penson and Keres lines.
529.	James Davis	50	Joining his own and Allison's survey.
530.	William Noeding	300	Joining Aaron Burlesons and Jonathan Birds land.
531.	Robert Gentry	375	On Little Limestone Creek.
532.	Samuel Wier	200	On the head waters of West Fork of Mill Fork of Big Limestone.
533.	Jordan Roach	400	Joining William Cobb and Callihans lines.
534.	David Miller	200	On both sides Little Limestone.
535.	James Davis	100	On a branch of Little Limestone joining Hugh Stevenson.
536.	Abraham Ripe	100	On a branch of Little Limestone.
537.	John Been	637	On both sides Watauga joining Ben Cobb's lines.
538.	Samuel Woods	87	On the branch of Cherokee Creek.
539.	Christian Brunk	250	Lying near the head of Weavers Spring.
540.	Hugh Stevenson	150	Joining Jones Davis and James Moores lines.
541.	Paul Cunningham	100	Joining William Cunningham and Greenby lines.
542.	Thomas Dungens ?	400	On the waters of Watauga including a mill on Brush Creek.
543.	James Stewart	350	On the west side of Big Limestone joining John Jacks lines.
544.	John Pable	200	On the waters Nolachucky joining Bakers.
545.	John Scott	150	Joining Weaver's lines.
546.	Owen Owens	150	On Sinking Creek waters of Nolachucky.
547.	John Tipton	150	Joining Casady and Huds lines.
548.	John Gillahan	400	On the head of Thomas Browns Creek.
549.	Reuben Bayles	200	On a drain of Brown's Branch.
550.	Samuel Moore	150	Near the head of Little Sinking Creek south McCartney's Nobbs.
551.	Charles Hayes	200	On Pensons Creek joining Aaron Burlesons.
552.	James Southern	300	Joining Horton's, Miers and Chamberlains lines.
553.	Joshua Kelly	130	Joining Jacob Chamberlains and Reeves land.

554.	Valentine Sevier Senr.	360	On Watauga River.
555.	Jeremiah Dungens	397	On both sides Watauga.
556.	John Robinson	100	On a hollow draft of Limestone.
557.	Robert Bailey	307	On both sides of Cherokee Creek.
558.	George Reaves	640	On the waters of Watauga and Middle Fork of Blevins Branch.
559.	John Prather	200	On Kendrick Creek.
560.	Edward Smith	600	On Iron Mountain on south bank of Watauga.
561.	Joseph Denton	335	On the waters of Brush Creek.
562.	James & Robert Stewart	150	On the North Fork of Cherokee Creek.
563.	William Horner	100	On Sinking Creek waters of Holston.
564.	Robert Guthrie	200	On the southside of Bullam Branch including a pond.
565.	Anna Hudden	100	On the middle fork of Big Limestone.
566.	Edwin Ingram	300	On the head spring of Buffalo Creek.
567.	William Ward	640	Joining his own lines.
568.	Thomas Smith	505	Joining Gideon Morris and John Howards lines.
569.	Edward Eagen	200	On a branch of Horse Creek.
570.	David Bayles	100	On the north fork of a branch called Cherokee.
571.	Joseph Davidson	200	On both sides of the reedy branch.
572.	Asahel Rawlings	30	On the southside of Sloans land.
573.	John Young	300	On the northwest corner of Robert Youngs place.
574.	Robert Armstrong	300	On an east branch of Little Limestone.
575.	John Calahan	400	On Nobbs Creek.
576.	Robert Cowan	300	On Nolachucky River.
577.	Samuel Tate	50	On Roanes Creek waters of Watauga.
578.	John Deyamond	300	On Camp Creek, south side of Nolachucky.
579.	Samuel Torbett	100	On the Northside of Watauga.
580.	John Layman	150	On the north fork of Cherokee Creek.
581.	Hezekiah Bayles	100	On the western side of Cherokee Creek.

582.	Jeremiah Jack	50	On the south side Nolachucky.
583.	James Graham	100	On the southside of Onion Branch.
584.	William Richey	200	On a small branch of Little Limestone.
585.	Alexander Campbell	200	On the waters of Big Limestone.
586.	Anthony Bewley	100	Beginning a little below the lick running into Nolachucky.
587.	Josiah Martin	100	Joining his own and Leroy Taylors lines.
588.	James Robeson	300	On Arnton's Fork of Lick Creek.
589.	William Persames ?	100	On a branch of Watauga.
590.	David Perry	200	On the waters of Kenetricks Creek.
591.	Thomas Talbott	60	On the south side of Roanes Creek.
592.	Ebenezer Serogs	300	Joining Alexander Matthews lines of Bakers Branch.
593.	William McBee	358	On Nobb's Creek.
594.	William Sharpe	600	On Little Doe of the Rones Creek.
595.	Robert Allison	100	On the north side of Watauga.
596.	Christopher Choote	300	On the waters of Brush Creek.
597.	Moses Meekes	100	On the waters of Kendricks Creek.
598.	Godfrey Kerchen	450	Below the Blue Spring joining the Iron Mountain.
599.	James Blythe	100	On the Rich Valley of Kendricks Creek.
600.	Samuel Tate	100	On the Buffalow Valley of Sinking Creek.
601.	Benjamin Holland	100	On the Buffalow Valley of Sinking Creek.
602.	Elijah Witt	100	On the waters of Sinking Creek.
603.	Walter Harr	100	On the waters of Cherokee.
604.	George Harr	100	On the waters of Little Limestone.
605.	Drury Morris	100	On the Middle Fork of Cedar Creek.

Washington County 1784

606.	John Arnold	100	On the east fork of Cobb Creek.
607.	Ezekiel Parramore	100	On the west side of Big Limestone.
608.	William Briley Smith	450	On the west side of Rones Creek.
609.	Samuel Kelsey	93	On Boones Creek joining John Hills lines.

610.	Godfaey Kirchen	640	Including the Blue Springs joining a big ridge.
611.	William Stone	406	On Boones Creek joining William Means Jr.
612.	John Swearone & David Miller	91	On a branch of Little Limestone.
613.	Absalom Hayworld	150	On the west side of Moores land joining Moores Meadows.
614.	Shadrach Hale	200	On the waters of Lick Creek and Hendricks Creek.
615.	John Redden	250	On Clarks branch joining Clarks line.
616.	Thomas Johnston	347	On the waters of Nolichuckey joining Asahel Rawlings.
617.	Samuel Moore	100	On Little Sinking Creek.
618.	Peter Kuykendale	150	On the waters of Sinking Creek.
619.	Josiah Martin	200	On the west side of Big Limestone.
620.	Alexander McKise	300	Joining John Clarks lines.
621.	Robert Lusk	260	On a branch of Buffaloe Creek.
622.	Emanuel Sudusky	640	On the waters of Horse Creek joining Beards lines.
623.	Emanuel Sudusky	100	Joining his former survey.
624.	Nehemiah Chamberlain	200	On the head of Riches branch.
625.	Hugh Beard	150	On the waters of Horse Creek joining Sedusky.
626.	Patience Cooper	300	On the waters of Watauga.
627.	John Clark	37	On Flanarys Fork of Rone's Creek.
628.	Thomas Payne	500	On Clarks Branch.
629.	Samuel Weaver	600	On a small branch of Little Limestone.
630.	James Hubbard	150	Joining Joseph Martin and William Nelsons lines.
631.	James Stewart	200	On the south fork of Lick Creek including McCartney's Camp.
632.	Thomas Payne	400	On Rones Creek.
633.	John Chisolm	200	On the head spring of Waldons Branch.
634.	Thomas Rogers	100	Joining Thomas Browns and Jo Wilsons land.
635.	Joseph Brown	200	On the head of Gipsons Branch.
636.	John Redden	100	Joining Emerys and Hannahs land.
637.	Christopher Cunningham	240	On the head of Sinking Creek known by Buffalo Valley.

No.	Name	Acres	Description
638.	Samuel Crawford	300	Joining Robertson and McCray's land.
639.	John Smith	100	On the waters of Little Limestone.
640.	Joseph Brown	200	On the waters of Nolachucky.
641.	John Carter	400	On the south side of the Synmie Mountain.
642.	Thomas Mandfield	606	Including the Old Indian Camp on the fork of Lick Creek.
643.	Randall Dupreast	100	On the north side Watauga.
644.	Rice Simms	100	Joining John Willis lines and Thomas Erwins.
645.	Richard Condry	100	On the Christian War Path.
646.	John Russell	400	On the waters of Boones Creek.
647.	Jacob Headrick	200	Joining William Shires and Kings lines.
648.	Archibald Sloan	200	On the Walnut Valley east side of his former intry.
649.	Matthias Talbot	400	On both sides of Gap Creek.
650.	Charles Roberson	500	On the north side of Nolachucky.
651.	Thomas West	85	Joining James Rogers and Owen Owens lines.
652.	Caleb Odle	80	Joining his own and Denton's lines.
653.	Christopher Choate	200	On the south fork of Hendricks Creek.
654.	Stephen Shelton	250	On the north fork of Kendricks Creek.
655.	John Ford	100	On Sinking Creek joining Joseph Duncan.
656.	James Campbell	100	On Dunham Spring Branch.
657.	Solomon Murphy	150	Joining Edmund and Horners lines.
658.	James Blythe	100	On the head of Kendricks Creek.
659.	Bartholomew Odeneal	200	On Kendricks Creek near the head of Bear Tree Hollow.
660.	Zachariah Coward	100	On the east side of Big Limestone Creek.
661.	William Powell	150	On Lick Creek including Prewitts improvement.
662.	Elijah Owens	100	On Sinking Creek joining Murray and Cavatts lines.
663.	John Hunter	300	Joining Hosea Rone on Cherokee Creek.
664.	Michael Woods	640	On the north side of Nolachucky River.

665.	William Noddy	500	On the waters of Little Limestone.
666.	Henry Earnest	600	On the south side of Nolachucky River.
667.	William Cox	500	On the south fork of Boones Creek.
668.	John Barron	150	On the waters of Sinking Creek.

Washington County 1785

669.	Charles Casun	300	On the waters of Watauga River.
670.	John Fuller Senr.	103	On the south side of Boons Creek.
671.	Jonathan Bird	200	Joining Kesiah Carr and Brooks lines.
672.	John Shields	100	On the east side of Cove Creek on the waters of Watauga.
673.	John Alexander	100	Joining Andrew Martins survey.
674.	John Alexander	50	Joining Moses Carsons lines.
675.	Ninean Chamberlain	135	Joining his former survey.
676.	Thomas Gillaspie	150	Joining his own lines.
677.	Roesdon Robinson	100	On the south side of a dry branch joining Thomas Talbots lines.
678.	John Carter	300	On Love Creek joining the Stone Mountain.
679.	Robert Carson	100	On the south side of Little Limestone.
680.	George Kerr	150	On the west side of Carricks Branch.
681.	David Kerr	150	On the north side of Nolachucky River.
682.	John Wear	100	Joining the Piney Mountain.
683.	Syras Broyles	28	On Little Limestone Creek joining Joseph Butten.
684.	William Steele	150	On the head of Sinking Creek.
685.	Daniel Dunn	200	On the waters of Watauga River.
686.	William Clark	100	On both sides of Nolachucky River.
687.	Richard Bullock	100	On the north spring of Dunhams Fork of Big Limestone.
688.	James English	100	Joining the War Path and English lines.
689.	James English	150	On the east side of his Mill Seat on Limestone Fork of Lick Creek.
690.	Moses Kennedy	100	On the waters of Lick Creek.
691.	William Bryan	110	Joining Woods and Roberson lines.

692.	George Doherty	100	On the Chestnut Road joining Emanuel Sedusky's lines.
693.	Meshech Hail	112	On both sides of Lick Creek.
694.	George Russell	100	Joining his own lines.
695.	Hosea Rose	100	On the north fork of Cherokee Creek.
696.	Josiah Lufsey?	640	On the southside of Watauga joining Sincolm? land.
697.	Robert Hampton	200	On the southside of Nolachucky joining a bluff of rocks.
698.	Robert Meaglen	200	On a large spring waters of Big Limestone.
699.	William Hale	200	Joining James Gibsons and Adam Wilsons lines.
700.	Shadrach Hale	100	On the waters of Lick Creek on Hollow Branch of Clear Creek.
701.	Samuel Tate	150	On the fork of a mountain joining Bermons plantation.
702.	Richard Bradcutt	165	On Cany Fork of a branch of Lick Creek waters of Watauga.
703.	Robert Steele	200	Below Joe Martin's entry.
704.	Edmund Williams	100	On Indian Creek waters of Nolachucky.
705.	Nathan Davis	31	Joining Samuel Dentons and Jesse Wilson's lines.
706.	William Payne	200	Joining Mark Michael's claim.
707.	Samuel Sparks	50	On Sinking Creek.
708.	James Walderon	217	Joining Joseph Duncan and William Grishams line.
709.	George Vanunt	150	Including a large spring joining Christopher Choles line.
710.	Edward Box	60	On the waters of Nolachucky River.
711.	Matthias Broils	200	Joining Francis Hughes lines.
712.	Jaob Wilder	50	On the waters of Watauga River.
713.	Benjamin Chole	100	On the waters of Kendrick's Creek.

Washington County 1786

714.	Moses Kennedy	100	Beginning in a large spring joining Leonard Adcocks line.
715.	Robert Oneal	200	On the southside of Nolachucky.
716.	William Fain	200	Joining William McMahan and John Blairs lines.
717.	William Gregory	90	On the Grassy Cove.

718.	Felix Walker	500	On the waters of Sinking Creek.
719.	Jacob Chamberlain	200	On the waters of Watauga.
720.	Richard Deakins	173	On the waters of Nolichucky River.
721.	William Ward	250	On both sides of Brush Creek.
722.	William Wells	100	On the north side of Watauga River.
723.	William Ward	200	Joining Jonas Littles line.
724.	William Sharp	400	On Casi Creek joining Matthias Talbott's line.
725.	Valentine Sevier	500	On the north bank of Watauga.
726.	John Humphrey	100	On the waters of Watauga.
727.	Samuel Bayles	74	Joining Isaiah Hamiltons line.
728.	Samuel Denton	229	Joining Joseph Tiptons line.
729.	Thomas Chapman	200	On the waters of Big Limestone.
730.	Samuel Piercefield	100	Including Jacob Hamilton's improvement.
731.	James Stuart	300	On Lick Creek joining the side of a mountain.
732.	John Saymond (Laymond?)	25	On the southside of Cherokee Creek.
733.	Samuel Fain	400	On a branch of Little Limestone.
734.	Robert Steel	150	On the east side on the head of Sinking Creek.
735.	Thomas Gillaspie	490	On the north side Big Limestone.
736.	William Reeves	200	Joining Moores and Wills lines.
737.	Robert Love	300	On both sides Indian Creek.
738.	John Saymond (Laymond?)	50	Joining Col. Robertson's land.
739.	Andrew Armstrong	300	On the southside Nolachucky.
740.	Thomas Robinson	200	Joining Reuben Rigland's land.
741.	John Laymond (Saymond?)	150	On Cherokee Creek joining David Huffmans line.
742.	John Conly	55	Joining John Lanes south line.
743.	Anne Moore	191	Joining Richeys and Caswells lines.
744.	Shadrach Hale	300	On the north fork of Limestone fork of Lick Creek.
745.	Robert Cowan	200	On the southside of Nolachucky.
746.	Jeremiah Dungin	200	On Cany Run and Brush Creek.
747.	Thomas Chapman	50	On the waters of Big Limestone.

748.	Benjamin Shaw	189	On the head of the Wolfe Branch.
749.	Samuel Pearcifield	100	Joining the land James Hamilton formerly lived.
750.	John Rider	100	On Sinking Creek.
751.	Abraham Heston	50	On the southside of Cherokee Creek.
752.	Cornelius ONeal	200	On the waters of Nolachucky joining another of his surveys.
753.	James English	100	On both sides of Limestone Fork of Lick Creek.
754.	James Alison	100	On the waters of Big Limestone.
755.	Cornelius Oneal	200	On the waters of Nolachucky River joining a bank of rock.
756.	Thomas Goin	225	On the waters of Cherokee Creek joining Tiptons line.
757.	Joseph Denton	350	On the waters of Cherokee Creek.
758.	Edward Smith	100	On the southside of the Iron Mountain.
759.	Peter Brown	200	On Boones Creek at the foot of the Indian Ridge.
760.	James Martain	100	Joining Joe Martins and Thomas Biddles lines.
761.	Jacob Light	100	Including Leaches improvement.
762.	John Everett	225	Joining his own and Richardson's lines.
763.	Charles Duncan	113	On the waters of Knobbs Creek.
764.	James Martain	60	Joining Thomas Beddys line.
765.	William Watson	100	Between Brush and Sinking Creeks.
766.	Robert Loxley Stubblefield	100	On the head of Gammons Branch.
767.	James Blithe	150	On Kendricks Creek.
768.	Christopher Chote	150	Joining Barrows and the Auston Chotes lines.
769.	Elisha Butler	200	Including Sinking Spring.
770.	Joseph Goodman	100	On the waters of Sinking Creek.
771.	John Clark	100	On the southside Nolachucky River.
772.	John Trotter	63	Joining Carsons line on the side of a nobb.
773.	David Stuart & Thomas Keef	200	On the Middle Fork of Buffalo Creek, waters of Holston River.
774.	Nicholas Hail	200	On the waters of Sinking Creek.
775.	Andrew Greer	200	On the waters of Watauga joining his own survey.

776.	Nathan Lewis	200	On the waters of Gap Creek.
777.	Christopher Chote	140	Joining Gates line.
778.	Matthias Little	100	On the waters of Gap Creek.
779.	Benjamin Holland	121	Joining Christopher Cunninghams and his own line.
780.	William Lucas	440	On Cedar Creek joining Pharoah Cobbs lines.
781.	Cothriel Bailey	100	Joining the Long Cain Brake line.
782.	James Cash	500	On the waters of Little Limestone.
783.	Landon Carter	150	On the northeast side of the big ridge of the Iron Mountain.
784.	John Tipton	600	Joining Joseph Dentons lines.
785.	John Hunter Senr.	170	Between Cherokee Creek and Buffalo Mountain.

Washington County 1787

786.	Ezekiel Buchannon	150	On the waters of Little Limestone.
787.	Morse Mattock	200	On the waters of Boones Creek.
788.	Peter Brown	300	On the waters of Boones Creek.
789.	David Greate	100	On the east side of Sinking Creek.
790.	Nicholas Hale	200	In the fork of Sinking Creek.
791.	Mary Duggard	226	On both sides Watauga.
792.	Moses Carson	50	On the waters of Big Limestone.
793.	William Watson	200	On the waters of Sinking Creek.
794.	Jacob Brown	640	On the south side of Nolachucky.
795.	Isaac Taylor	300	On the west side of Gap Creek.
796.	Thomas Brummett	200	Joining John Reddens line.
797.	Andrew Greer	363	On the north side of the mouth of Stoney Creek.
798.	Thomas Gillaspie	150	On Rock House Branch.
799.	Andrew Greer	394	Bounded by his own lines and the Iron Mountain.
800.	John Davis	100	On the north fork of Davis Creek.
801.	Matthias Little	200	On the north side of the Mountain Path.
802.	Thomas Gillaspie	150	On the Rock House Branch.
803.	Isaac Lincoln	265	On the waters of Watauga River.
804.	Sebastian Hatler	400	Joining his own and Broyles line.
805.	William Brown	100	Joining Joseph Brown Senrs. lines.

806.	John Davis	200	On the north side of Watauga.
807.	Benjamin Ward	300	On the southside of Watauga opposite Cobe Creek.
808.	John Reiley	100	On the northeast side of the big ridge of Iron Mountain.
809.	Thomas Gillaspie	100	On the rockhouse branch joining a former survey.
810.	Thomas Carrey	300	On the southside Watauga.
811.	Joseph Greer	415	On the east side of Doe River joining John Carters lines.
812.	William Campbell	254	On Cedar Branch of Big Limestone.
813.	John Hunter	57	On Orhew(?) Cherokee Creek.
814.	James Eden	100	Joining his own survey on Gap Creek.
815.	Jacob Tipton	100	On west side of Doe River.
816.	Edmond Williams	100	Joining Robert McAfees lines on Buffalow Mountain.
817.	James Robertson	200	On Arenton's Fork of Lick Creek.
818.	John Allison	640	On Clark's Branch joining John Hannah's line.
819.	John Thomas	200	Joining Callahan and Roaches line.
820.	John Torbett	200	On the northside Watauga.
821.	James Eden	100	On waters of Gap Creek in valley above the big Spring.

Washington County 1788

822.	John Anderson	99	On waters of Big Limestone.
823.	Samuel Wilson	200	On northside of Holstein opposite mouth of Hynnecutts Creek.
824.	Daniel McCray	200	On Pensons Creek joining Birds...
825.	Samuel Garland	300	On Flag Pond Branch...Watauga
826.	Pharoah Cobb	300	On East Fork of Nobb Creek.
827.	Godfrey Carrygin	300	On Buck Creek above the war road.
828.	Thomas Carney	220	On the waters of Watauga.
829.	Joseph Parron	200	On the waters of Sinking Creek...
830.	Robert Carson	100	On waters of Big Limestone.
831.	John Moore	50	On north side Watauga.
832.	Shadrach Murray	150	On the banks of Sinking Creek...
833.	John Allison	400	On Clark's Branch joining Weavers line.
834.	John Buller	100	Joining Thomas McCullocks line.
835.	Jacob Hedricks	220	On west side of Doe River.
836.	Henry French	150	On waters of Cherokee Creek.
837.	Edmund Williams	100	On east side of dry creek.

838.	Benjamin Cobb	600	On Nobb Creek joining Pharoah Cobb's lines.
839.	James Owens	87	On Cedar Creek joining James Holleys lines.
840.	Pharoah Cobb	640	On the east fork of Nobb Creek.
841.	Andrew Greer	575	On waters of Watauga joining John Shebby (Shelby?) Jrs. lines.
842.	John Allison	191	On waters of Big Limestone on Cedar branch.
843.	Charles Asher, Senr.	300	On both sides of Watauga.
844.	James & Robert Stuart	200	In the Limestone Cove under foot of Iron Mountain.
845.	James & Robert Stuart	100	(Same as above) on waters of the Nolachucky.
846.	James & Robert Stuart	200	(Same as above)
847.	Francis Hodge	500	On northside of Watauga.
848.	John Clark	640	On waters of Nolachucky.
849.	George Milhorn	200	On waters of Watauga above Sholes plantation.
850.	Barbard Caffery	100	On Lick Creek below Nathaniel Davis's.
851.	James Givin	522	On Cove Creek below the Rock House
852.	Ezekiel Rawlings	200	On Limestone Fork of Lick Creek.
853.	Ezekiel Rawlings	200	On waters of Lick Creek.
854.	Ezekiel Rawlings	100	Joining Stevensons, Pickens and Hadons lands.
855.	Charles Asher	300	On north bank of Watauga.
856.	John Whatlook	100	On draughts of Kendricks Creek.
857.	William Hollaway	200	On Kendrick's Creek.

Washington County 1789

858.	Andrew Beard	200	On southside of Nolachucky joining Boxes(?) line.
859.	Nicholas Broyles	100	On west side of Little Limestone.
860.	Samuel Harris	480	On waters of Boones Creek.
861.	Benjamin Ward	300	On southside of Watauga.
862.	Adam Gunn	200	On east side of Steep Spur Nobbs joining Camp Creek.
863.	Adam Wilhight	200	On waters of Nolachucky.
864.	Joseph Bullar	150	On Little Sinking Creek.
865.	Michael Rawlings	50	On waters of Big Limestone.
866.	Mordecai Price	400	On Sinking Creek, waters of Watauga.
867.	William Holloway Junr.	200	Including branches of Kendricks Creek.
868.	John Shields	66	On southside of north fork of Cherokee Creek.
869.	John Bayles	150	On the north fork of Cherokee Creek.

870.	John Bayles	150	On the north fork of Cherokee.
871.	Larkin Wisdom	300	On the south side of Holston.
872.	John Ryan	100	On the Clear Fork of Lick Creek.
873.	William Dotson	100	On the North Fork of Sinking Creek.
874.	George Martin	100	On the waters of Lick Creek.
875.	Anne Moore	240	Joining Richey's & Caswells.
876.	Thomas Hughes	99	Between Watauga and Holston.
877.	Andrew Neally	300	On the southside of French Broad River opposite the mouth of the Nolachucky.
878.	John Neally	640	On the southside of French Broad River opposite the mouth of the Nolachucky.
879.	John Been	200	On the south side of Watauga.
880.	James Campbell	600	On the north side of Watauga west end Clinch Mountain.
881.	Isaac Perkens	100	On Campbell's Creek joining Perkins land.
882.	William Colyer	200	On Bumpen Creek the south side of Nolachucky.
883.	William Dotson	75	Joining Joseph Duncans former entry.
884.	John Peveshouse	100	On the south fork of Cobbs Creek waters of Watauga.
885.	John Lynch	100	On the draughts of Watauga.
886.	John Peveshouse	100	On the south fork of Cobbs Creek, waters of Watauga.
887.	George Gabbard	640	On Little Doe a fork of Rones Creek.
888.	Patrick Morrison	200	On Lick Creek the mouth of Cedar Creek.
889.	Joseph Brown	150	On the waters of Cherokee Creek.
890.	Thomas Murray	300	On the south fork of Sinking Creek, waters of Holston.
891.	James Cash	100	On the waters of Cherokee Creek joining Bennet's line.
892.	David Waggoner	112	On the waters of Roans Creek joining Richard Whites survey.
893.	Roland Jenkins	240	On Roans Creek by Phillip Koons line.

Washington County 1790

894.	Drury Morris	100	On Cedar Creek joining his own entry.

895.	James Barrow	50	On a draught of Sinking Creek including a spring.
896.	Joseph English	160	On the northside of Nolachucky.
897.	John Bell	100	On the north fork of Sinking Creek.
898.	John Peoples	100	On a branch of Buffalo Creek.
899.	Abraham Anthony	200	On the southside of Nolachucky.
900.	John Whealock	100	On a draft of Kendricks Creek.
901.	Nathaniel Davis	200	In the fork of Watauga and Holston Rivers.
902.	Thomas Miller	200	On Stoney Creek.
903.	William Colyer	150	On Bumpers Cove the southside of Nolachucky.
904.	Jacob Bealer	200	On Stoney Creek.
905.	William Bell	50	On the waters of Big Limestone.
906.	Charles Young	200	Joining William Meeks line.
907.	John Hammer	200	Joining John Chisolm's line.
908.	John Hammer	200	On Knob Creek joining John Chisolm lines.
909.	Samuel Tate	78	On Little Dove a fork of Boones Creek.
910.	Samuel Tate	100	On Elk Creek a branch of Watauga.
911.	Robert Blackley	200	Joining a survey of William Richey.
912.	Christopher Taylor	100	On the southeast fork of Stoney Creek.
913.	James Phillips	200	On the southeast fork of Stoney Creek.
914.	Daniel Rawlings	300	On Lick Creek at the mouth of the ford.
915.	William Casson	200	On the north fork of Sinking Creek.
916.	Thomas Entree	35	On the northside of Nolachucky.
917.	Hosea Rose	320	Joining Robert Seviers line.
918.	Abednego Hail	200	On the fork of Sinking Creek.
919.	Morgan Murrey	50	On the waters of Boones Creek waters of Watauga.
920.	John Lyon	100	On the waters of Boones Creek waters of Watauga.
921.	George Emmout	300	Joining Marshes line and the knobbs.
922.	James Martain	100	Joining his first entry and Thomas Biddles lines.

923.	John Tate	50	On Elk Creek a branch of Watauga.
924.	William Griffin	200	On Rones Creek joining Jacob Heathericks lines.
925.	Joseph Barron	130	On the fork of Sinking Creek on the south side.
926.	Abraham Anthony	200	On the east fork of Cherokee Creek.
927.	Joseph Duncan	200	Joining John Jistes lines.
928.	Hains Hetherly	100	On Little Doe the waters of Rones Creek.
929.	Samuel Tate	50	On Elk Creek a branch of Watauga.
930.	Michael Tully	300	On Doe River a branch of Watauga.
931.	Thomas Smith	100	On the waters of Carricks Creek on the Stand Fork.
932.	John Saymon	200	On the waters of Nolachucky.
933.	Charles Robinson	38	On the waters of Nolachucky.
934.	James Barron	75	On the dividing ridge joining Thomas Murrey.
935.	Francis Baker	100	Joining Abraham Dunlaps lines.
936.	Charles Robinson	50	On the waters of Nolachucky.
937.	George Perkins	100	On the first fork of Little Doe the waters of Rones Creek.
938.	Edmund Stevens	50	On the waters of Limestone Creek.
939.	Thomas Murrey	90	Including a big spring joining Murrey's line.
940.	William Dotson	100	On the northside of Sinking Creek waters of Holston.
941.	James Condray	200	On a branch of Lick Creek below George Martins.
942.	James Cox	90	Joining Scotts and Millhorns line.
943.	Richard White	270	On the waters of Rones Creek known as Ambroses old line.
944.	Philip Koons	233	On a fork of Rones Creek.
945.	Thomas Payne	132	On Roan's Creek and waters of Watauga.
946.	Jacob Heathrick	107	On Roan's Creek joining Griffins lines.
947.	Thomas Smith	100	On the waters of Big Limestone.
948.	Robert Mason	100	On the island fork joining McKennies lines.
949.	William Bean	100	On the northside of Boons Creek.
950.	Henry Massingale	150	On the waters of Watauga joining Cobbs and Allisons lines.

951.	John Gilleland	200	On the southside of a branch of Bush Creek.
952.	Thomas Tadlock	120	On a branch of the clear fork of Lick Creek.
953.	John Gilleland	640	On the south side of Spring Branch of Bush Creek.
954.	John Carter	300	Joining the Stone Mountain and Cove Creek.
955.	Samuel Tate	500	On the waters of Watauga at the mouth of Elk Creek.
956.	Joseph Crouch	100	On a small branch of Sinking Creek.
957.	George Barkley	145	Joining his own and Lains lines.
958.	William Bean Senr.	400	On the north side Boones Creek waters of Watauga.
959.	John Ford	170	On the head waters of Sinking Creek.
960.	Moses Gambill	400	On the north side of the Watauga.
961.	John North	100	On the south side of Cherokee Creek joining Pensons entry.
962.	David Waggoner	460	On Rone's Creek joining Philip Horns (Koons) lines.
963.	Charles Young	240	Joining Robert Youngs and his own lines.
964.	Lewis Jordan	400	On the waters of Little Limestone.
965.	William Colyer	200	On both sides of Nolachucky River.

Washington County 1791

966.	Anthony McNitt	35	On the waters of Limestone joining his own lines.
967.	Landon Carter	640	On Stoney Creek called Caldwells Improvement.
968.	Archibald Sloan	640	Joining his own lines beginning at a white oak and sourwood.
969.	Thomas Gillaspie	200	On the west side of Nolachucky.
970.	George Gillaspie	100	On the west side of Big Limestone.
971.	Landon Carter	280	Joining Parkins and his own survey on Stoney Creek.
972.	Landon Carter	200	On Stoney Creek joining his own survey.
973.	Landon Carter	200	On Stoney Creek joining his 280 acre survey.
974.	Landon Carter	200	On Stoney Creek joining his own lines.

975.	Landon Carter	200	On Stoney Creek joining Peters and his own lines.
976.	Landon Carter	200	On Stoney Creek joining his own lines.

Sullivan County 1782

977.	James Glasgow	477	Joining Charles Campbells line at the first of the Nobbs.
978.	James Glasgow	640	On the waters of Sinking Creek near the Virginia Line.
979.	Richard Caswell	640	On both sides Beach Creek.
980.	Richard Caswell	640	On both sides Beach Creek including the first fork on the north side.
981.	William Caswell	640	On the southside of Beach Creek near the Chimney Top Mountain.
982.	William Caswell	640	On both sides Beach Creek joining Col. Martin Caswell's lines.
983.	George Little	237	On the north side of Holston River.
984.	Stokeley Donaldson	300	On the southside of Holston River at Robertsons Creek.
985.	Nathaniel Lyon	300	On the waters of Holston River.
986.	Stephen Renfro	200	On the northside of Holston at the mouth of Beaver Creek.
987.	Stokeley Donaldson	500	On Honeycutt's Creek.
988.	John Owens	200	Joining the westside of Cole's Ridge.
989.	Philemon Nauter	100	Including a small island and at the foot of a Nobb.
990.	Gilbert Christian	250	On the northside of Holston at the mouth of Reedy Creek.
991.	Stephen Rentfro	70	On the southside of Holston River.
992.	George Bond	412	In Carters Valley.
993.	Stokeley Donelson	400	On Robertson's Creek.
994.	Stokely Donelson	340	On Dodsons Creek.
995.	Henry Hues	200	Joining the High Ridge beginning at a hicory and beech.
996.	Jacob Hedrack	300	Joining Adam Patres lines near a small brook.
997.	Mary Leiper	250	On the waters of Holston River.
998.	Samuel Doak	300	On the waters of Ruby Creek near the gap of a ridge.

999.	Timothy Acuff	386	Joining Robert Grays and William Rodgers lines.
1000.	John Shelby	100	On Sinking Creek.
1001.	Philemon Vawter	55	On Holston River joining James Ofilon lines.
1002.	Daniel Grant	350	On the big creek joining McMurray lines.
1003.	David Bragg	270	On Walkers Fork a branch of Horse Creek.
1004.	Stokley Donaldson	400	On the head of Robertsons Creek.
1005.	Solomon Cole	200	On Lindal Creek.
1006.	Stephen Easley	500	On Horse Creek on both sides of a fork of said creek.
1007.	Joseph Smith	50	Joining John Crawfords lines.
1008.	Daniel Miller	640	On a branch of Beaver Creek joining John Bealers lines.
1009.	William Payne	420	On the right hand fork of Dobsons Creek.
1010.	Samuel McMurray	236	On the south fork of Big Creek.
1011.	David Mahau	236	On a branch of Burr Creek.
1012.	James Patterson	265	On the waters of Fall Creek and the north side of Holston.
1013.	Benjamin Looney	200	On the waters of Sinking Creek.
1014.	Henry Huse	200	On a branch of Reedy Creek.
1015.	James Hollis	200	On Fall Creek.
1016.	John Adams	292	Joining John Snodgrasses lines and his own lines.
1017.	Joseph Wallace	200	On the north side of Holston.
1018.	Adam Biffle	154	On the south side of Holston River.
1019.	Benjamin Merritt	200	On Dillinghams old place on Horse Creek.
1020.	Moses Cavatt	50	On the south side of Holston River.
1021.	Jesse Maxwell	300	On the south side of Muddy River.
1022.	John Cotter	200	Lying in the fork between Holston and the north fork.
1023.	Anderson Smith	250	On Kendricks Creek joining Christopher Chotes corner.
1024.	George Maxwell	200	On Sinking Creek joining James Brighams corner.
1025.	John Sharpe	620	Joining McFarrons and Dossetts lines.

1026.	David Wade	100	On Holston River joining John Baileys lines.
1027.	Robert Gray	560	On the waters of Muddy Creek.
1028.	Abraham McClennon	405	On Beaver and White Top Creek.
1029.	William Pemberton	200	On both sides of Sinking Creek.
1030.	Thomas Ramsey	500	On Fall Creek joining his own lines.
1031.	Shadrach Hicks	317	On the northside Holston.
1032.	Joseph Kinkaid	250	On the southside of Holston.
1033.	George Ridley	200	On the southside of Holston.
1034.	Arnold Shell	450	On the southside of Holston River.
1035.	James Hollis	200	On the waters of Fall Creek.
1036.	Stephen Easley	300	On Horse Creek of Holston River.
1037.	Joseph Smith	30	On the Big Ridge between Crawford and Waldropes lines.
1038.	John Cox Junr.	220	On the north side of Holston River.
1039.	Matthias Little	120	On the southside of Holston on Indian Creek.
1040.	William Calvitt	600	On the northside of Holston joining Frederick Calvitts lines.
1041.	Robert Poge	150	On Youngs Run joining Cockrans lines.
1042.	David Wade	100	Joining his own and Baileys lines.
1043.	Andrew Forges	400	On Possum Creek in Stanley Valley.
1044.	James Harris	86	On Sinking Creek joining Grubbs lines.
1045.	Hugh Crafford	227	On the head of Possum Creek.
1046.	Lewis Shelton	285	On Horse Creek joining John Mullins lines.
1047.	James Waldrop	50	On Jarrold's Branch the southside of Holston.
1048.	Jonathan Douglass	450	On the north side of Holston River.
1049.	Peter Smith	300	Joining a large ridge Henry Huses lines.
1050.	Rodger Topp	170	On the south side of Holston.
1051.	Andrew Little	300	On the south side of Holston River.
1052.	Valentine Little	100	On the south side of Holston River.
1053.	Jonathan Douglass	200	On both sides Carley Valley Road.

1054.	John Miner	250	On the north side of Holston.
1055.	John Melone	200	On the waters of Beaver Creek.
1056.	James Cain	260	On both sides of Big Creek.
1057.	Samuel Smith	630	On Hicory Creek the south side of Holston River.
1058.	George Beale	250	On the waters of Beaver Creek the north side of Holston.
1059.	John Cochran	250	On Young Branch the north side of Holston.
1060.	John Adair	400	On the north side of Holston River both sides the mountain.
1061.	Willery Bealer	150	On Beaver Creek the northside of Holston River.
1062.	Abraham Grub	210	On the north side of Holston River on Sinking Creek.
1063.	Josiah Ramsay	200	On the north fork of Rentfroes Creek.
1064.	William Patterson	187	In Carters Valley.
1065.	John King	400	On the northside of Holston River.
1066.	Robert Corvan	180	On the northside of Holston River.
1067.	John Looney	160	On Possum Creek in Stanley Valley.
1068.	Benjamin Webb	240	On the southside of Holston River.
1069.	Robert Steel	400	On the northside of Holston River.
1070.	David Webb	575	On the southside of Holston River.
1071.	James Hollis	500	On the waters of Fall Creek joining Blantons lines.
1072.	William Wallace	300	On the northside of Holston River joining George Littles lines.
1073.	Henry Copoh?	100	On the southside Holston on Indian Creek.
1074.	Thomas Banks	479	Joining John Rogers and his own lands.
1075.	Brewer Russell	640	On the northside of Holston River.
1076.	Robert Young	500	On White Top Creek.
1077.	Robert Patterson	250	On the northside of Holston River.
1078.	Andrew Leeper	240	On the northside of Holston River.
1079.	John Provines	300	On the banks of Sinking Creek.
1080.	David Ervin	440	On the southside Holston waters of Fall Creek.
1081.	William Bailey	175	On Beavers Creek the northside of Holston.

1082.	Patrick Shoulds	50	On Clear Fork of Horse Creek.
1083.	Joseph Cloud	300	On the southside of Holston.
1084.	Edmund Davis	160	On the waters of Fall Creek north side of the Holston.
1085.	Coonrod Peters	587	On the waters of White Top Creek.
1086.	Samuel Smith	250	On the southside of Holston River.
1087.	Thomas Caldwell	347	On the northside of Holston River joining his first survey.
1088.	Arnold Shell	200	On the southside of Holston River.
1089.	Robert Young	200	In Carters Valley.
1090.	William Melone	100	On the waters of Beaver Creek.
1091.	John McMurray	200	On the South Fork of Big Creek.
1092.	James Offield	200	On the south fork of Holston River.
1093.	John Chastain	400	On a little creek of Horse Creek.
1094.	Joseph Cole	50	Joining a large hill.
1095.	John Moorfield	177	On the mouth of Horse Creek.
1096.	William Caswell	640	On both sides of Brick Creek above Shoathe House.
1097.	Alexander Laughlin	720	On both sides of Sinking Creek.
1098.	James Harris	370	On the waters of Sinking Creek.
1099.	James Laughlin	456	On the northside of Holston River.
1100.	Elizabeth Young	500	On the northside of Holston River.
1101.	Joseph Smith	150	On the Clear Fork of Horse Creek including the flat spring.
1102.	Robert Gray	400	On the head of Hings Branch.
1103.	Thomas Harrison	400	On Horse Creek joining Lewis Sheltons corner.
1104.	John Webb	622	On the southside of Holston River.
1105.	John Scott	220	On the northside of Holston River.
1106.	John Rhea	400	On both sides Caney Creek the northside of Holston.
1107.	Martan Rowler	312	On Fall Creek.
1108.	John Good	33	On the southside of Holston River.
1109.	Isaac Fitsworth	206	On Horse Creek.
1110.	George Ridley	400	On the southside of Holston River.
1111.	James Brigham	600	On the southside of Muddy Creek.
1112.	Christopher Rodesand & John Manefield	1500	On the North Fork on the north side of Holston.

1113.	Marke Chambers	400	On the northside Holston River.
1114.	James McCarning	300	On Muddy Creek on the northside of Holston.
1115.	John Long	640	In Carters Valley.
1116.	John Craig	430	On the north side Holston River.
1117.	John Scott	100	On the north side Holston River.
1118.	William Delaney	640	On the south side of Holston.
1119.	John Sharpe	700	On the north side Holston River.
1120.	Jesse Vanters	550	Joining his own and Chambers line.
1121.	Mark Mitchell	200	On Honneycutt's Creek.
1122.	Mark Mitchell	300	On Dodson's Creek.
1123.	Mark Mitchell	300	On Dodson's Creek.
1124.	Mark Mitchell	300	On Hunneycutts Creek.
1125.	Mark Mitchell	300	On Hunneycutts Creek.
1126.	Mark Mitchell	600	On the head of Bent Creek.
1127.	John Hail	200	On John Hunneycutts Creek.
1128.	Mark Mitchell	340	On the south side Holston River.
1129.	Mark Mitchell	400	On Hunneycutts Creek.
1130.	Joab Mitchell	540	On the southside Holston River.
1131.	Joab Mitchell	640	On the southside Holston River.
1132.	Joab Mitchell	300	On the southside Holston River opposite the mouth of Clouds Creek.

Sullivan County 1783

1133.	John Hail	640	On the east side of Bent Creek.
1134.	Elijah Robertson	447	Near the mouth of Caney Creek.
1135.	Elijah Robertson	329	On the south side of Holston River at the mouth of Cloud's Creek.
1136.	Elijah Robertson	490	On the south side Holston River.
1137.	Bryant Ward Nawlin	640	On the waters of Holston River.
1138.	William Armstrong	240	On the north side Holston on Carters Valley.
1139.	George Burdwell	27	On the south side Holston opposite the mouth of Fall Creek.
1140.	Alexander Cavell	94	On the north side Holston called Burntship.
1141.	David Looney	179	Joining James Brighams lines.
1142.	Andrew Willoughby	342	On both sides Sinking Creek.

1143.	William Jennings	120	Joining Moses Looneys lines.
1144.	John Carothers	220	On the north side Holston River.
1145.	Samuel McKinley	150	Joining Creesly Weavers lines.
1146.	Henry Turney	300	On Big Creek waters of Holston.
1147.	John Scott	100	On the southside of Holston joining his own lines.
1148.	Moses Looney	300	On the head spring of Divers Run.
1149.	John Crockett	200	On Sewell Creek.
1150.	Benjamin Looney	260	On the head of Possum Creek.
1151.	John Scott	100	On the south side Holston River.
1152.	William Delaney	100	On both sides Riddley's Mill Creek northside of Holston.
1153.	Nathaniel Clark	164	On Stewarts Branch below the Island.
1154.	Nathaniel Clark	83	Joining George Russells lines.
1155.	Vachel? Dillingham	940	On Horse Creek the southside of Holston River.
1156.	Charles Gates	372	On Stewarts Branch.
1157.	Andrew Kincannon	483	In the Hicory Cove of Big Creek.
1158.	Thomas Titsworth	400	On Horse Creek.
1159.	Thomas Copenhafer	960	On the northside Holston River.
1160.	Loyd Ford	371	On Sinking Creek.
1161.	Adam Orth	640	On the northside Holston River.
1162.	James Blyth	275	On Fall Creek joining George Cooks lines.
1163.	James Blyth	264	On Fall Creek.
1164.	Robert Gray	640	On Caney Creek.
1165.	William Scott	300	On the south side of Holston.
1166.	Joseph Marten	400	On the north side of Holston in the Long Island.
1167.	Joseph Smith	44	On the waters of Horse Creek.
1168.	Michael Craft	92	Joining Stephen Easley's survey on Horse Creek.
1169.	Stephen Easley	320	On the east side of George Ridley's survey.
1170.	Richard Gammon	400	On the north side of Holston.
1171.	Moses Looney	303	Joining William Jennings lines.
1172.	Andrew Kincannon	220	On a place called Nettle Place.

1173.	Peter Morrison	300	On the north side Holston in Carters Valley.
1174.	William Scott	200	On the south side Holston in the spring of Hogans Branch.
1175.	Peter Morrison	630	On the northside Holston River.
1176.	George Webb	613	On Beaver Creek.
1177.	Adam Orth	600	On the northside Holston River.
1178.	John Laughlin	400	On the northside Holston River.
1179.	John Laughlin	320	Joining Abraham Grubbs corner line.
1180.	William Routledge	450	On a branch of White Top Creek.
1181.	Garrett Fitzgerald	63	On Horse Creek.
1182.	James Chastian	300	On Indian Camp Creek.
1183.	Joseph Bragg	200	On the southside of Walkers Fork on a branch of Horse Creek.
1184.	John Barnatt	600	On Bush Creek below Chotes Horse Slump.
1185.	Garrett Fitzgerald	400	On Lick Creek at the mouth of the Limestone Fork.
1186.	Bryant Ward Nawlen	200	On a branch of Horse Creek.
1187.	Adam Orth	350	On the northside Holston River.
1188.	Francis Holt	300	On the southside of Holston River.
1189.	Joseph Martin	400	On the southside Holston River.
1190.	Adam Orth	640	On the Sinking Creek on the northside of Holston.
1191.	John King	400	On the northside of Holston.
1192.	Adam Orth	320	On the northside of Holston.
1193.	Adam Orth	640	On the northside of Holston at the mouth of Big Creek.
1194.	Loyd Ford	200	On both sides of Cavett's Mill Creek.
1195.	Peter Morrison	80	On the east side of the north fork of Holston.

Sullivan County 1784

1196.	Meshack Morrison	30	On the north side of Holston.
1197.	Isaac Litsworth	400	On the Flatt Branch waters of Horse Creek.
1198.	Levi Murphy	100	On a branch of Holston River.
1199.	James Daniel	100	On the northside Holston River.
1200.	Thomas Ames	100	On both sides of Big Creek.

No.	Name	Acres	Location
1201.	William Delaney	56	On a small creek of Holston River.
1202.	Weight Stubblefield	95	Joining Fitzgerald's and his own lines.
1203.	George Brooks	200	On the northside Holston River.
1204.	Moses Cabbafeety	50	On the southside of Holston and a draft of Sinking Creek.
1205.	William Tredway	300	On the northside of the North Fork of Holston.
1206.	Walter Johnston	260	In Stanley's Valley.
1207.	William McCormack	100	On the southside Holston River.
1208.	Nicholas Edwards	200	In Stanley's Valley on Big Creek.
1209.	James McWhiter	142	In Carter's Valley.
1210.	Joseph Rogers	640	On the northside Holston River.
1211.	James Odam	200	On a branch of Cavatt's Mill Creek.
1212.	Edward Wade	35	On Jarrott's Branch.
1213.	George Maxwell	160	On the northside Holston River.
1214.	George Ridley	179	On the waters of Horse Creek.
1215.	William Thomas	440	Joining John Shelby's lines.
1216.	John McFarlan	100	On the head of the clear fork of Horse Creek.
1217.	Adam Dinsmore	380	Joining David Shelbys and Thomas Hughes lines.
1218.	Isaac Fitrell	100	On Weaver Creek the southside of Holston.
1219.	William Anthony	500	Joining Thomas Harrison line.
1220.	James Cooper	300	In Stanley's Valley.
1221.	Elisha Dodson	200	On the southside Holston River.
1222.	Henry Waggoner	500	On the southside Holston River.
1223.	Christian Rhodes & John Manifield	640	On the westside the north fork of Holston River.
1224.	Peter McCall	300	Joining William Anderson lines.
1225.	Solomon Smith	400	On Indian Creek the southside Holston River.
1226.	Robert Young	150	In Carters Valley on the northside of Holston.
1227.	John Miller	150	On the waters of Possum Creek.
1228.	John Gates	75	On a branch of Horse Creek.
1229.	Christian Weaver	540	On the southside Holston River.
1230.	Garret Fitzgerald	100	In the Sugar Tree Valley.

1231.	Peter Cocke	250	On the southside Holston River.
1232.	Julius Hacker	640	On both sides Beaver Creek waters of Holston.
1233.	Charles Gates	200	On the waters of Horse Creek.
1234.	Robert Sellars	200	On the waters of Horse Creek a little creek on an old War Road.
1235.	David Looney	600	In Stanleys Valley both sides of Possum Creek.
1236.	John McBroom	282	On the northside of Carters Valley.
1237.	Robert Crockett	281	On the northside of Holston.
1238.	John Crawford	100	On the Clear Fork of Horse Creek.
1239.	William Anderson	200	Joining Peter McCalleys lines.
1240.	Thomas Caldwell	400	On Caldwells Creek.
1241.	Samuel McFettors	300	On the southside Holston River.
1242.	Robert Coyle	321	On the huny (honey?) cove northside Holston River.
1243.	John Tally	145	Joining James Copelands and his own survey.
1244.	Thomas Gibbons	640	On northside Holston in Stanley Valley on Possum Creek.
1245.	Elijah Chrisham	220	On both sides Dodsons Creek.
1246.	John Shute	600	On the north fork of Buck Creek.
1247.	William Lane	100	On the southside Holston River.
1248.	John Leeper	450	On the northside Holston River.
1249.	Charles Campbell	140	On the northside Holston River.
1250.	Peter Cocke	300	On Buck Creek a branch of Holston.
1251.	David Gambill	200	In Standleys Valley on Big Creek.
1252.	George Delay	100	Joining George Vincints lines.
1253.	Henry Simpson	100	On the waters of Rudy Creek.
1254.	Joseph Kincade	970	In Carters Valley.
1255.	John Snodgrass	174	Joining William Rogers line.
1256.	David Looney	200	On Widow Kirk's Mill Creek.
1257.	Francis Kenar	500	On the northside Holston opposite Dotsons Ford.
1258.	Henry Simpson	200	On the waters of Reedy Creek.
1259.	Robert Young	300	On the northside Holston River.
1260.	James Smith	200	On the northside Holston River.
1261.	Mordecai Haywood	300	On the northside Holston River.

1262.	William Dyke	640	On Buck Creek above Shotes Horse Camp.
1263.	Henry Hughes	200	On northside Holston near the mouth of Kendricks Creek.
1264.	Robert Campbell	140	In Carters Valley northside Holston.
1265.	William Anderson	250	On the north side of Holston.
1266.	John Blanton	600	On the north side of Holston.
1267.	Levy Murphy	100	Near Holston River.
1268.	David Grimes	200	On Fall Creek.
1269.	John Jackson	180	In Carter's Valley.
1270.	George Ridley	200	Including the Pond Spring.
1271.	James Gates	150	Joining Samuel Jobe's lines.
1272.	John Pemberton	306	Joining John Hickwoods lines.
1273.	Thomas King	640	Northside Holston River.
1274.	Patrick Cragon	170	On Indian Creek.
1275.	Samuel McFeeters	640	On Duncans Branch.
1276.	Peter Cocke	300	On Caney Creek.
1277.	Joseph Moore	150	On the south bank of Holston River.
1278.	James Cooper	163	In Carters Valley.
1279.	Stephen Bennett	150	On the flat branch of Horse Creek.
1280.	Davis Shelby	100	On the northside Holston River.
1281.	Edward Ward	100	On Jarrotts Branch above Jarrotts Camp.
1282.	Stockley Donelson	385	On the north side Holston.
1283.	Edward Cox	292	On the north side Holston.
1284.	Thomas Caldwell	220	On the north side Holston.
1285.	Augustine Willson	200	On the Middle Fork of Horse Creek.
1286.	George Roberts	505	On both sides Robesons Creek.
1287.	James Campbell	365	In Carters Valley.
1288.	Jacob Gardener	280	Between Sinking Creek and Dukes Branch.
1289.	William Smith	41	On the south side Holston River.
1290.	Alexander Poole	200	On Indian Creek.
1291.	Henry Colpoh	150	On the Blue Spring.
1292.	Bartlett Lime	90	On the north side of Holston.
1293.	Thomas Maxwell	612	On the north side of Holston.

1294.	John Sharpe	116	On both sides Holston River.
1295.	John Aronware	600	On the north side of Holston River.
1296.	James Copeland	300	On the north side of Holston.
1297.	Charles Gentrey	510	On a branch of Kendricks Creek.
1298.	James Hollis	420	On the north side of Horse Creek.
1299.	Michael Craft	100	On the north side of Horse Creek.
1300.	Thomas Sharp	593	On the north side of Horse Creek.
1301.	Jonathan Douglass	200	On both sides Carters Valley.
1302.	Garratt Fitzgerald	200	Joining William Russells lines.
1303.	John Dever	537	On the waters of Fall Creek.
1304.	David Shelby	200	Between Stephen Rentfroes and his own lines.
1305.	George Burdwell	100	On the north side of Holston.
1306.	Jacob Cox	200	On the head of Horse Creek.
1307.	John Cooper	180	On the northside Holston River.
1308.	Aaron Lisbey	125	On the waters of Horse Creek.
1309.	William Lisbey	187	On the Fall Branch of Horse Creek.
1310.	John Mullins	200	Joining Thomas Titsworth lines.
1311.	Joseph Gates	150	On Kendricks Creek.
1312.	Archibald Fisher	300	On the north side of Holston.
1313.	Henry Rice	643	On the north side of Holston River.
1314.	John Carney	400	On the north fork of Holston River.
1315.	George Russell	74	On Russells Creek.
1316.	Joseph Johnston	200	Joining John Gillihan's lines.
1317.	John Tally	350	On the north side Holston.
1318.	Henry Mock	200	On the north side Holston.
1319.	Patrick Morrison	300	On both sides of Jarrotts Branch.
1320.	John Bailey	383	On Jarrotts Branch the south side of Holston.
1321.	Lewis Widener	200	On Possum Creek.
1322.	Nathaniel Davis	200	On the north side of Holston.
1323.	Jane Carr	450	Joining William Blacks lines.
1324.	Thomas Wallace	250	On Beaver Creek.
1325.	James Thompson	150	In Carters Valley.

Sullivan County 1787

1326.	Daniel Duggan	248	Joining William Rogers line.
1327.	James Patterson	226	On the south side of the big road.
1328.	James Patterson	200	In the fork of Fall Creek.
1329.	Michael Weaver	500	On the north side of Holston.
1330.	William Latham, William Richardson & Spencer McCoy	500	On Reedy Creek.
1331.	William Latham, William Richardson & Spencer McCoy	640	On Reedy Creek joining John Cochrans lines.
1332.	William Latham, William Richardson & Spencer McCoy	300	On Reedy Creek joining John Cochrans lines.
1333.	William Latham, William Richardson & Spencer McCoy	500	On Reedy Creek.
1334.	William Latham, William Richardson & Spencer McCoy	300	On Reedy Creek.
1335.	William Latham, William Richardson & Spencer McCoy	300	On Reedy Creek.
1336.	John Graig	200	On the head of Freelands Creek north side of Holston.
1337.	Elisha Wallen	461	On the northside of Holston.
1338.	David Hughes	150	On White Top Creek.
1339.	James Hughs	200	On White Top Creek.
1340.	William Duff	200	Joining Sharpes and Kings lines.
1341.	John Henderson	600	On the northside of Holston.
1342.	Jonathan Douglass	456	On the northside of Holston.
1343.	John Roberson	640	On the northside of Holston.
1344.	James Cooper	1280	In Carters Valley.
1345.	Elijah Chesham	250	On the southside of Holston.
1346.	John Morrill	87	On the southside of Holston.
1347.	Alexander Grant	200	On the northside of Holston.
1348.	William Blevens	312	On the northside of Holston.
1349.	Robert Hambleton	125	On southside of Holston at the head of the big bend.
1350.	John Harrold	400	On the north side of Holston.
1351.	Robert Topp	200	On both sides Rices Mill Creek.
1352.	Anthony Bledsoe	400	At the mouth of the north fork of Holston.

1353.	James Carlisle	200	On the southside of Holston.
1354.	Thomas Murrill	150	On the northside of Holston.
1355.	Abraham Cox	307	On a stoney branch southside Holston.
1356.	Anthony Bledsoe	500	On the North Fork of Holston.
1357.	John Gilbert	236	On the waters of Beaver Creek.
1358.	Thomas Bencent	100	On the north fork of Horse Creek.
1359.	Samuel Billingsbee	100	On the waters of Holston joining John Clarks line.
1360.	Lambeth Lain	316	On the southside Holston River.
1361.	Robert Williams	400	In Carters Valley waters of Holston.
1362.	James Hyland	300	On Calwell's Creek waters of Holston.
1363.	John Cocken	170	On the southside of Reedy Creek.
1364.	Nathaniel Lewis	450	On Beaver Creek.
1365.	William King	270	On the waters of Reedy Creek.
1366.	Joseph Wallen	640	On the north side Clinch River.
1367.	Henry Spar	200	On the head of South Reedy Creek.
1368.	John Sheets	400	On Steels Creek joining Anthony Bledsoe's lines.
1369.	Acquilla Lain	100	On the southside Holston River.
1370.	Christian Road & John Manifee	1280	On Reedy Creek northside of Holston.
1371.	John Hall	640	Joining Mooneys lines.
1372.	Richard Lain	100	On the southside of Holston.
1373.	Robert Samuel Broshare	300	On the north branches of Reedy Creek.
1374.	David Adare (Adams?)	200	Joining Snodgrasses lines.
1375.	Joseph Jack	207	In Carter's Valley on Big Creek.
1376.	Nathaniel Maxwell	150	On the west side of Spring Creek.
1377.	Frederick Caler	640	On the southside Holston.
1378.	William Latham, William Richardson David & Spencer McCoy	640	On Reedy Creek on the southside of Holston.
1379.	John Cox	400	On the southside of Holston.
1380.	Garrott Fitzgerald	100	Joining Vances lines.
1381.	William Hall	500	In Powell's Valley.
1382.	Moses Cavatt	63	On the flatt branch of Horse Creek.

1383.	Frances Berry	10	On both sides Sinking Creek between the great Nobbs.
1384.	James Whealer	100	Between Horse Creek and Lick Creek.
1385.	John Murphy	100	Joining Nathaniel Bonuns lines.
1386.	David Ross	200	On the southside Holston River.
1387.	Richard Green	640	On Clinch River below Black Water.
1388.	William Coplan	150	On the northside Holston River.
1389.	Edmund Lyne	640	In Powell's Valley.
1390.	Samuel Billingsbee	100	Joining Charles Robertsons lines.
1391.	William Smith	100	On the southside of Holston River above the Long Island.
1392.	James Roberts	100	On the waters of Reedy Creek.
1393.	Charles Morgan	640	In Powells Valley on Powells River.
1394.	Roger Topp	170	Joining Julius Haws lines.
1395.	Garrott Fitzgerald	100	On the southside of Holston.
1396.	William Hall	500	On the south side Powell River in Powell's Valley.
1397.	William Hall	500	In Powell's Valley on Gap Creek.
1398.	James Cooper	380	In Carters Valley the northside of Holston.
1399.	James McDaniel	140	On the waters Hannahs Creek.
1400.	James McWherter	320	In Carters Valley.
1401.	John Johnston	211	On the waters of Beaver Creek.
1402.	Ann Palate	147	Joining Moses Looney line.
1403.	Jacob Grub	200	On both sides little Sinking Creek.
1404.	John Holloway	50	On the south side the north fork
1405.	Martin Shutts	160	On the southside Holston River.
1406.	John Manifee	250	On the waters of Reedy Creek.
1407.	James Hamilton	170	On Pattersons Creek.
1408.	Nathaniel Lewis	200	Joining George Hines lines.
1409.	Andrew Winnegar	203	In Carters Valley northside Holston.
1410.	Jason Cloud	300	In Carters Valley.
1411.	William Tredway	150	On the southside the North Fork of Holston.
1412.	Gigan Leeper	640	On the northside Holston.
1413.	Robert Campbell	130	In Carters Valley.

1414.	Arthur Campbell	600	On the northside Holston River.
1415.	Honey Harkleroad	640	On Beaver Creek.
1416.	Arthur Campbell	640	On a large creek that empties into Clinch.
1417.	John Belar	260	On the waters of Beaver Creek.
1418.	Daniel Miller	248	On the waters of Beaver Creek.
1419.	Frederick Keiller	640	On the southside of Holston.
1420.	John Belar	300	On the waters of Beaver Creek.
1421.	James Brigham	470	Joining David Looneys lines.
1422.	John Rhea	209	On the southside Holston River.
1423.	Joseph Bealer	248	On the waters of Beaver Creek.
1424.	Jacob Nedeaver	400	Opposite the mouth of Richland Creek.
1425.	Jacob Nedeaver	1050	On both sides Indian Creek.
1426.	William Blevins	120	On the northside Holston River.

Sullivan County 1788

1427.	John Baley	150	On Stewarts Branch above the Watauga Road.
1428.	Nicholas Houzer	50	On both sides Cherokee Creek.
1429.	Thomas King	2000	On the northside of Holston River.
1430.	Arthur Gilbreath	70	In Carters Valley.
1431.	John Houzer	97	Includes the double spring and Clark's muster ground.
1432.	Jacob Nedeaver	200	On both sides Colboths Creek.
1433.	William Good	200	On the northside of Walkers Gap.
1434.	Matthias Little	100	Joining Sol Smiths lines.
1435.	William Roberts	3000	On the Rich Valley on the watery of Reedy Creek.
1436.	John Thompson	200	On Cales Branch.
1437.	Samuel Wilson	300	On Poole Valley Creek northside Holston.
1438.	Joseph Rodgers	500	On the southside of Holston.
1439.	Lewis Whitnee	300	On Stanley Valley.
1440.	Walter Bailey	230	Joining Thomas Taylors lines.
1441.	William Good	100	On the head of Lick Creek.
1442.	Martin Warrick	150	Joining Shells lines.
1443.	Moses Looney	394	On the northside Holston River.
1444.	Richard Shipley	400	On the waters of Fall Creek.

1445.	Richard Gammon	640	On Debers branch.
1446.	Samuel Smith	57	Joining John Reiley's lines.
1447.	William Elliott	300	On Reedy Creek.
1448.	Jason Cloud	200	On the southside of Holston.
1449.	William Goad	200	On the waters of Horse Creek.
1450.	Mordecai Ford	100	On Sinking Creek.
1451.	John Robertson	100	On the northside Holston River.
1452.	Thomas Amis	150	On both sides Big Creek northside Holston.
1453.	William King	400	On the waters of Holston River.
1454.	John Anderson	630	On the southside of the north fork of Holston.
1455.	James Blair	300	On the northside of Holston.
1456.	James Thompson	200	On the northside of Holston.
1457.	John Shelby	300	At the mouth of Carters Valley.
1458.	William Payne	300	On the left hand fork of Dodsons Creek.
1459.	Christian Weaver	300	On Underwood Branch waters of Holston.
1460.	Robert Koil	400	On Stock Creek a branch of Holston.
1461.	Charles Payne	100	On the northside of Holston.
1462.	William Spurgin	400	On Painters Creek the south side of Holston.
1463.	William Payne	300	On Painters Creek the south side of Holston.
1464.	Thomas McBroom	233	In Carter's Valley.
1465.	Anthony Bledsoe	600	On the waters of Steels Creek.
1466.	Anthony Bledsoe	300	On the waters of Steels Creek.
1467.	Anthony Bledsoe	300	Joining the main road that leads from the head of Holston.
1468.	John Shelby	200	In Carter's Valley.

Sullivan County 1789

1469.	William Spurgen	300	On the southside Holston.
1470.	Lawrence Ketrene	1276	On the southside Holston.
1471.	Henry Hirkleroad	640	On both sides Beaver Creek.
1472.	Joseph Cole Senr.	363	On Beaver Creek.
1473.	Benjamin Money	401	On the southside Holston River.
1474.	Joseph Cole	72	On Lenvill Creek.

1475.	Henry Herkleroad	625	On both sides Beaver Creek.
1476.	The road (written like this)	290	On both sides Beaver Creek.
1477.	William McMullen	252	On the waters of Fall Creek in a branch of Holston.
1478.	Felix Walker	640	On Buck Creek.
1479.	John Cox	100	On the southside Holston River.
1480.	Martin Myers	386	On the waters of Beaver Creek.
1481.	Rawleigh Dodson	150	On the left fork of Dodsons Creek.
1482.	John Sharp	146	On the waters of Holston River.
1483.	Carr Bayley	89	On both sides Holston River.
1484.	William Payne	200	On the southside of Holston River.
1485.	Robert Locksley	100	On the waters of Sinking Creek.
1486.	John Blanton	114	On the northside Holston.
1487.	William Warren	100	On the Sinking Spring of Lains Creek.
1488.	William Stubblefield	160	On the southside Holston.
1489.	Rawleigh Dodson	150	On the southside Holston.
1490.	Jacob Belar	74	On the waters of Sinking Creek.
1491.	Lazarus Dotson	300	On the southside of Holston.
1492.	John Miller	270	On the northside of Holston.
1493.	Solomon Cole	386	On both sides Beaver Creek.
1494.	William McCormack	100	On the southside Holston.
1495.	Jacob Eller	100	On the southside Holston.
1496.	Joseph Crockett	85	On both sides Beaver Creek.
1497.	Jacob Gross	300	On the path that goes from Nancy Chotes to Burlieos.
1498.	Peter Huffman	312	On both sides of Horse Creek.
1499.	Larkin Peirpoint	83	Joining Thomas Braggs lines.
1500.	Moses (Moore?) Mattock	200	On the Clear Fork of Horse Creek.
1501.	Margaret Venus	400	On the waters of the North Fork of Holston.
1502.	David Looney	150	Joining his first survey.
1503.	David Looney	230	On the northside Holston River.
1504.	Anthony Sharpe	100	On the north side of Holston.

Sullivan County 1790

1505.	Phelix Walker	640	On Beech Creek.

1506.	Moses Robinson	620	On Horse Creek.
1507.	William Buckner	300	On Horse Creek.
1508.	James Morrison	300	On the waters of Rich Creek.
1509.	Henry Clark	200	On a branch of Hendricks Creek.
1510.	Abraham Britain	100	Joining William Kees lines.
1511.	Garrett Fitzgerald	40	Joining Lloyd Ford's survey.
1512.	Richard Messer	200	On Beach Creek.
1513.			
1514.	(The numbers skipped)		
1515.			
1516.	John Duncan	400	On Falling Branch of Horse Creek.
1517.	Samuel Curry	200	On south fork of Beech Creek.
1518.	William Black	190	On northside of Holston.
1519.	Thomas Barton	100	On the waters of Holston.
1520.	John Young	300	On a branch of Reedy Creek.
1521.	Brice Russell	150	On the northside of Holston.
1522.	Moses Calvett	326	On the southside Holston River.
1523.	William Snodgrass	100	Joining James Steeles lines.
1524.	Robert Burdwell	200	On Clear Creek waters of Holston.

Sullivan County 1791

1525.	Henry Simpson	200	On the waters of Reedy Creek.
1526.	Thomas Morrison	54	On the waters of Reedy Creek.
1527.	John Gentrey	240	Joining Nicholas Gentry lines.
1528.	Peter Clike	150	On Possum Creek.
1529.	Jacob Duvall	150	Lying on Shuckers fork.
1530.	George Roberts	150	On the northside of Holston River.
1531.	John Young	350	In Carters Valley.
1532.	Nicholas Gentry	200	Joining Robert Kings lines.
1533.	David Perry	450	On Hendricks Creek.
1534.	Thomas King	100	In two Islands opposite the mouth of Sinking Creek.

Greene County 1786

1535.	Martin Caswell	640	On the northside Nolachucky River.
1536.	Josiah Seath	640	On French Broad River.
1537.	Alexander Outlaw	640	On the southside of Nolachucky.
1538.	Alexander Outlaw	640	On the southside of Nolachucky.
1539.	Alexander Outlaw	640	On the north side of Nolachucky.
1540.	Alexander Outlaw	5,000	On the north side of Tennessee.
1541.	John Heritage	640	On the northside of Nolachucky River.
1542.	Jesse Henley	420	On the northside of Nolachucky River.
1543.	James Lee	210	In the Cany Valley south side Holston.
1544.	Charles Hodges	450	On the waters of Bent Creek.
1545.	David Stuart & Adam Willson	420	On the northside of Holston River.
1546.	David Campbell	640	On the waters of Nolachucky.
1547.	Alexander Outlaw	400	On both sides Bent Creek.
1548.	Silas George	150	On the northside French Broad River.
1549.	David Campbell	270	On Flatt Creek.
1550.	David Campbell	600	On Flatt Creek.
1551.	Francis Alexander Ramsay	400	On Connerin Mill Creek.
1552.	George Gillespie	200	On the northside Nolachucky.
1553.	William Nellson	300	On the northside Nolachucky.
1554.	James Hubbard	1,000	On the northside of Tennessee River.
1555.	Thomas Gillaspie	200	On Dumplin Creek.
1556.	Thomas Gillaspie	100	On Dumplin Creek.
1557.	Andrew Henderson	236	On the northside of French Broad River.
1558.	Abednego Inman	200	On the southside of Holston.
1559.	Isaac Taylor	600	On the southside of Holston.
1560.	Robert Kerr	300	Joining Robert Hoods lines.
1561.	James Walker	200	On the northside of French Broad River.
1562.	Alexander McMillen	500	On the southside of Holston.
1563.	Nicholas Steel	200	On the waters of Clear Creek.
1564.	John Webb	100	On the southside of Nolachucky.

1565.	Samuel Dunwoody	300	On Delaneys Creek.
1566.	John Sevier & Richard Caswell	357	Including the island in French Broad.
1567.	Andrew Chamberlain	3,750	On Richland Creek the northside of Holston.
1568.	Francis Alex. Ramsey	200	On Common Mill Creek Valley.
1569.	John Crow	150	On Sinking Creek.
1570.	John Wood	1,820	On the northside of Holston.
1571.	Elijah Witt	200	On Long Creek.
1572.	Anthony Moore	100	On the head of Stoney's Creek.
1573.	Thomas Ishabell	100	On the waters of Lick Creek.
1574.	Garrett Fitzgerald	300	On the north side of French Broad River.
1575.	William Ansly	640	On the waters of Prices Creek.
1576.	Alexander Outlaw	640	On the southside of Holston.
1577.	Thomas Gillaspie	2200	On Nolachucky opposite the mouth of Camp Creek.
1578.	Alexander McFarlin	200	On the meadows.
1579.	George Gillaspie	200	On the northside of Lick Creek.
1580.	James Hubbard & William Terrel Lewis	600	On the northside French Broad River including the mouth of Coper Creek.
1581.	Joseph Hardin	400	On Big Gap Creek.
1582.	William Wilickson	150	On the waters of Dumplin Creek.
1583.	Thomas Jarnagin	200	On the northside of Nolachucky.
1584.	David Stuart	400	On the northside Tennessee.
1585.	Isaac Taylor	100	On the south side of Clear Creek.
1586.	Joseph Hixon	100	On the south side of Clear Creek.
1587.	Isaac Taylor	200	On a branch of French Broad River.
1588.	William Nelson	640	On the southside Nolachucky.
1589.	Isaac Taylor	500	On both sides of Holston.
1590.	Thomas Joniken	640	On Nolachucky River.
1591.	David Stuart	400	On the north side of Tennessee.
1592.	Ananias McCoy	500	On the north side of Tennessee.
1593.	Joseph Witt	160	On French Broad River.
1594.	William Reed	100	On the waters of Little Chucky.
1595.	James Allison	222	On Dumpling Creek.
1596.	Abraham Swaggerty	200	On Clear Creek.

1597.	Thomas Stockton	400	On the north side French Broad River.
1598.	Samuel Vance	250	On Little Chucky.
1599.	Jeremiah Jack	300	On the southside of Nolachucky River.
1600.	James Roddye	640	On the waters of Bent Creek.
1601.	Frederick Swaggerty	450	On Clear Creek joining his former survey.
1602.	Alexander Kelly	500	On the southside Nolachucky River.
1603.	Abraham Swaggerty	300	On Clear Creek.
1604.	Joshua Gist	200	On the north side French Broad River.
1605.	Joseph Harden	600	On both sides Big Gap Creek.
1606.	John Murphy	640	On both sides of Lick Creek.
1607.	Joseph Dunham	500	On the northside of Nolachucky River.
1608.	James Roddy	220	On Bent Creek at the junction.
1609.	Henry Farnsworth	655	On Richland Creek.
1610.	Hugh McClung	800	On the northside Tennessee River.
1611.	James Roddy	267	On the waters of Burnt Cabin branch.
1612.	James Ashmore	300	On both sides Lick Creek.
1613.	Frederick Swaggerty	200	On a branch of French Broad River.
1614.	George Ewing	487	On the northside of Holston.
1615.	Isaac White	200	On Long Creek at the mouth of Sinking Creek.
1616.	Garrott Fitzgerald	150	On the southside of Nolachucky.
1617.	Francis Alexander Ramsey	100	Joining Joseph Lusk's lines.
1618.	William Rainey	300	On the northside of French Broad River.
1619.	John Trimble	500	On the south side of Nolachucky.
1620.	Major Temple	240	On a branch of Richland Creek.
1621.	Abednego Inman	150	On the southside of Holston.
1622.	James Houston	200	On the northside of Nolachucky.
1623.	Francis Alexander Ramsey	300	On Dumpling Creek.
1624.	Robert Armstrong	300	On the southside Nolachucky River.
1625.	Francis Alexander Ramsey	90	Joining Washington County line.
1626.	Aquilla Lane	240	On the northside French Broad.
1627.	Isaac Taylor	200	On the northside of Tennessee.

1628.	Thomas Gillaspie	100	On Middle Creek.
1629.	George Gillaspie	50	Lying on McCartney's Branch.
1630.	Gideon Richey	250	On the northside of Nolachucky.
1631.	Jeremiah Chamberlain	1,000	On the northside of Holston.
1632.	James Hill	400	On the northside of Nolachucky.
1633.	Nenian Chamberlain	500	On the northside of Holston River.
1634.	Jeremiah Chamberlain	400	Joining Copelands line.
1635.	Thomas Isbell	200	On both sides Lick Creek.
1636.	Joseph Lusk	200	Joining Solomon Reed's line.
1637.	John Smith	300	On the northside Nolachucky.
1638.	Ananias McCoy	500	On the northside Tennessee.
1639.	Thomas Jarnagin	1,000	On the southside of Holston.
1640.	Garrett Fitzgerald	600	On the north side of French Broad River.
1641.	James Ashmore	300	On Lick Creek near the mouth of Lick Run.
1642.	Amos Byrd	400	On the northside of Chuckey River.
1643.	David Taylor	200	On the northside of Nolachuckee.
1644.	John Corbett	100	On the northside of Nolachucky.
1645.	Richard Woods	150	On Cedar Creek.
1646.	John Smith	500	On the southside of Holston River.
1647.	John Walker	250	On the waters of French Broad River.
1648.	Hezekiah Balch	250	On Richland Creek.
1649.	James Hubbard	600	On French Broad River.
1650.	John Chamberlain	250	Joining John Trimble's lines.
1651.	Elijah West	200	On the north side Nolachucky.
1652.	James Fulchart	400	On the northside of French Broad River.
1653.	John Crow	300	On both sides of Sinking Creek.
1654.	Joshua Gist	135	On the waters of Dumplin Creek.
1655.	Henry Conway	600	On the northside Nolachuckee.
1656.	John Toole	100	Joining Joseph Fowlers.
1657.	William McGaughey	200	On Limestone Fork of Lick Creek.
1658.	James Hayes	30	On Limestone Fork of Lick Creek.
1659.	John Callom	100	On the waters of Dumplin Creek.
1660.	Andrew Kerr	5,000	On the northside of Tennessee River.

1661.	Francis Alexander Ramsey	200	On the waters of Holston.
1662.	Francis Alexander Ramsey	300	Joining the other survey.
1663.	James Hubbart	400	On the northside French Broad.
1664.	John Balch	200	On the north side French Broad.
1665.	Isaac Taylor	4,000	On northside Tennessee River.
1666.	William Annesley	640	On the northside Nolachucky River.
1667.	David Craig	300	On the northside French Broad River.
1668.	David Kerr	150	On the northside Nolachuckee.
1669.	James Hill	78	On the northside Nolachuckee.
1670.	Caleb Witt	200	On a branch of Long Creek.
1671.	Thomas Hackett	253	On the northside of Tennessee River.
1672.	Amos Balch	400	On Long Creek.
1673.	James Roddy	400	On Bent Creek.
1674.	William Conway	600	On the northside of Nolachuckee.
1675.	Adam Meek	600	On the southside of Holston.
1676.	Adam Meek	100	On the southside of Holston.
1677.	Harwood Jones	2,500	On Mossy Creek a branch of Holston.
1678.	John Sevier & Richard Caswell	2,500	On Mossy Creek a branch of Holston.

Greene County 1787

1679.	Adam Meek Junr.	200	On the northside of Tennessee River.
1680.	David Stuart	200	On the northside of Tennessee River.
1681.	Adam Meek	100	On the northside of Tennessee River.
1682.	Adam Meek	600	On the northside of Holston.
1683.	Adam Meek	480	On a valley between Sinking Creek.
1684.	Adam Meek	200	On the southside Holston River.
1685.	William Robertson	478	On Big Creek on northside Holston.
1686.	William Black	640	On the northside Tennessee River.
1687.	Thomas Goodin	150	On a draught of Lick Creek.
1688.	John Hackett	800	On the northside of Clinch River.
1689.	John Crockett	640	In Cumberland Valley on Clear Creek.

1690.	Joseph Bullard	400	On a branch of Lick Creek.
1691.	Joseph Bullard	3,000	On the southside of Holston River on Loss Creek.
1692.	Joseph Bullard	1,000	On a branch of Nolachucky River.
1693.	John Lloyd	200	On a branch of Nolachucky River.
1694.	James Graham	29	On the southside Nolachuckee River.
1695.	John Harden	400	Between Holston and French Broad.
1696.	John Harden	100	On Roseberry's Creek.
1697.	Samuel Thompson	200	On the northside French Broad River.
1698.	John Hackett	600	On the northside Tennessee River.
1699.	Andrew Miller	300	On both sides Cove Creek southside Nolachuckee.
1700.	John McAdams	300	On Mossy Creek the southside Holston.
1701.	James Moore	200	Below the mouth of Mossy Creek.
1702.	Joseph Eaten	200	On the Mirey Branch.
1703.	Joseph Bullard	100	On the southside Holston.
1704.	David Stuart	200	On the northside Tennessee.
1705.	Abednego Inman	100	On the southside Holston.
1706.	William Donelson	250	On Little Sinking Creek.
1707.	James White	800	On the northside Clinch.
1708.	David Stuart & John Hill	300	On the south side of French Broad River.
1709.	Thomas Flippen	200	On the northside of Holston River.
1710.	Shadrach Inman	200	On the northside Nolachuckee.
1711.	William Doak	300	On the northside Holston River below Roseberry Creek.
1712.	Jeremiah Chamberlain	640	On the northside Holston River.
1713.	John Waddle	600	On the west side of the mouth of McCalls Creek.
1714.	Abner Chapman	400	On the southside Powell's River.
1715.	Acquilla Lain	400	On Bent Creek.
1716.	Acquilla Lain	270	On a branch of the Roaring Fork.
1717.	John Harden	200	On the southside Holston River.
1718.	Thomas Flippen	200	On the northside of Holston River.
1719.	Kince Johnston	200	On the northside of Holston River on Flatt Branch.

1720.	Joseph Bogle	236	On Little Chuckey the mouth of Delaneys Branch.
1721.	Robert McNutt	200	On the northside Holston River near Richland Creek.
1722.	Joseph McRandels	130	On the northside Nolachucky River.
1723.	David Stuart	300	On the northside of Holston.
1724.	Joseph Lang	300	On the southside Clinch River in Hindes Valley.
1725.	John & Joseph Harden	300	On Flatt Creek on the northside of Holston.
1726.	William Roseberry	200	On Roseberry Creek the northside of Holston.
1727.	Thomas Love	300	On the southside Nolachucky.
1728.	David Rankin	200	On the head of Stories Creek.
1729.	William Doak	300	On the southside Holston River.
1730.	John Beard	100	On the southside Holston River.
1731.	Robert Hood	175	Joining Beards and his own lines.
1732.	John Hornback	100	On the southside of Holston.
1733.	James McGill	260	On Sinking Creek joining Jonathan Evans lines.
1734.	James Lackey	276	On French Broad River.
1735.	John Hackett	214	On the East Fork of Little Sinking Creek.
1736.	James Hubbard	250	On the northside of French Broad River.
1737.	Joseph Bullard	400	On the southside Holston River.
1738.	James Conner	1,000	On the northside Clinch River opposite the Buffalo Creek.
1739.	Stokeley Donelson	1,000	On the northside Tennessee on Neals Fork of Deep River.
1740.	Stokeley Donelson	5,000	In Pleasant Garden Valley north side of Tennessee.
1741.	Stokeley Donelson	1,000	In Cumberland Valley north side of Tennessee.
1742.	Joseph McCulloch	500	On the southside Holston River.
1743.	Stokeley Donelson	1,000	In Cumberland Valley on Richland Creek.
1744.	Abraham Utter	300	On the northside Clinch River.
1745.	Joseph Bullard	140	On the northside of Lick Creek.
1746.	Stokeley Donelson	400	In a small valley on an east branch of Piney River.
1747.	Stokeley Donelson	200	In Cumberland Valley on Westfork of Richland Creek.

1748.	Stokeley Donelson	400	In a small valley on an east branch of Piney River.
1749.	Isaac Taylor	200	On the waters of Sinking Creek.
1750.	James Crosby	2,000	In Pleasant Garden Valley northside Tennessee.
1751.	Stokeley Donelson	1,000	In Cumberland Valley northside Tennessee.
1752.	Stokeley Donelson	640	In Cumberland Valley northside Tennessee.
1753.	Stokeley Donelson	600	In Cumberland Valley northside Tennessee.
1754.	Stokeley Donelson	600	In Cumberland Valley northside Tennessee.
1755.	John McDonald	400	On a branch of Richland Creek.
1756.	Amos Bird	500	On the northside Tennessee River.
1757.	Joseph Bullard	500	On Beaver Dam Creek.
1758.	William Black	640	On the northside Clinch River.
1759.	David Stuart	200	On the waters of Russells Creek.
1760.	John Newman	600	On the waters of Lick Creek.
1761.	John Adair	200	On the southside Holston River.
1762.	Samuel Sample	150	On the southside Holston River.
1763.	William Johnston	150	On the waters of Mossy Creek.
1764.	Andrew Leper	250	On the northside of Nolachucky.
1765.	Benjamin Jameson	100	On the waters of Hollies Creek.
1766.	John Newman	50	On the waters of Lick Creek.
1767.	Michael Woods	300	On Meadow Creek southside of Nolachucky.
1768.	James Moore	130	On the northside of Holston.
1769.	George Russell	300	On the head of Fall Creek.
1770.	David Stuart	640	On the southside of Holston.
1771.	John Hornback	300	On the southside of Holston.
1772.	John Mahan	300	On both sides of Lick Creek.
1773.	James Woods Lackey	300	On the northside Tennessee.
1774.	Michael Woods	200	On Cove Creek the southside Nolachucky.
1775.	Alexander McMillan	200	On the southside of Holston River.
1776.	David Stuart	160	On the northside Buffalo Creek.
1777.	Claudius Bailey	100	On a branch of Lick Creek.
1778.	Claudius Bailey	300	On a branch of Lick Creek.

1779.	John Bags	100	On the eastside of Little Chucky.
1780.	Thomas West	300	On the southside Holston River.
1781.	Isaac Taylor	400	On the northside of Tennessee River.
1782.	Joseph Eatton	200	On the northside Holston River.
1783.	John Newman	100	On the waters of Lick Creek.
1784.	William Cock & David Stuart	400	On the waters of Clinch River and War Creek.
1785.	Joseph Bullard	150	On a branch near McCartneys Mountain.
1786.	David Stuart	300	On the southside Powell's River in the Cedar Branch.
1787.	David Stuart	400	On the Sinking Fork of Russells Creek.
1788.	David Stuart	500	On the northside of Tennessee.
1789.	David Stuart	470	On Russells Creek the waters of Powell's River.
1790.	John Patterson	200	On a branch of Lick Creek.
1791.	Thomas Ray	150	On Little Chucky.
1792.	George Brock	211	On the northside of Nolachucky River.
1793.	David Eagleton	500	On Little Chucky.
1794.	William T. Lewis	300	On the west fork of Flatt Creek the waters of Nolachucky.
1795.	John Blackburn	400	On Long Creek.
1796.	James Hobbart	100	On Dumplin Creek.
1797.	Robert Blackburn	200	On Richland Creek northside Nolachuckee.
1798.	Henry Farnsworth	224	On the waters of Burnt Cabbin.
1799.	Claudius Bailey	200	On a south branch of Lick Creek.
1800.	Benjamin Guest	400	On the northside of Nolachuckee.
1801.	John Corbit	200	On the northside of Nolachuckee.
1802.	Samuel Sample	200	On the southside of Holston.
1803.	Joseph Harden	200	On the southside of Holston.
1804.	George Russell	600	On Fall Creek.
1805.	John Terrill	200	On the northside of Holston River.
1806.	Abraham Faulkner	500	On the northside of French Broad River.
1807.	George Daugherty	400	On the southside of Nolachucky.
1808.	David Coffman	200	On the southside of Lick Creek.

1809.	Jonathan Hicks	300	On the northside of Nolachucky.
1810.	Robert Coile	100	On the northside of Holston.
1811.	Nathaniel Evans	600	On the northside French Broad River.
1812.	Matthew Peat	72	On the northside of Nolachucky.
1813.	James Delaney	200	On Delaneys Creek.
1814.	Abraham Fulkerson	500	On the northside of the French Broad River.
1815.	John Morris	100	Joining James Hawkins lines.
1816.	James Gilbert	200	On the southside Holston River.
1817.	John Wagoner	200	On a fork of Camp Creek.
1818.	William Ashort	123	On the Rocky Spring of Hines Branch.
1819.	John Shores	170	On the waters of Lick Creek.
1820.	William Cocke	470	On Russells Creek the waters of Powell's River.
1821.	Abraham Fulkerson	500	On the northside of French Broad River.
1822.	John Lyons	250	On the southside of Holston River.
1823.	John Gillaspie	450	On the waters of Lick Creek.
1824.	Jesse Riggs	70	On Fall Creek on the southside of Holston.
1825.	Benjamin Goodin	230	On both sides Big Gap Creek.
1826.	Alexander Brown	300	On the southside Holston.
1827.	Moses Carson	200	On the waters of Lick Creek.
1828.	Daniel Carter	400	On both sides of Lick Creek.
1829.	Edward Wright	200	On Pigeon Creek.
1830.	John Parrett	640	On Clear Creek a branch of French Broad River.
1831.	John Weer	200	On the northside of Nolachuckee.
1832.	Thomas Gilbreath	640	On Little Chucky.
1833.	Andrew Coffman	200	On the west side of Lick Creek.
1834.	Austin Brumley	100	On the waters of Nolachucky.
1835.	Michael Reed	132	On the Buffalo Branch of Pigeon Creek.
1836.	Joseph Wilson	300	On Little Chucky.
1837.	George Daugherty	300	On the southside of Lick Creek.
1838.	John Casteel	311	On Penchen Camp Creek.
1839.	John Carter	100	On the roaring fork of Lick Creek.

1840.	William Whitfield	2,500	On the northside of Tennessee River.
1841.	James Buddle?	300	On Little Chucky.
1842.	Pleasant Dake	200	On the southside of Holston River.
1843.	George Halmark	350	On both sides of Lick Creek.
1844.	John Johnston	100	On Clay Lick Creek waters of French Broad River.
1845.	Jacob Carter	200	On the roaring fork of Lick Creek.
1846.	John Patterson	100	On the head waters of Holleys Creek.
1847.	George Hayworth	300	On the waters of Nolachucky.
1848.	Robert Orr	223	On the southside of Nolachuckee.
1849.	Brittain Smith	200	On the south side of Holston.
1850.	James Armstrong	200	On the waters of the Dry Fork of Lick Creek.
1851.	Robert Gentry	475	On the head of Holleys Mill Creek.
1852.	Matthew Wallace	200	On Little Gap Creek.
1853.	William Walker	272	On the north side French Broad River.
1854.	James Nicholas	400	On the north bank of Holston.
1855.	William Reed	400	On Beaver Dam Creek.
1856.	Thomas Tower	150	On Clay Creek.
1857.	Smith Hutchins	200	On the waters of Lick Creek.
1858.	David Haley	315	On the north side Holston on Richland Creek.
1859.	James Ballinger	95	On Pigeon Creek.
1860.	Robert Greer	200	On the northside Nolachucky.
1861.	Michael Halfacre	239	On the northside French Broad River.
1862.	John Tool	29½	On Browns Creek.
1863.	Henry Haggard	300	On Sisles Creek.
1864.	James Randolph	600	On the northside French Broad River.
1865.	James Blair	100	On the northside Holston in the first bend above the Hazel?
1866.	William McBroom	400	On the northside Holston in the head west fork of Flatt Creek.
1867.	Benjamin Goodin	400	On the roaring fork of Lick Creek.
1868.	James Willis	200	On the southside Holston River on Island Creek.

1869.	Robert Seypeart	600	On Slate Creek between French Broad and Nolachucky.
1870.	Joseph McMurtree	300	On both sides of Camp Creek.
1871.	James Blair	200	On the head of Roseberrys Branch near Clinch Mountain.
1872.	Bryant Bryan	400	On both sides Lick Creek.
1873.	William Goforth	350	On Richland Creek.
1874.	Andrew McPhearn	400	On the waters of Long Creek.
1875.	John Gass	400	On both sides of Lick Creek.
1876.	John Carter Junr.	250	On Lick Creek and the Dry Fork.
1877.	Abram Carter	275	On Lick Creek of Dry Fork.
1878.	James Gillaspie	150	On Lick Creek of Dry Fork.
1879.	William Reed	400	On Beavers Dam Creek.
1880.	George Wagoner	400	On both sides Lick Creek.
1881.	Patrick McCleary	100	On Sinking Creek.
1882.	Joseph McFarlan	228	On the southside Nolachucky.
1883.	Claudius Bailey	320	On a south branch of Lick Creek and Lick Creek.
1884.	Brittain Smith	500	On the southside Holston River and Bowmans Branch.
1885.	William Roseberry	250	On the Grassy Plains of Roseberrys Creek north side Holston.
1886.	Pleasant Duke	80	On the northside of Holsteen.
1887.	William Whitlock	187	On the southside Chucky on the head Meadow Creek.
1888.	James McDonald	100	Near the south end of Clinch Mountain near Richland Creek.
1889.	James Mahan	300	On Lick Creek.
1890.	George Daugherty	100	Joining his own lines.
1891.	James White	112	In the first island in Holston below the mouth of French Broad.
1892.	James Milliken	150	In the southfork of Cedar Branch of Lick Creek.
1893.	James Galbreath	31	Joining Robert Pause and David Campbell's lines.
1894.	Alexander Outlaw & William Terrill Lewis	5,000	On the north side of Tennessee River.
1895.	Andrew Mitchell	200	On Lick Creek.
1896.	James Pearce	129	On the southside Nolachucky.
1897.	William Owens	200	On the northside Holston.
1898.	David Reed	200	On the waters of Little Chucky.

1899.	John Spurgeon	100	On the southside Nolachucky.
1900.	Hugh Cavenaugh	100	On Dunham's Branch.
1901.	Permanas Taylor	200	On the waters of Lick Creek.
1902.	William Bigham	100	On the southside Nolachucky.
1903.	Robert Orr	100	On the southside Nolachucky.
1904.	William Clark	180	On the northside French Broad River.
1905.	John Kiney	300	On the waters of Nolachuckee.
1906.	Robert Parress	100	On Sinking Creek.
1907.	James Henderson	200	On the southside Nolachuckee River.
1908.	Richard Martin	300	On the waters of Clinch River.
1909.	John McAdon	50	On the Chesnut Ridge.
1910.	David Prewitt	115	On Little Chucky.
1911.	John Olliphan	50	On McCartney's Creek.
1912.	William McBroom	100	On Burnt Cabbin Spring.
1913.	Matthew Pate	100	On the northside Nolachucky.
1914.	John Richardson	240	On Grassy Branch waters of Lick Creek.
1915.	George Daugherty	38	Opposite the mouth of Little Pigeon on an island in French Broad.
1916.	John Blair	100	On Poor Valley Creek.
1917.	John Campbell	300	On southside Holston on Sinking Creek.
1918.	Joseph Tipton	400	On Lick Creek.
1919.	Archibald Blackburn	400	On Little Lick Creek southside Nolachucky.
1920.	Matthias Peat	200	On the northside of Nolachucky.
1921.	Drury Hodges	300	On Lick Creek.
1922.	Robert King	200	Southside Holston on Lyons Creek.
1923.	William Hughlet	600	On the White Horn Fork of Bent Creek.
1924.	John Patterson	300	On the west fork of Flatt Creek north side of Holston.
1925.	Joshua Tadlock	100	On Cany Branch waters of Lick Creek.
1926.	Joseph Ray	150	On the head of McCartneys Branch.
1927.	Nicholas Smith	335	On White Horn Fork of Bent Creek.
1928.	Robert Hunter	200	On Richland Creek northside Holston.

1929.	John Gass	200	On the waters of Lick Creek.
1930.	Alexander Colbreath	50	On Sinking Creek.
1931.	Isaac Davis	125	On one of the branches of Little Gap Creek.
1932.	William Garrett	100	On Lick Creek.
1933.	Nicholas Lee	200	On Robinson's Creek the south side of Holston.
1934.	Thomas Brown	120	On Browns Creek.
1935.	Thomas Brown	300	At the mouth of Flatt Creek.
1936.	Alexander Blair	200	On the northside Holston River.
1937.	Abraham Fulkerson	224	On the northside French Broad River.
1938.	Ebenezar Byran	300	On the headwaters of Little Chucky.
1939.	Marshall Lovelady	100	On the Cedar Branch.
1940.	John Leatherdale	200	On the northside of Nolachucky.
1941.	Andrew Hampton	640	On the westside of French Broad River.
1942.	James Miller	150	On both sides Hoopers Creek.
1943	James Miller	640	On both sides French Broad River.
1944.	James Miller	640	On both sides French Broad River.
1945.	James Miller	640	On both sides Cany Creek and Coopers Creek.
1946.	James Miller	348	On both sides French Broad River.
1947.	James Miller	312	On both sides French Broad River.
1948.	John Hitchcock	125	On the north side of Chucky.
1949.	John Caldwells	498	In Bald Valley the north side of Clinch.
1950.	John Hitchcock	82	On the bank of Little Chucky.
1951.	John Patterson	100	On the head of Holley's Creek.
1952.	John Wolsey	100	Joining Nathaniel Davis' lines.
1953.	David Copeland	200	On the east fork of Turkey Creek southside Holston.
1954.	Hosea Stout	100	On Lick Creek the southside of Nolachuckee.
1955.	Thomas Henderson	350	On the head of German Creek northside of Holston.
1956.	William Cloud	640	On the upper end Cloud's Valley northside of Holston.
1957.	Charles Hays	500	On the waters of Swift? Creek north side of Tennessee.

1958.	Edward Rigges	1,000	On the southside Holston on Dumpling Creek.
1959.	James Galbreath	50	On the Reedy Fork of Sinking Creek.
1960.	Jacob Tipton	200	Joining his 500 acre survey.
1961.	John Beard	400	On Deep Creek the northside of French Broad River.
1962.	Jason Cloud	640	On the waters of Lick Creek.
1963.	John Fenn	150	On the waters of Lick Creek.
1964.	David Lindsay	400	On the waters of Lick Creek on Plumb Creek.
1965.	James Bradley	400	On the southside of Holston.
1966.	Richard Webb	150	On the northside of Chucky opposite Cany Branch.
1967.	Benjamin Goodin	120	On the head of Swan Pond Creek.
1968.	Robert Boyd	300	On Meadow Creek the northside Nolachucky River.
1969.	Benjamin Anderson	600	On the Roaring Fork of Lick Creek.
1970.	Moses Carson	100	On the waters of Lick Creek.
1971.	James McAmish	800	On the head of Fall Creek southside of Holston.
1972.	William Moore	100	On Holleys Creek waters of Nolachucky.
1973.	William Rainey	200	On the southside of Holston.
1974.	Abel Lanham	200	On Bent Creek waters of Nolachucky.
1975.	James Gibson	200	On the head branch of Pigeon Creek.
1976.	Daniel Harberson	400	On Bent Creek waters of Nolachucky.
1977.	Joseph McCullak	140	On the southside of Holston.
1978.	John Patterson	200	On a small branch of Lick Creek.
1979.	Robert King	300	On the southside of Nolachucky.
1980.	Robert Coile	50	On the mouth of Clouds Creek northside Holston.
1981.	John Delaney	100	On the waters of Sinking Creek.
1982.	John Watson	100	Joining Edwards lines.
1983.	William Morrow	170	On the southside Nolachucky.
1984.	John Howard	200	On a branch of Long Creek.
1985.	Nathaniel Davis	200	On Lick Creek.
1986.	Nathaniel Curtis	150	On Little Lick Creek southside of Nolachucky.

1987.	Isaac Hammer	200	On the Limestone Fork of Tuckahoe.
1988.	John Walker	175	On Meadow Creek.
1989.	Archibald McCalleb	150	On the head of Seetths Branch waters of French Broad.
1990.	Moses Shanks	500	On Punchen Camp Creek waters of Lick Creek.
1991.	William McPherron	250	On the northside Nolachuckee.
1992.	John Moore	100	On the southside Nolachuckee including the Horseshoe Bent.
1993.	Thomas Lee	520	On the southside Holston River in the Carters Valley.
1994.	John Lisler	280	On the southside Nolachuckee.
1995.	James Goodin	200	On both sides Lick Creek.
1996.	Joseph Gist	200	On Gisses Creek.
1997.	Corbin Lane	150	Joining James McCartneys lines.
1998.	William Gilbreath	200	On Cubb Creek waters of Holston.
1999.	William Cocke	320	On Cedar Branch waters of Powells River.
2000.	Abner Chapman	640	On White Horn Creek.
2001.	William Cocke	400	On a Sinking branch waters of Powells River.
2002.	David Copeland	200	On Cedar Creek southside Holston.
2003.	Isaac Bullard	640	On Lick Creek.
2004.	Thomas Christian & Joseph English	200	On Clay Lick Creek.
2005.	Gideon Morris	400	On Fawn's Camp Branch.
2006.	George Sample	160	On the waters of Little Chucky.
2007.	Jesse Cheat	595	On the head of Fall Creek.
2008.	Edmund Boez	60	On the west fork of Dodsons Creek.
2009.	William Cloud	640	On Poor Valley Creek.
2010.	William Blount	5,000	On Emery's River northside Clinch River.
2011.	Alexander Moore	400	On Meadow Creek.
2012.	David Lindsay	640	On Plumb Creek and Churn Camp Creek.
2013.	David Haley	250	On the northside Holstein at the mouth of Richland Creek.
2014.	Jeremiah Meek	400	On Lick Creek.
2015.	Thomas Goin	300	On Lick Creek including his improvement.

2016.	Thomas Stockton	100	On the north side French Broad River.
2017.	Benjamin Crow	300	On Meadow Creek south side Nolachucky.
2018.	Lewis Robeson	200	On the northside Holsten.
2019.	Henry Rice	640	On both sides Loss Creek in Bald Valley.
2020.	Andrew Simpson	250	On the south branch of Lick Creek.
2021.	Joseph Stuart	400	On White Horn Branch of Bent Creek.
2022.	John Baldwin	200	On the dry fork of Lick Creek.
2023.	John Bradshaw	200	On the head of Dumplin Creek.
2024.	Samuel Graig	200	On Meadow Creek.
2025.	Robert Coile	100	Opposite the mouth of Clouds Creek northside Holston.
2026.	Andrew McFerron	250	On the west side of Richland Creek.
2027.	William Cock	200	On the waters of Clinch River near the Copper Ridge.
2028.	Thomas Brumley	100	On Little Sinking Creek.
2029.	David Copeland	300	On the head spring of Falling Creek.
2030.	Hugh Brown	200	On Flagg Branch southside Nolachucky.
2031.	Edward Riggs	445	On the northside the Nobbs that divide the Holston and French Broad.
2032.	Thomas Standfield	300	On a branch of Lick Creek.
2033.	Elisha Baker	640	On the northside Holston River.
2034.	Edmund Roberts	300	On Cedar Branch.
2035.	Thomas Davis	200	On Camp Creek southside Nolachucky.
2036.	Andrew Kincaid	200	On the northside Holston River.
2037.	Andrew English	200	On the waters of Lick Creek joining Chimney Top Mountain.
2038.	John Allen	300	On the southside Holston River.
2039.	William McGill	200	On Sinking Creek northside Nolachucky.
2040.	Hugh Cavenaugh	100	On Dunhams Branch.
2041.	Michael Borden	250	On the southside Nolachuckee.
2042.	Samuel Cox	500	On the southside Holston.
2043.	Robert Bigges	300	On the Sinking Fork of Long Creek.

2044.	Reuben Webster	200	On the southside Holston on the
2045.	Thomas Caldwell	400	On the northside Holston.
2046.	Joseph Carter	250	On Grassy Creek a branch of Lick Creek.
2047.	James Dixon	100	On the northside Holston River.
2048.	Nicholas Hayes	100	On a branch of Sinking Creek.
2049.	Robert Coile	250	On the northside Holston.
2050.	Philip Babb	100	On the south branch of Lick Creek.
2051.	George Daugherty	100	On the northside Nolachuckee.
2052.	George Irwin	1,040	On the northside Holston.
2053.	Ephraim Cox	400	Joining John Patterson's lines on Nolachucky.
2054.	William Patterson	500	On the northside Holston River.
2055.	Charles Brantley	150	On the northside Holston River.
2056.	Robert Paress	100	On Sinking Creek.
2057.	William Menon	327	On Richland Creek.
2058.	William Wyatt	520	On Lick Creek.
2059.	Benjamin Ray	320	On Richland Creek.
2060.	Abraham Fulkerson	500	On the northside French Broad.
2061.	Thomas Graham	200	Joining Farnsworth and his own land.
2062.	Joseph Bird	300	On Oven Creek southside Nolachuckee.
2063.	Joseph Hough	200	On the eastside of French Broad River.
2064.	Jacob Jackson	200	On the northside of Long Creek on Sinking Creek.
2065.	John Uzzell	300	On the northside of Nolachuckee.
2066.	Acquilla Sherrer (Sherrill)	300	On Cove Creek.
2067.	Adam Sherrer (Sherril)	300	On the southside of Nolachuckee.
2068.	Caleb Carter	500	On Lick Creek including his improvement.
2069.	Welcome Hodges	300	On both sides Lick Creek.
2070.	John Smith Senr.	500	On the southside Holston on a branch of Fall Creek.
2071.	Thomas Lusk	400	On the northside French Broad at the mouth of Sinking Cave.
2072.	William English	640	On Horse Creek.
2073.	William Moore	300	On Meadow Creek.
2074.	Jonathan Evans	500	On Little Sinking Creek.

No.	Name	Acres	Location
2075.	Samuel Hibbard	246	On the waters of Lick Creek.
2076.	Jacob Fishback	400	On Cedar Branch north side Nolachucky.
2077.	Jacob Johnston	200	On the northside Nolachuckee.
2078.	Robert Caldwell	300	On the southside Nolachuckee.
2079.	James White & James Cozby	2,100	On Spring Creek in the Grassy Valley northside of Holston.
2080.	Benjamin Cox	140	On Sinking Branch on the waters of French Broad.
2081.	James Johnston	600	On the southside of Nolachuckee.
2082.	Hossa Stouth	200	On the southside of Nolachuckee.
2083.	Thomas Eshmeal	200	Joining John Franciscos lines.
2084.	William Bigham	500	On the northside French Broad.
2085.	Charles Gilgore (Kilgore)	300	On the northside Nolachuckee River.
2086.	Thomas Henderson	286	On German Creek northside of Holston.
2087.	Joseph Ballard	600	On Lick Creek joining Levi Carters line.
2088.	Peter Fine	200	At the mouth of Clear Creek northside of French Broad River.
2089.	Hugh Bryson	200	On Richland Creek.
2090.	John Pearry	121	On the southside of Holston above the mouth of Spring Creek.
2091.	Thomas Lee	540	In Carter's Valley southside Holston.
2092.	Henry Dunham	200	On Pidgeon Creek.
2093.	John Lee	220	On Flag Branch the southside Nolachuckee.
2094.	Nicholas Davis	300	On Little Chuckey.
2095.	Frethias Wall	317	On Cove Creek the southside Nolachucky.
2096.	Jacob McConnell	200	On Clear Creek the waters of French Broad River.
2097.	John McNabb	432	On Big Pidgeon River.

Greene County 1788

No.	Name	Acres	Location
2098.	Stokeley Donelson	1,000	On the northside of Tennessee.
2099.	Stokeley Donelson	1,000	On the northside Clinch River.
2100.	Stokeley Donelson	640	On the northside Clinch River.
2101.	Stokeley Donelson	640	On the northside Tennessee.
2102.	Stokeley Donelson	500	On the northside Tennessee.

2103.	William Moore? & Thomas Hutchins	2,000	On the northside of Clinch and both sides of Blounts Creek.
2104.	John Donelson	1,500	On the northside Tennessee.
2105.	Thomas King & Stokeley Donelson	5,000	On Spring Creek waters of Wolf River.
2106.	Thomas King & Stokeley Donelson	5,000	On Brimstone Creek the waters of Wolf River.
2107.	Thomas & Robert King	1,000	On Stewart's Creek northside of Tennessee.
2108.	Thomas & Robert King	400	On Brimstone Creek the waters of Wolf River.
2109.	Thomas & Robert King	1,000	On Buckeye Creek southside Clinch River.
2110.	Thomas King	640	On the west fork of Sinking Creek.
2111.	George Ridley Senr.	500	On the northside Holston River.
2112.	Benjamin Maeden	500	On the southside Holston River.
2113.	Hugh Kelsey	225	On the northside French Broad River.
2114.	Annanias McCoy	400	On Tenants Creek southside Clinch River.
2115.	John Hackett	225	On the northside Tennessee west fork of Richland Creek.
2116.	William Bryant	500	On the northside French Broad including an island.
2117.	John Toole	640	On the northside Holston River.
2118.	John Toole	400	On the northside Holston River.
2119.	Stokeley Donelson	2,000	On the northside Tennessee River in Cumberland Valley.
2120.	James Henry	1,000	On the eastside of Clinch including the mouth of Buffalo Creek.
2121.	John Hackett	500	On the northside Clinch River.
2122.	Thomas Bayley	320	On the waters of Little Gap Creek.
2123.	James Conner	500	On the southside Clinch River above the Island Ford.
2124.	James White	320	On the northside Holston.
2125.	Thomas King	400	On the north side Holston West Fork of Third Creek.
2126.	Thomas King	100	On the north side of Holston.
2127.	Anannias McCoy	640	On Camp Creek northside of Tennessee.
2128.	Anannias McCoy	200	On the northside Clinch River.
2129.	Samuel Dunwoody	200	On the southside of Little Chucky.
2130.	John Hackett	640	On the northside of Holston.

2131.	Joseph Bullard	100	On Little Sinking Creek.
2132.	Joseph Bullard	250	On the waters of Loss Creek.
2133.	Abraham Swaggerty	600	On the northside Clinch River.
2134.	James Cresswell	50	On the southside Holston.
2135.	Stokeley Donelson	400	Near the end of Clinch Mountain including Pond Spring.
2136.	John Hackett	640	On Sinking Creek northside of Holston.
2137.	John Hackett	250	On the southside Clinch River.
2138.	James Hubbard	400	On the northside French Broad River.
2139.	Thomas Gillaspie	200	On the northside Clinch River.
2140.	Joseph Bullard	100	On the southside of Holston River.
2141.	Joseph Bullard	400	On the southside of Holston River.
2142.	Ananias McCoy	640	On the northside Clinch River.
2143.	Thomas Beardon	400	On the waters of Long Creek.
2144.	Jacob Smencer	100	On Holleys Creek the waters of Nolachucky.
2145.	Isaac Taylor	250	On Dumpling Creek including the Beaver dam.
2146.	Isaac Thomas	100	Joining Lanes and Morris lines.
2147.	James Robinson	100	On the southside Clinch River.
2148.	John Shorres	250	On the dry fork of Caney Branch.
2149.	John Evans	150	On the southside Holston.
2150.	Thomas Engles	100	On the eastside of McCartneys Branch.
2151.	James Woods Lackey	300	On the southside Clinch River.
2152.	Thomas Galliher	600	On the southside Clinch River.
2153.	Martin Armstrong & Stokeley Donelson	500	On the northside Tennessee River.
2154.	Joseph Bullard	200	On the head of Loss Creek.
2155.	John Hackett	500	On the first bottom below the mouth of Little River.
2156.	Isaac Taylor	640	On the southside Clinch River.
2157.	James White	100	On the northside French Broad River.
2158.	Stokeley Donelson	1,000	In Cumberland Valley southside of Tennessee.
2159.	Stokeley Donelson	1,000	In Pleasant Garden Valley southside of Tennessee.
2160.	John Hackett	2,000	Northside of Tennessee River.

No.	Name	Acres	Location
2161.	Thomas Gillaspie	300	On the southside Clinch River.
2162.	William Lenoir & William T. Lewis	3,500	On the northside Tennessee River.
2163.	Joseph Martin & John Hackett	500	On the southside Clinch River.
2164.	James Roberts	50	On Big Limestone.
2165.	Stokeley Donelson	600	On the southside Clinch River above the mouth of Buffalo Creek.
2166.	Stokeley Donelson	640	On the southside Clinch River opposite the mouth of Beaver Creek.
2167.	James Conner	500	Including the mouth of Conners Mill Shole Creek.
2168.	Archibald McSpadden	100	On the northside of French Broad River.
2169.	Stokeley Donelson	600	On the waters of Flatt Creek.
2170.	John Kellum	500	On the northside of Tennessee River.
2171.	John McSpadden	300	On the northside French Broad River.
2172.	James White	1,000	On the northside Holston River on Whites Mill Creek.
2173.	John McGirt?	165	On the waters of French Broad River.
2174.	William Be ore?		On Clear Creek.
2175.	Abraham Swaggerty	1,000	On the mouth of Big Creek on the waters of Clinch.
2176.	Abraham Swaggerty	640	On Hicory Creek southside Clinch River.
2177.	John Darmond	200	On the north fork of Emmery's River.
2178.	Isaac Taylor	200	On the west fork of Flatt Creek.
2179.	Robert King	200	On the northside of Holston River.
2180.	John Evans	112	On the Northside of Holston River.
2181.	Edward George	400	On the northside French Broad River.
2182.	Elisha Dotson	200	On the northside of Holston opposite the Chimney rock.
2183.	Thomas Gillaspie	200	On Swan Pond in the fork of Holston and French Broad.
2184.	David Walker	100	On the east fork of Third Creek.
2185.	John Hackett	100	On the northside of French Broad River.
2186.	James Robertson	200	On Cedar Branch.

2187.	John Hough	400	On the northside French Broad.
2188.	James Richardson	640	On the southside of Nolachucky.
2189.	John Kelly	100	On the southside of Nolachucky.
2190.	Henry Conway	300	On the northside French Broad River.
2191.	David Stuart	250	On the northside French Broad River.
2192.	Charles Robertson (Where Solomon Lutheran Church is. G.F.B.)	300	On the southside Nolachucky on Cove Creek.
2193.	James Hubbard	200	On the northside Dumplin Creek.
2194.	Joseph Green	100	On a prong of Bull Run westside of Copper Ridge.
2195.	James Green	400	On Flatt Creek westside of Clinch Mountain.
2196.	John King Fitzgerald	400	On a branch of French Broad River.
2197.	Michael Box	150	On both sides of Camp Creek.
2198.	John Blair	1,008	On Brimstone Creek waters of Wolf River.
2199.	Thomas White	350	On the eastside of Big Pidgeon River.
2200.	Robert Goodlo Harper	5,000	Joining Hendersons lines on Bull Run.
2201.	Edward Riggs	200	On the dry fork southside Holston.
2202.	William Coleman	150	On the northeast side of Big Pidgeon River.
2203.	William Colliar	130	On the northside of Nolachucky River.
2204.	Spencer Rice	347	On Clay Lick Creek the southside of Nolachuckee.
2205.	David Brown	200	On Cane Branch between Lick Creek and Clear Creek.
2206.	William Cocke	640	On Richland Creek.
2207.	John Stevenson & Henry Jones	500	On the eastside of Big Pidgeon River.
2208.	William Hoover	150	On the southside of Nolachuckee.
2209.	Gasor Dagy	200	On the southside French Broad River.
2210.	Joel Lewis & Benjamin Goodin	300	On Big Gap Creek.
2211.	Constantine Perkins	640	On the northside of Holston River.
2212.	Joseph Green	500	On a prong of Bull Run southside Clinch River.

No.	Name	Acres	Location
2213.	Joseph Green	400	On both sides of the north fork of Bull Run.
2214.	Nathan Athenson	1,000	On the headwaters of Bull Run that makes into Clinch.
2215.	Nathan Athenson	400	On the headwaters of Bull Run.
2216.	Needham Whitfield	500	Between Clinch Mountain and the Clinch River.
2217.	Needham Whitfield	400	On a prong of Bull Run.
2218.	Needham Whitfield	400	On both sides of the north fork of Bull Run.
2219.	John Gilliland	66	On the southside French Broad River.
2220.	James Baldridge	5,000	In the fork of Big Pidgeon and French Broad River.
2221.	Benjamin Athenson	314	On Clinch River below Clinch Mountain.
2222.	Elizabeth Green	400	On Flat Creek the westside of Clinch Mountain.
2223.	Elizabeth Green	400	On a prong of Bull Run.
2224.	William Whetfield	400	On both sides the north fork of Bull Run.
2225.	James Bunch	200	On the northside Holston River below Poor Valley Creek.
2226.	Benjamin Douglass	200	In the valley between Clinch Mountain and Cooper Ridge.
2227.	William Terrill Lewis	500	On Alexander Branch the waters of Nolachucky.
2228.	Matthias Wilhite	200	On Dumplin Creek.
2229.	Needham Whitfield	400	On the waters of Bull Run.
2230.	William Whitfield	400	On the west side Copper Ridge on a prong of Bull Run.
2231.	Nathan Atkinson	400	On the head of the North Fork of Bull Run waters of Clinch.
2232.	William T. Lewis	2,500	Joining Hendersons and Compy line.
2233.	William Shores	200	On Grassy Creek.
2234.	William Cocke	300	On the northside Holston River.
2235.	Nathan Athenson	300	On Flatt Creek between Clinch Mountain and Clinch River.
2236.	John Green Junr.	400	On the headwaters of Bull Run.
2237.	Joseph Green Junr.	400	On Flatt Creek between Clinch Mountain and Clinch River.
2238.	Henry Speer	200	On Bent Creek the waters of Nolachuckee.
2239.	Philip Hall	100	On the northside of Nolachuckee.

2240.	William Stevens	220	On a creek that makes into Clinch River.
2241.	William Whitfield	400	On both sides the North Fork of Bull Run.
2242.	John Green	400	On the west side of Clinch Mountain.
2243.	Joseph Green	500	On both sides the North Fork of Bull Run.
2244.	Joseph Green	1,000	On the east side of Flatt Creek below the end of Clinch Mountain.
2245.	James Green	400	On the heads of Bull Run that makes into Clinch.
2246.	Nathan Athenson	300	On Clinch River.
2247.	William Greene	500	On Flatt Creek the westside of Clinch Mountain.
2248.	Mark Mitchell	300	On the southside Holston River.
2249.	John Rice	300	On the northside of Clinch River.
2250.	Abraham Fulkerson	500	On the northside of French Broad River the waters of Dumplin Creek.
2251.	William Job	500	On the northside of French Broad River.
2252.	Furnifold Green	400	On the westside of Clinch Mountain.
2253.	Phillemon Green	200	On the northside Holston River.
2254.	William Green	400	On Flatt Creek on the westside of Clinch Mountain.
2255.	Nathan Athanson	300	On Flatt Creek on the westside of Clinch Mountain.
2256.	Nathan Athanson	400	On Flatt Creek on the westside of Clinch Mountain.
2257.	Samuel Reed	400	On Big Creek on the south side of Nolachuckee.
2258.	Jordan Rock	640	On Holston River including the Rock House on Cove Spring.
2259.	Philip Hatler	100	On the southside Nolachucky.
2260.	James Cameron	200	On the southside Nolachucky River.
2261.	Hugh Wier	200	On the northside Nolachucky River.
2262.	Christopher Ludspeak	122	On the southside of Chucky.
2263.	David Stuart & Compy	155	On the fork of Big Pidgeon and French Broad Rivers.
2264.	John Byrd	100	On the northside French Broad River.
2265.	John Keeneys	67	On the northside French Broad River.
2266.	Thomas Lee	120	On the head of Flatt Creek.

#	Name	Acres	Location
2267.	John Gilliland & David Stuart, John Ward & James Turnen	200	On the head of a branch the waters of French Broad River.
2268.	Augustin Brumley	200	On the northside of Nolachucky.
2269.	Richard Byrd	200	On the head spring of the shelving rock creek southside Holston.
2270.	David Stuart and Benjamin Taylor	640	On the southside Holston waters Hornbeaks Creek.
2271.	John McCoskey	100	On the northside of Nolachucky River.
2272.	George Vincent	100	On both sides of Cherokee Creek southside Holston.
2273.	(Skipped in book)		
2274.	Jason Isbell	100	On southside French Broad River above Big Pidgeon.
2275.	William Whitson	282	On the northeast side of Big Pidgeon.
2276.	John McCrosky	200	On the westside of Holley's Creek.
2277.	Jonathan Douglass	250	On the southside of Holston River.
2278.	Frederick Whittenbarger	300	On the northside Nolachucky.
2279.	William Cocke	300	On the northside Nolachucky.
2280.	John Cunningham	100	On the southside of Nolachucky.
2281.	Jesse Bean	2,000	On German Creek the first fork below said creek.
2282.	William Crowson	400	On the northeast side of Big Pidgeon River.
2283.	Henry Lutz	200	On the northside of Holston River.
2284.	John Gilliland	240	Between the War Ford of French Broad and Big Pidgeon.
2285.	Samuel Wilson	300	On the southside of Nolachucky.
2286.	Benjamin Goodin & Joel Lewis	600	On a draught of Lick Creek.
2287.	Low Todd	300	On the southside of Nolachucky.
2288.	William Cocke	200	On the southside of Richland Creek.
2289.	David Copton	300	On the northside of Nolachucky River.
2290.	Job Simms	574	On Lick Creek.
2291.	Godfrey Cariger	2,000	On Richland Creek.
2292.	Joseph Kyler	200	On the northeast side of Cove Creek southside Nolachuckee.
2293.	Henry Thompson	2,000	On the southside French Broad River.

2294.	John Gilliland	100	On the lower end of the first island below the war ford.
2295.	Thomas Chapman	200	On the northside of Holston.
2296.	Benjamin Goodin	600	On the watery fork of Bent Creek.
2297.	Samuel Wilson	150	On the southside of Nolachucky River and Cove Creek.
2298.	Garett Fitzgerald	400	On the northside of Holston.
2299.	Garett Fitzgerald	300	On Richland Creek.
2300.	John Gilliland	640	On French Broad River at the mouth of Big Pigeon.
2301.	George Daugherty	1,500	On the first Indian Path below Turkey Creek.
2302.	Martin Armstrong	1,000	On the northwest side of Clinch River below Clinch River.
2303.	Martin Armstrong & George Daugherty	1,000	On the first creek that empties into Holston.
2304.	Martin Armstrong & George Daugherty	800	On both sides Mountain Creek of Clinch River.
2305.	Martin Armstrong & George Daugherty	400	On the northwest side of Clinch River below Lick Creek.
2306.	Martin Armstrong & George Daugherty	1,000	On Mountain Creek of Lick Creek.
2307.	Martin Armstrong & George Daugherty	1,000	On Revells Creek of Clinch River.
2308.	Martin Armstrong & George Daugherty	900	At the southside of Tennessee.
2309.	Martin Armstrong & George Daugherty	300	On the southside of Clinch River.
2310.	Martin Armstrong & George Daugherty	1,000	On the southside of Clinch River including the mouth of Lick Branch.
2311.	Martin Armstrong & George Daugherty	1,000	On the first Creek that empties into Holston above the Tennessee.
2312.	Martin Armstrong & George Daugherty	320	On the first creek below the junction of Holston River.
2313.	Martin Armstrong & George Daugherty	500	On the southeast side Clinch River.
2314.	Martin Armstrong & George Daugherty	700	On a bald creek that empties into Clinch.
2315.	Martin Armstrong & George Daugherty	1,000	Near the Pilot Nobb on the North West side of Clinch River.
2316.	Martin Armstrong & George Daugherty	1,000	In the Beaver Dam Valley on Beaver Dam Creek.
2317.	Martin Armstrong & George Daugherty	1,000	On both sides the southwest fork of Lick Creek.
2318.	Martin Armstrong & George Daugherty	320	On the northeast side of Clinch River.

2319.	Martin Armstrong & George Daugherty	1,000	On the head branches of small Sinking Creek.
2320.	Martin Armstrong & George Daugherty	1,000	On both sides Beaver Dam Creek.
2321.	Martin Armstrong & George Daugherty.	1,000	On the northside of Holston.
2322.	Martin Armstrong & George Daugherty	800	On the first creek below the junction of Holston.
2323.	Martin Armstrong & George Daugherty	1,000	On the west fork of White's Creek.
2324.	Martin Armstrong & George Daugherty	1,200	Joining Daughertys 1,500 acre survey on Turkey Creek.
2325.	Martin Armstrong & George Daugherty	1,000	On a small creek that empties into Holston.
2326.	Martin Armstrong & George Daugherty	1,000	On Reeds Creek.
2327.	Martin Armstrong & George Daugherty	500	On the southeast side Clinch River on the Lick Branch.
2328.	Martin Armstrong & George Daugherty	1,000	On a large spring that runs across the Indian Path.
2329.	Martin Armstrong & George Daugherty	1,000	On a small creek that empties into Holston.
2330.	Martin Armstrong & George Daugherty	1,400	On a large spring that crosses the Indian Path.
2331.	Martin Armstrong & George Daugherty	1,000	Joining their former survey near the Pilate Nobb.
2332.	Thomas Hall	400	On the northside Holston River.
2333.	Thomas King	600	On the head of McCrays Creek.
2334.	Thomas King	1,200	On the northside of Holston River.

Greene County 1789

2335.	John McIntire	640	On the headwaters of Grassy Creek in Grassy Valley.
2336.	Samuel Gragg	100	On the North side of Meadow Creek.
2337.	James King	50	On Blairs Branch northside Holston.
2338.	Ephraim Dunlap	600	On the West Fork of White's Creek northside Tennessee.
2339.	Joseph Perrin	200	On the northside Holstein River.
2340.	James Bryan	200	On a branch of Copelin's Creek.
2341.	Francis Dean	50	On the northside French Broad River.
2342.	James McEnnis	200	On the westside of Sinking Creek.
2343.	John Hackett	250	On the fork of Tennese and Clinch Rivers.

2344.	Henry Rowan	550	On Tuckehoe Creek the waters of French Broad River.
2345.	Andrew Lewis	640	On French Broad River.
2346.	Josiah (Leath or Seath)	225	Joining his former survey of 640 acres.
2347.	Robert McFarland	200	On the southside Nolachuckee.
2348.	Michael Hatter	200	On the southside Nolachuckee.
2349.	John Douglass	250	On the waters of French Broad River.
2350.	Jonathan Langdon	200	On the waters of French Broad River.
2351.	Ananias McCoy	300	On the northside Clinch River.
2352.	George Daugherty	20	On an island in French Broad River.
2353.	Robert Young	120	On the northside of Holston.
2354.	John Long	640	On the northside of Holston.
2355.	James Paul	250	On the west bank of Little River.
2356.	James Casey	300	On the northside of Lick Creek.
2357.	Isaac Bullard	100	On the northside of Lick Creek.
2358.	Joseph Bullard	200	On southside Holston.
2359.	Joseph Bullard	200	On southside Holston.
2360.	Joseph Bullard	400	On southside Holston.
2361.	James Stinson	150	On the fork of Lick Creek.
2362.	Abner Chapman	400	On the waters of Clinch.
2363.	William Eliot	100	Joining McKeer's lines.
2364.	Stephen Cobb	200	On Nolachuckee River.
2365.	Thomas Blackburn	200	On Camp Creek the waters of Nolachuckee.
2366.	Daniel Perkins	140	On Mossy Creek joining Johnston lines.
2367.	William Largan	150	On the southside of Nolachuckee.
2368.	Benon Perryman	200	On the northside Holston River.
2369.	Joseph Brown	100	On French Broad River.
2370.	Joseph Brown	200	On Punchin Camp Creek waters of Nolachucky.

Greene County 1790

2371.	Daniel Rice	200	On Big Creek southside Nolachuckee.
2372.	Garrett Fitzgerald	640	On the waters of French Broad River.

2373.	Garrett Fitzgerald	300	On the waters of French Broad River.
2374.	John Gilbreath	100	On Sinking Creek.
2375.	James McDonald	100	On the west fork of Richland Creek.
2376.	James Robinson	200	On Robinsons Creek the southside of Holston.
2377.	Robert Qunan?	370	On the northside of Clinch River.
2378.	David Rankin	100	On the head of Sinking Creek.
2379.	John Singleton	300	On the southside of Clinch River.
2380.	Joseph Conway	200	On Clay Lick Creek southside of Nolachuckee.
2381.	Isaac Davis	100	On the double Lick Fork of Lick Creek.
2382.	Alexander Moore	200	On Cedar Creek.
2383.	Abraham McLeary	100	On the northside French Broad River.
2384.	John Ramsay	100	On the northside Nolachuckee.
2385.	Robert Clark	200	In the fork of French Broad and Big Pidgeon Rivers.
2386.	John Shield	200	On the southside of Nolachucky.
2387.	Zophar Johnston	100	Joining William Hannahs lines.
2388.	Christopher Myers	100	On both sides of Long Creek.
2389.	Joseph McMurtree	100	Joining Carters Valley.
2390.	Lewis Christian	250	On the Lick Fork of Bent Creek.
2391.	John Ring	1,011	On the waters of Duck River.
2392.	William Branch	5,000	On the waters of Duck River.
2393.	Samuel McCamey	375	On the watery fork of Cany Branch.
2394.	John Branch	5,000	On the waters of Duck River near Nashville and Chicomogo Tram?
2395.	James Blair	200	On the waters and westside of Poor Valley Creek.
2396.	John Gibson	200	On the headwaters of the west fork of Holley Creek.
2397.	John Jones	960	On a creek of the westfork of Stones River.
2398.	William Jones	1,000	On a creek of the westfork of Stones River.
2399.	Robert Lamb	640	In Beech bottoms the North side of French Broad River.
2400.	James Hutcheson	100	On the southside Nolachucky.
2401.	John Coleman	1,000	On a creek of the west fork of Stones River.

2402.	Isaiah Vinsent (Van sandt)	350	Joining Hutchison's lines on the top of a long ridge.
2403.	Phillip Hale	100	Including an island on the southside of Nolachuckee.
2404.	Joseph Brown & Harry Rowan	250	On Grassy Creek joining Hugh Browns lines.
2405.	George McNutt	50	On the southside Holston.
2406.	Peter Huff	300	On the northside French Broad River opposite Big Pidgen.
2407.	William Hannah	99	On the waters of McCartney Creek.
2408.	Alexander Wilson	100	On Franck's Creek.
2409.	Hugh Nelson	66	On the northside Nolachucky.
2410.	Benjamin Allen	100	On Athen's Creek the northside French Broad River.
2411.	James Paul	640	On the northside of Holston River.
2412.	Hugh Kirkpatrick	100	On Bowman's Branch a fork of Bent Creek.
2413.	Robert Biggs	200	Between the Cedar Branch and Sinking Fork of Long Creek.
2414.	Enos Johnston	200	On the east branch of Buffalo Creek northside of Holston.
2415.	William Conway	25	On the northside Nolachucky joining his own lines.
2416.	James Allison	200	On Dumplin Creek.
2417.	Solomon Cox	250	On the southside of Holston River the waters of Long Creek.
2418.	John Ward	400	On the southside of French Broad River.
2419.	Henry Grigg	400	On the head Clear Creek northside French Broad River.
2420.	Tilghman Smith	164	Joining Peter Kings lines.
2421.	Joseph Conway	70	On the southside Nolachucky River.
2422.	David Johnston	44	On the fork of Long Creek between French Broad River and Chucky.
2423.	Thomas Johnston	640	On Bent Creek including the big lick.
2424.	Sebert Sellers	200	On the head waters of Meadow Creek.
2425.	Alexander Wilson?	100	On Holley's Creek.
2426.	William Campbell	150	On the east fork of Spring Creek.
2427.	William Tate	100	On the north side French Broad River.
2428.	Robert Kirkpatrick	300	On Plumb Creek including the War Path.

2429.	John Gillaspie	50	On McCartney's Branch joining Isaac Bullard.
2430.	James Daniel	700	On the southside of Holston River.
2431.	Daniel Robertson	100	On the waters of Big Creek northside of Holston River.
2432.	Hugh Kelsey	100	On the northside French Broad River.
2433.	Amos Balch	200	On the northside French Broad River joining Kerrs lines.
2434.	Isaac Wright & James Pierce	200	On Cove Creek northside of Nolachuckee River (but it is southside – G.F.B.)
2435.	Isaac Vanzant	585	On Cove Creek northside of Nolachuckee River.
2436.	Robert Boyd & William Logan	600	On the northside of Nolachuckee.
2437.	John Reeives	80	On the head of a branch of Little Chucky.
2438.	Parmenas Taylor	65	On the northside French Broad River.
2439.	William Hutchison	155	On the waters of Cove Creek southside of Nolachuckee.
2440.	John Wilson	100	Joining Samuel Wilsons lines.
2441.	Thomas Love	80	On the southside Chucky River.
2442.	James McNare	200	On the southside Holston opposite the mouth of German Creek.

Greene County 1791

2443.	Joseph Lovelelly	100	On the sinking fork of Oven Creek southside Nolachucky.
2444.	Isaac Taylor	200	On the northside French Broad River.
2445.	Andrew Evans	37	Including an island on French Broad River.
2446.	Joseph White	953	At the Buffalo Ford on Lick Creek.
2447.	Joseph Copeland	640	On the southside French Broad River.
2448.	Francis Green	200	On the waters of Bent Creek.
2449.	David Johnstone	300	On the northside French Broad River.
2450.	John Patterson	300	On the southside of Holstein River.
2451.	James Callison	600	On the southside of Holstein River.
2452.	Evan Evans	200	On the northside Nolachucky.

2453.	John Bennett	300	On a branch of Richland Creek.
2454.	Lawrence Glaze	250	On the southside of Nolachucky.
2455.	William Hambleton	229	On the northside of Holstein River.
2456.	David Johnston	200	On the northside French Broad River.
2457.	William Walker	100	On the waters of Lyons Creek.
2458.	George Hopkins	200	On the Sinking Cave northside French Broad.
2459.	Richard Morgan	100	On the waters of Dumplin Creek northside French Broad.
2460.	Evan Evans	40	On the northside of Chucky River.
2461.	William Boylston	200	On Sinking Cane Creek north side French Broad River.
2462.	James Pierce	150	Joining Moses Moore's lines.
2463.	William Murphy	150	On an island northside French Broad River.
2464.	James Johnson	150	On the southside Nolachucky River.
2465.	Charles Gentry	400	On the northside French Broad River.
2466.	John Hornbeck	200	On a valley between Hornsback Creek and Lost Creek.
2467.	Thomas Ranken	150	On Dumplin Creek.
2468.	Lawrence Glaze	247	On the southside Chucky River.
2469.	James Cox	173	On the southside of Nolachucky.
2470.	Henry Seatten (Peatten?)	300	On the bank of Clear Creek between Mill Shoal and ___?___ Creek.
2471.	Jesse Dodson	300	On the northside of Holstein River.
2472.	William Davidson	305	On the mouth of a creek at the lower end of the Painter Bottoms.
2473.	Francis Rowan	100	On Clay Creek.
2474.	John Bradshaw	475	On the waters of Dumplin Creek.
2475.	John Rees	200	On Pigeon Creek.
2476.	John Hackett	150	On the north side French Broad River.
2477.	Daniel Reed	250	On Pidgeon Creek northside of Chucky River.
2478.	John Duncan	300	In the fork between Holston and French Broad Rivers.
2479.	Joseph Nation	113	On Little Chucky Creek at the head of the Blue Spring.

2480.	Samuel Lewis	100	On the head of McCartneys Branch.
2481.	John Johnston	120	On the head of Collins Creek.
2482.	John Bearde	400	Joining Stokeley Donelsons lines.
2483.	Joseph Bird	300	On the southside of Nolachucky including the mouth Oven? Creek.
2484.	Hugh Beard	300	On the waters of Emerys River joining Blounts S? line.
2485.	Thomas Pearce	640	On the west bank of Little River.
2486.	Sparling Bowman	300	On the southside of Nolachucky River.
2487.	John Mires	200	On the waters of Nolachucky.
2488.	Robert Kerr	200	Joining his old survey.
2489.	Benjamin Rector	200	On the west side of Lick Creek.
2490.	John Fulkerson	100	On Sinking Spring waters of Painters Creek.
2491.	Daniel Britton	200	On a branch of Lick Creek.
2492.	John Gwinn	100	On the southside of Dumplin Creek.
2493.	Benjamin Lucas	640	On the waters of Holston at the mouth of French Broad.
2494.	Thomas Wilkinson	100	On the waters of Nolachucky.
2495.	Samuel Humber	50	On the waters of Lick Creek.
2496.	Jonathan Langdon	100	On the waters of French Broad River.
2497.	David Jonston	100	On the southside of Chucky River.
2498.	Jasper Miller	200	Joining Lanty Armstrong lines.
2499.	Andrew Fox	300	On the southside Chucky.
2500.	Joseph Rainey	100	On Dumplin Creek.
2501.	Edward Osburn	200	On the northside French Broad River.
2502.	Robert Hammill	200	On the waters of Little Chucky River.
2503.	Hugh Brown Junr.	200	On the waters of Lick Creek.
2504.	David Lyles	320	Joining Charles Gentereys lines.
2505.	Joseph Scates	640	On Bent Creek.
2506.	Richard Rankin	300	Joining John Bradshaws lines.
2507.	Christopher Ellis	100	On the southside of a large Nobb.
2508.	James Seeton	200	On the northside French Broad.
2509.	David Walker	200	On the northside of Lick Creek.

2510.	Abraham McCleary	300	On the northside French Broad River.
2511.	not shown		
2512.	Franklen Bownon?	200	On the northside French Broad River.
2513.	Laurence Glaze	150	On the southside Nolachucky.
2514.	William Bryan	200	On a fork of Little Chucky.
2515.	William Nelson	200	On Sinking Creek north side of Chucky River.
2516.	John Jones	200	On the east side of Lick Creek.
2517.	Joseph Taylor	200	Joining Daniel Reeds lines.
2518.	William Ewing	300	On the northside of Holston River.
2519.	John Fien	200	On the northside of French Broad.
2520.	John Brumley	40	On the south side of Nolachucky.
2521.	Alexander McMullin	200	On the east fork of Swann Pond Creek.
2522.	Kezia Bowen	100	On the west side of Lick Creek.
2523.	Joseph Pryor	200	On Cove Creek.
2524.	Henry Cross	100	On the Long Fork of Lick Creek.
2525.	George Brock	200	In the fork of Holston and French Broad rivers.
2526.	Benjamin Carter	100	On the Roaring Fork of Lick Creek.
2527.	John Hackett	300	On the southside of Clinch River.
2528.	John Coulter	300	On the north bank of Holston.
2529.	John Gillaspie	177	On McCartneys Creek.
2530.	James Cox	35	Above the mouth of Flatt Creek.
2531.	William Goforth	100	Joining his own lines.
2532.	Thomas Morgan	50	On the southside of Nolachuckee.
2533.	John Loyd	150	On the waters of Nolachucky.
2534.	James Montgomery	220	On the north side French Broad River.
2535.	Augustine Brumley	100	On the northside of Chucky.
2536.	Nehemiah Pettit	35	On the waters of Lick Creek.
2537.	Andrew Martin	100	On the head of the Second Creek.
2538.	James Hubbart	300	On the northside of French Broad River.
2539.	James Peirce	300	On the northside of Nolachucky.
2540.	James Hubbart	200	On Dumplin Creek.
2541.	Landon Carter	640	On Bords Creek.

2542.	Abraham Haworth	500	On Nolichucky River.
2543.	James Blair	300	On the Big Meadows.
2544.	John Woods	150	On Little Nolachucky River.

Hawkins County 1788

2545.	James McCarty	300	On the southside of Holston River.
2546.	Stephen Richards	158	On the southside Big Creek.
2547.	Stephen Richards	315	On the north side Clinch Mountain.
2548.	John Rhea	193	On the northside of Holston northside Richland Creek.
2549.	Stokeley Donelson	2,300	On the northside of Tennessee on the long reach.
2550.	Stokeley Donelson	500	On the northside of Holston.
2551.	Stokeley Donelson	5,000	Opposite the mouth of Highwassie on the northside of Tenessee.
2552.	Stokeley Donelson & Martin Armstrong	500	On the northside of Tennessee below the mouth of Clinch.
2553.	Stokeley Donelson & Martin Armstrong	640	On the northside Tennessee at the mouth of Deep River.
2554.	Joshua Gist	50	On the southside Clinch river.
2555.	Moses Ballinger	300	On the northside Holston river.
2556.	Thomas & Robert King	1,000	On Brimstone Creek.
2557.	Thomas & Robert King	1,280	On Wolf River near the Great Salt lick.
2558.	Thomas & Robert King	?	On the Meadow Fork of Big Creek.
2559.	Thomas & Robert King	?	On the Meadow Fork of Big Creek.
2560.	Thomas Ingles	400	On the south side Holston River.
2561.	John Arnwine	640	In Cumberland Valley on the Cainy Fork of Lick Creek.
2562.	Isaac Taylor	200	On the south bank of Holston on the top of a bluff of rocks.
2563.	Robert King & Thomas King	600	Joining Alexander Blair's lines on Brimstone Creek.
2564.	Robert King & Thomas King	1,280	On Wolf River.
2565.	James Cresswell	1,000	On both sides West Fork of Turkey Creek.
2566.	William Parker	580	On the northside of Clinch River.

2567.	Landon Carter	640	On the North Fork of Deep River northside of Tennessee.
2568.	James Glasgow	5,000	On the northside Clinch including the north of Emerys river.
2569.	Samuel Wilson	513	On the hecory Cove on a branch of big creek.
2570.	Hawson Keener	254	On the southside of Holston river.
2571.	Cornelius Carmack	295	In Carters Valley on the Northside big Creek.
2572.	David Ross	100	On the southside Holston river.
2573.	Cornelius Cormack	400	In Carters Valley Northside Big Creek.
2574.	Landon Carter	640	On Gap Creek Valley southside Clinch river.
2575.	Landon Carter	640	On Gap Creek southside Clinch.
2576.	Joshua Guest	200	On the north side Clinch River.
2577.	Thomas Gibbons	300	In Carter's Valley on both sides of Big Creek.
2578.	George Ridley	200	On the head of Russells Creek.
2579.	William Terrill Lewis	400	On the northside Clinch.
2580.	William Terrill Lewis	500	On a creek that runs into Clinch above the mouth of Emerys River.

Hawkins County 1789

2581.	John Groves Senr.	400	On the side of Big Creek in Carters Valley.
2582.	Robert Coile	199	On the head branch of Cany Fork.
2583.	James Brigham	340	On the north side of Clinch River.
2584.	Cornelius Carmack	290	On both sides Big Creek northside of Holston.
2585.	Thomas Jackson	200	On the southside of Holston.
2586.	John Carmack	156	On the northside of Holston River.
2587.	Stokeley Donelson	75	On the northside of Holston River.
2588.	Stokeley Donelson	300	On the southside Clinch River.
2589.	William Terrill Lewis	400	On the north side Clinch River.
2590.	Thomas Gibbons	300	In Carters Valley on the eastside a big creek.
2591.	Thomas McLaughlin	400	On Sinking Creek northside of Holston.
2592.	John McMin	250	On the north side Holston River.
2593.	William Terrill Lewis	500	On the southside of Clinch River.

2594.	James Randols	200	On the northside Holston on the waters of Flatt Creek.
2595.	William Terrill Lewis	500	On the southside Clinch River.
2596.	John McBroom	100	In Carters Valley joining Thomas Gibbons lines.
2597.	James Hayland	131	On the northside of Holston.
2598.	Samuel Wilson	640	On Poor Valley Creek.
2599.	Arthur Galbreath	271	In Carters Valley northside Holston.

Hawkins County 1790

2600.	Stokeley Donelson	400	On the northside of Holston River.
2601.	Stokeley Donelson	250	On the southside of Holston River.
2602.	Jarrot Winningham	100	On both sides the west fork of Flatt Creek.
2603.	covered		At the mouth of Creek southside of Holston.
2604.	William Roseberry	500	On both sides Roseberry Creek northside of Holston.
2605.	William Robinson	500	On the waters of Flatt Creek.
2606.	John Reddick	150	On the southside Holston River.
2607.	Bartholomew Donahoe	100	On Merrish? Creek southside Holston.
2608.	James Hyland	344	On the southside Holston River.
2609.	William Roseberry	400	On both sides Caney Creek northside of Holstein.
2610.	John Groves	400	On the northside of Holstein River.
2611.	William Anderson	400	In Caney Creek waters of Clinch River.
2612.	William Lea	300	On the northside Holston River.
2613.	John Criner	200	On Poor Valley the northside of Holston.
2614.	Thomas Caldwell	200	On Buck Creek southside Holston.
2615.	John Criner	200	On both sides Poor Valley northside of Holston.
2616.	John Criner	400	On both sides Poor Valley northside of Holston.
2617.	John Hunt	100	On the eastside Rentfroe Creek northside of Holston.
2618.	Jacob Bayley	348	On the southside Holston on the waters of Mossy Creek.
2619.	Joseph Bullard	150	On Buffaloe Creek southside Holston River.

2620.	Joseph Bullard	100	On the southside of Holston River on the head of Loss Creek.
2621.	Gideon Morris	200	On the northside Holston River.
2622.	Robert Demott	400	On the head of Woods Creek waters of Holston.
2623.	Matthew Wellaba	640	On the head of Panther Creek southside Holston.
2624.	Hugh Johnston	200	On the waters of Holston joining Jesse Riggs.
2625.	Matthew Willaba	200	In Powell's Valley.
2626.	Matthew Willaba	640	On Powell's Valley on the waters of Lick Creek.
2627.	James Moore	100	On the upper fork of Possum Creek in Cane Valley.
2628.	James Glasgow	1,000	On the westside of Emery River.
2629.	William Campbell	400	On the east fork of Spring Creek.
2630.	Alexander Laughlin	300	On the northside of Holston on Cumberland Camp.
2631.	David Hamblen	100	On the northside of Holston.
2632.	James Caldwell	63	In Carters Valley.
2633.	John Bunn	200	On the southside of Holston River.
2634.	Welcome Hodges	500	On the southside of Holston River on Hodges Creek.
2635.	Ralph Shelton	200	On the southside of Holston River at a big bluff.
2636.	Joseph Ake?	188	On Richland Creek northside of Holston.
2637.	Michael Morrison	200	On the northside Holston River.
2638.	John Cotter	200	Including the Lick Spring.
2639.	Joseph McCullak	399	On Bull Run southside Clinch.
2640.	Jacob Kennedy	400	On Honeycutt's Creek southside Holston.
2641.	John Rice	100	On the northside of Holston River.
2642.	John Looney	200	On both sides Sinking Creek north side of Holston.
2643.	Alexander Blair	150	Joining William Smith lines.
2644.	Robert Kyles	200	On Cany Creek.
2645.	David Haley	150	On Richland Creek northside of Holston.
2646.	James Patterson	100	On both sides Roseberry Creek northside of Holston.
2647.	William Armstrong	50	On the head of the west fork of Rentfroes Creek.

2648.	Robert Coyles	111	On Coales Ridge.
2649.	Stokeley Donelson	3,000	On the northside of Clinch River.
2650.	William Daniel	150	On the southside of Holston on Ganies? Creek.
2651.	John Rice	640	On the southside of Clinch River.
2652.	Isaac Taylor & Robert Young	640	On the northside of Tenessee River.
2653.	Robert Coyles	100	On Cany Creek.
2654.	William Smith	200	In the Piney Valley.
2655.	Robert Coile	100	On the northside of Holston River.
2656.	Elisha Walling	200	On Fowlers Fork of Bush Creek.
2657.	William Armstrong	100	Joining his own survey on the Rentfroe Creek.
2658.	Stephen Richards	400	On McMurry's Creek northside Clinch Mountain.
2659.	Alexander Montgomery	300	On the southside of Holston River.
2660.	Elizabeth Young	400	On the northside Clinch River.
2661.	Henry Marshall	450	On the northside of Holston.
2662.	John Rice	300	In Standley Valley.
2663.	Alexander Smith	100	On the southside of Holston.
2664.	Robert Coyle	400	In Cany Creek.
2665.	Thomas Lain	1100	In Gravilly Valley on Rentfroe Creek.
2666.	John Rice	640	On the southside Clinch River.
2667.	John Adair	200	On Whites Creek.
2668.	Stokeley Donelson	640	On the northside of Holston river.
2669.	John Skitmore	178	On the northside of Holston river.
2670.	John Richards	100	On the northside of Holston river.
2671.	Belford Wood	250	On both sides Bigg Creek southside Holston.
2672.	Thomas Brooks	400	On Clouds Creek joining Coils lines.
2673.	Devirres Gilliham	640	On the southside of Holston River.
2674.	John Hornback	200	In a valley between Hornback's Creek and Lost Creek.

Hawkins County 1791

2675.	William Hird	300	On the head of War Creek and fish creek.
2676.	Thomas & Robert King	300	On the northside Holston River.

2677.	John Evans	400	On or near the head of Panther Creek.
2678.	Richard Mitchell	640	On German Creek.
2679.	John Long	225	On the northside of Holston River.
2680.	Robert Bean	640	On German Creek.
2681.	Robert King	300	On the northside of Holston.
2682.	Frances Mabry	607	On the northside of Holston.
2683.	Wallis Balley	200	Joining John Long's survey.
2684.	Francis Maberry & Thomas Jackson	250	On the east fork of Dotsons Creek.
2685.	Matthew McKee	200	On the southside of Holston River.
2686.	William Horde	300	In Powell's Valley below Cumberland Gap.
2687.	Robert King	500	On the southside of Holston River.
2688.	Elijah Danthen	640	On Youngs Creek.
2689.	William Ward	200	On both sides Powells Valley.
2690.	Burwell Scott	150	Joining his own lines on a former survey.
2691.	John Ebenezer	300	On Loss Creek.
2692.	John Evans	640	Opposite the head of Panther Creek.
2693.	John Crawford	150	On the head branches of Beaver Creek.
2694.	David Sutherland	150	On the southside of Holston River.
2695.	Samuel Smith	50	On an island in Holston River.
2696.	Peter Turney	200	On the northside of Holston.
2697.	Robert King	600	On the Sinking Spring joining the Virginia line.
2698.	John Mulsbey	300	On the southside Holston River.
2699.	David Davies	200	On the northside Holston River.
2700.	James King	300	On the head of Richland Creek.
2701.	Stokeley Donelson	400	On the southside Clinch River in Hernsey's Valley.

Eastern District 1788

2702.	Stokeley Donelson	400	On the northeast side Bluff Creek.
2703.	Stokeley Donelson	3,000	On Bluff Creek on Clinch River.
2704.	Stokeley Donelson	1,000	On the north side Tenessee above the mouth of Clinch.
2705.	Stokeley Donelson	640	On both sides Clinch River.
2706.	Stokeley Donelson	640	On the waters of Bull Run.
2707.	Stokeley Donelson	500	On Bears Dam Creek and Grassy Fork.
2708.	Stokeley Donelson	1,000	On Bluff Creek.
2709.	Stokeley Donelson & Thomas Hutchins	500	On the northeast side of Clinch River.
2710.	Stokeley Donelson & Thomas Hutchins	2,000	On Bluff Creek of Clinch River.
2711.	Stokeley Donelson & Thomas Hutchins	640	On the waters of Bluff Creek.
2712.	Stokeley Donelson & Thomas Hutchins	1,000	On the east fork of Bluff Creek.
2713.	Stokeley Donelson & Thomas Hutchins	1,200	On the east fork of Bluff Creek.
2714.	Stokeley Donelson	640	On the north side of Clinch in Bald Valley.
2715.	Stokeley Donelson	640	On White's Creek on Holston River.
2716.	Thomas Hutchings	640	On McCray's Creek of Holston River.
2717.	Thomas Hutchings	400	On Beaver Dam Creek.
2718.	Thomas Hutchings	640	On McCray's Creek on Holston River.
2719.	Thomas Hutchings	640	On Beaver Dam.
2720.	Thomas Hutchings	640	On Sinking Creek, James Whites survey adjoining.
2721.	Thomas Hutchings	500	On Beaver Dam Creek.
2722.	Thomas Hutchings	640	On the waters of Sinking Creek.
2723.	Thomas Hutchings	300	On Beaver Dam.
2724.	Thomas Cox & William Hankins	500	On the northside Clinch River in Bald Valley.
2725.	Moses Poor	300	On Beaver Dam Creek including the Cedar Spring.
2726.	Seth Johnston	100	On Beaver Dam Creek joining Poors survey.
2727.	John Adair	300	On the northside Beaver Dam Creek.
2728.	John Adair	640	On the head of White's Creek.

2729.	John Adair	400	On Bull Run of Clinch River.
2730.	John Adair	300	On the southside of Beaver Dam Creek.
2731.	Frances Maberry	640	On the southside of Beaver Dam Creek.
2732.	Spruce McCoy	5,000	On Beaver Dam Creek joining Hendersons and Camp P Grant?
2733.	Joseph Hinds	400	On Bull Run.
2734.	Joseph Hinds	500	On Bull Run.
2735.	Levy Hinds	200	On the waters of Beaver Dam Creek.
2736.	Jesse Harper	1,250	On the head of Bull Run and Beaver Dam Creek.
2737.	John Rhea	1,000	On a large creek of Clinch River.
2738.	Augustey Wilson	640	On Bull Run of Clinch River.
2739.	Ebenezer Byrum	400	On Beaver Dam Creek including a large spring.
2740.	William Gaily	300	On the waters of Beaver Dam Creek.
2741.	Ebenezer Byrum	400	On the waters of Beaver Dam Creek.
2742.	Ebenezer Byrum	400	On the waters of Beaver Dam Creek.
2743.	David Campbell	500	On Turkey Creek.
2744.	Alexander Caswell	400	On Beaver Dam Creek.
2745.	Martin Armstrong	300	On Plumb Meadow fork of Beaver Dam Creek.
2746.	Martin Armstrong & Stokeley Donelson	1,000	Joining John Donelsons lines near the Indian Camp.
2747.	David Kincaid	200	On the southside of Clinch River.
2748.	Martin Armstrong & Stokeley Donelson	1,000	On the northside of Holston river.
2749.	Martin Armstrong & Stokeley Donelson	640	On the southside of Clinch river.
2750.	Martin Armstrong & Stokeley Donelson	400	On the southside of Clinch river.
2751.	Martin Armstrong & Stokeley Donelson	2,000	On the Northside of Tennessee river.
2752.	Martin Armstrong & Stokeley Donelson	200	On the Northside of Clinch River.
2753.	Martin Armstrong	400	On Beaver Dam Creek.
2754.	Martin Armstrong & Stokeley Donelson	400	On Beaver Dam Creek.
2755.	Martin Armstrong & Stokeley Donelson	600	On the Northside of Tennessee.

2756.	Martin Armstrong & Stokeley Donelson	100	On the Northside of Tenessee.
2757.	Martin Armstrong & Stokeley Donelson	640	On Camp Creek.
2758.	Martin Armstrong & Stokeley Donelson	640	On the meadow fork of Big Creek.
2759.	Martin Armstrong & Stokeley Donelson	600	In Bald Valley.
2760.	Martin Armstrong & Stokeley Donelson	600	On Beaver Dam Creek.
2761.	Martin Armstrong & Stokeley Donelson	640	On Beaver Dam Creek.
2762.	Martin Armstrong & Stokeley Donelson	640	On the Northside Clinch river.
2763.	Martin Armstrong & Stokeley Donelson	1,000	On the first large creek northside Holston.

Eastern District 1789

2764.	Martin Armstrong & Stokeley Donelson	1,000	On the northside Tennessee River.
2765.	Martin Armstrong & Stokeley Donelson	200	On the Beaver Dam Creek.
2766.	Stokeley Donelson	5,000	On the northside Clinch River.
2767.	Thomas Amess	100	On the southside of Holston.
2768.	Thomas Amess	100	On the northside of Holston.
2769.	Nathaniel Lyon	100	Joining Bradley's lines on Holston River.
2770.	John Barritt	150	On the southside Holston River.
2771.	Thomas Caldwell	400	On Sinking Branch southside Clinch River.

Eastern District 1790

2772.	Gideon Morris	200	On the northside Holston River.
2773.	Robert Demott	400	On the head of Woodses Creek waters of Holston.
2774.	Matthew Willaba	640	On the head of Panther Creek waters of Holston.
2775.	Hugh Jonston	400	On the southside Clinch River.
2776.	Joseph Rogers	200	On Dry Creek southside Holston.
2777.	David Shultes	50	On the waters of Honeycutts Creek.
2778.	Joseph McCulloch	150	On the southside of Clinch.
2779.	John Ireland	50	On the north side of Holston.
2780.	Simon Fletcher	100	On the southside of Holston.

2781.	James Manesco	300	On the waters of Dry Creek southside Holston.
2782.	James Manesco	300	On the southside Holston River on the White Horse fork.
2783.	Stokeley Donelson	640	On Poplar Creek.
2784.	Stokeley Donelson	640	On Poplar Creek.
2785.	John Crawford	500	On the waters of White's Creek.
2786.	John Crawford	300	On the waters of White's Creek.
2787.	Mark Chambers	140	On Forrells Creek southside Holston.
2788.	Moses Justice	250	On the waters of Big Creek.
2789.	John Parton	200	On the southside of Holston River.
2790.	William Roseberry	150	On the northside Holston.
2791.	Mark Chambers	150	On the northside Holston.
2792.	Mark Chambers	150	On Ferrell Creek.
2793.	Thomas Caldwell	200	On the headwaters of Shelbys Creek.
2794.	George Mooney	199	On the southside Holstein River.
2795.	Charles Payne	200	On the southside Holstein River.
2796.	Francis Maberry	150	On the northside Holston River.
2797.	Andrew Crockett	280	On the southside Clinch River.
2798.	James Dixon	125	On the northside Holstein River.
2799.	Thomas Jackson	400	On the southside Clinch River.
2800.	Thomas Caldwell	200	On the northside Holstein River.
2801.	Joseph McCullok	492	On the northside of Clinch River.
2802.	John Adair	640	On both sides of White's Creek.
2803.	William Barnett	188	On the southside Clinch River.
2804.	James Teenan	620	On the southside Clinch River.
2805.	Adam Peek	1,000	On the southside Holstein River.
2806.	Elijah Patten	1,000	On Nobb Creek northside Duck River.
2807.			

2

Eastern District 1791

2808.	David Adair	250	On the waters of Whites Creek.
2809.	James Lea	500	On the northside Holstein River.
2810.	David Walker	200	On the northside Holstein River on the East Fork of Third Creek.
2811.	David Walker	250	On the northside Holstein River on the East Fork of Third Creek.

2812.	Henry Payne	150	On the head of McCarey's Creek northside of French Broad River.
2813.	Mary Ann Elizabeth Armstrong	2,000	On the northside of Tennessee River.

Middle District 1788

2814.	James Brown	3,980	On Lyles Creek southside Duck River.
2815.	William Gilbreath	1,000	On the eastside Sugar Creek southside Duck River.
2816.	Griffith Rutherford	5,000	On the southside Duck River below Tom Bigby's Creek.
2817.	John Hardin	1,000	On the east side Tennessee River on Swift Creek.
2818.	Ezekiel Polk	2,000	On the North Branch of Elk River.
2819.	Thomas Polk	5,000	On the headwaters of Harpeth River.
2820.	Thomas & Robert King	1,000	On a branch of Wolf River.
2821.	John Sevier	1,000	On both sides Buffalo River.
2822.	Anthony Sharpe & Thomas Dugan	1,000	On the southside of Duck River west of Sugar Creek.
2823.	Samuel Patten Junr.	520	On Duck River above the mouth of Sugar Creek.
2824.	John Sumner	1,470	On the east waters of Richland Creek of Duck River.
2825.	Demsey Powell	1,977	On Duck River.
2826.	Thomas Tolbott	2,000	On Duck River.
2827.	Hardy Murfro	5,000	On the headwaters of Harpath River.
2828.	marked out on fold.		
2829.	George Martin, Richard Martin & Associates	3,234	On Duck River southside of __?__ Sugar Creek.
2830.	John Sevier	2,115	On Duck River on both forks of Rich Creek.
2831.	Alexander Robertson	2,000	On Duck River five miles above the forks of Rich Creek.
2832.	James Bradshaw, Charles McConnon & Amos Balch	5,000	On the southside Duck River on both sides Sugar Creek.
2833.	Elijah Robertson	5,000	On Richland Creek of Elk River.
2834.	Robert McCarmick	2,000	On the southside Duck River eastside Sugar Creek.

2835.	William Rainey	4,000	On Richland Creek the waters of Elk River.
2836.	Amos Balch	1,000	On the northside Duck River.
2837.	Hezekiah Balch	1,000	On the eastside Tenessee River on Swift Creek.
2838.	Joseph Kerr	1,850	On the northside Duck River on both forks of Spring Creek.
2839.	James Polk	5,000	On the northside Duck River.
2840.	Thomas Polk	5,000	On the southside of Duck River.
2841.	Thomas Temple Armstrong	2,000	On the waters of Elk River on Lime Creek.
2842.	Joseph Dickson	5,000	On both sides of the North Fork of Duck River.
2843.	William Hardin	1,700	On the northside of Duck River.
2844.	James Wall	1,000	On the southside of Duck River on Cedar Creek.
2845.	Martin Armstrong	3,000	On the southside of Duck River near the head of Sinking Creek.
2846.	Thomas & Samuel Thompson & John Cootes	4,260	On the northside of Duck River on both sides Mill Creek.
2847.	Matthew Lock	5,000	On both sides of the North fork of Duck River.
2848.	David Vance	1,000	On the head of the Eastern branch of Stones River.
2849.	Richard Locke	2,000	South of Lytles Big Spring.
2850.	Michael Robertson	1,500	On the northside of Duck River.
2851.	Martin Phifer	2,373	On the northside of Duck River above Falling Creek.
2852.	Thomas Polk	5,000	On the waters of Elk River and the Richland Creek.
2853.	Samuel Pattens Junr.	1,000	On the southside of Duck River.
2854.	Thomas & Alexander Greers	5,000	On the southside of Duck River.
2855.	John Marr	1,000	On the waters of Elk River.
2856.	Ebenezer Alexander	3,000	On a branch of the North Fork of Duck River.
2857.	James Robertson	3,000	On Weakley's Creek waters of Richland Creek.
2858.	Thomas Polk	5,000	On Elk River waters of Richland Creek.
2859.	Wikoff & Clarke	250	On Elk River waters of Richland Creek.
2860.	William Sherrin	750	On both sides Duck River.
2861.	Thomas Polk	5,000	On Elk River of Richland Creek.

2862.	Thomas Polk	3,000	On the North Branch of Richland Creek.
2863.	Thomas Sharpe	250	On Weakley's Creek waters of Elk River.
2864.	Stokeley Donelson	2,300	On the northside of the Tennessee.
2865.	John Nelson	5,000	On the headwaters of Robertsons and Richland Creek.
2866.	George Daugherty	5,000	On the Richland the waters of Elk River.
2867.	Thomas & Robert King	5,000	On Spring Creek on Brimstone Creek.
2868.	Robert Fenner	4,038	On the southside of Richland Creek of Elk River.
2869.	John Sevier	1,000	On the north prong of Duck River.
2870.	Samuel Patten	1,500	On the southside of Duck River and Sugar Creek.
2871.	Robert Weakley	2,000	On a west fork of Richland Creek of Elk River.
2872.	Joseph Horton	3,000	On the northside of Tennessee River.
2873.	Samuel Lockhart	3,000	On the southside of Elk River.
2874.	John Graham	2,000	On the southside Duck River.
2875.	William Gilbreath	1,000	On the southside Duck River.
2876.	Theophilas Hunter	2,316	On the southside Duck River on both sides Creek.
2877.	Anthony Sharpe	1,000	On the southside Duck River on both sides Creek on Sugar Creek.
2878.	Charles Polk Jun.	5,000	On the waters of Elk River.
2879.	William T. Lewis	5,000	On Big Creek waters of Elk River.
2880.	Samuel Lockhart	2,000	On the Northside of Elk River.
2881.	William T. Lewis	5,000	On the west side of Richland Creek.
2882.	Martin Armstrong	250	On the headwaters of Weakleys Creek of Elk River.
2883.	Mark Robinson	5,000	On the northside of Duck Creek.
2884.	Robert & Thomas King	2,500	Between the north of Holston and ford of Wolf River.
2885.	Martin Armstrong	5,000	On the northside of Elk River and headwaters of Big Creek.
2886.	Joseph Kilpatrick	800	On both sides of Duck River
2887.	James Holland	5,000	On both sides of Duck River.
2888.	Ezekiel Polk Jun.	5,000	On the northside of Duck River.

2889.	Joshua Nichols & John Webb	1,900	On the southside of Duck River.
2890.	Anthony Sharpe & Thomas Dugen	1,000	On the southside of Duck River on the west side of Sugar Creek.
2891.	Samuel Kerr	1,000	On Duck River on both sides the north fork.
2892.	Henry Montford	5,000	On the northside of Duck River.
2893.	Thomas Gillaspie	4,000	On the southside of Duck River on both sides of Long Creek.
2894.	Robert Hays	1,000	On the northside of Duck River on Caney Spring Creek.
2895.	Joseph Hinds	5,000	On both sides Duck River.
2896.	James Brandon	1,000	On both forks of Spring Creek.
2897.	Joseph Kerr	2,000	On the north side of Duck River.
2898.	Thomas Gill	1,860	On the southside of Duck River on Fountain Creek.
2899.	William T. Lewis	5,000	On the southside of Duck River on Globe Creek.
2900.	David Vance	1,000	On the southside of Duck River.
2901.	Richard Graham	2,000	On the southside of Duck River on Little Tom Bigbys Creek.
2902.	Martin Armstrong	2,000	On the southside of Duck River.
2903.	James Brandon	2,000	On both sides the North Fork of Duck River.
2904.	James Kerr	1,000	On the north side of Duck River on Spring Creek.
2905.	Thomas & Ezekiel Polk	5,000	Joining Carters Creek and spring branch.
2906.	Walter Braley	3,000	On the head waters of Spring Creek.
2907.	Thomas Allison	4,000	On Flatt Creek northside of Duck River.
2908.	Elijah Robertson	5,000	On the southside of Duck River on the head of Fountain Creek.
2909.	Martin Armstrong	5,000	Lying on Richland Creek waters of Elk River.
2910.	James Robertson & Hugh Leeper	2,034	On the northside of Duck River.
2911.	David Wilson	1,096	On the northside of Duck River on Cane Spring Creek.
2912.	George Alexander	1,000	On the west side of Alexanders Creek.
2913.	Nathaniel Jones	1,350	On the southside of Duck River.
2914.	Samuel Barton	500	On the northside of Duck River.

2915.	Caleb Phifer	3,000	On Fall Creek.
2916.	Richard Trotter	4,000	On Falling Creek.
2917.	Martin Phifer	5,000	On Falling Creek.
2918.	Robert Hays	5,000	On Richland Creek of Elk River.
2919.	Elijah Robertson	5,000	On the southside Duck River on both sides Fountain Creek.
2920.	George Cathey Sen.	2,500	On the southside of Duck River on both sides Rich Creek.
2921.	Robert Weakley	2,000	On the northside Duck River both sides Caney Spring Creek.
2922.	John Rutherford	5,000	On the southside of Forked Deer River.
2923.	William Gilbert	5,000	On both sides of Fountain Creek.
2924.	Thomas Polk	2,000	On the southside of Duck River the head of Sinking Creek.
2925.	Thomas Polk	5,000	On the northside of Duck River.
2926.	William Cocke	5,000	On the northside of Duck River on both sides Bear Creek.
2927.	James McKesseck	1,000	On the southside of Duck River on the east side of Sugar Creek.
2928.	John Nelson	5,000	On the west waters of Richland Creek.
2929.	John Armstrong	5,000	On Richland Creek of Elk River.
2930.	Thomas Polk	5,000	On Richland Creek of Elk River.
2931.	John Nelson	5,000	On Robertson's Creek a fork of Richland Creek.
2932.	Micajah G. Lewis	5,000	On Richland Creek joining John Armstrongs lines.
2933.	William Terrell Lewis	5,000	On Big Creek waters of Elk River.
2934.	William Cathey	4,000	On the southside of Duck River on Cathey's Creek.
2935.	Robert Walker	700	On Elk River and on a fork of Richland Creek.
2936.		Middle District 1789	
2936.	Felix Robertson & John Jackson	4,000	On the northside of Duck River.
2937.	Martin Armstrong	5,000	On Richland Creek of Elk River.
2938.	William Lanier?	1,500	On the northside of Duck River.
2939.	Anthony Numan	5,000	On the northside of Duck River.
2940.	Martin Armstrong	2,050	On Weakley's Creek west fork of Richland Creek.

2941.	Thomas Sharpe	400	On Weakley's Creek west fork of Richland Creek.
2942.	William Hardy Murphee	5,000	On the southeast side of Richland Creek.
2943.	Tignall Jones	2,100	On the southside of Duck River.
2944.	Peter Short	1,076	On the waters of Duck River and flat creek.
2945.	George Cathey Sen.	3,000	On the northside of Duck River and on Nobb Creek.
2946.	Joel Laine	2,000	On the southside of Duck River.
2947.	Thomas Polk	5,000	On the headwaters of Richland Creek.
2948.	John Wilson	626	On Falling Creek.
2949.	Henry Rutherford	5,000	In the fork of Forked Deer River.
2950.	William Terrell Lewis	5,000	On the southside Duck River on Globe Creek.
2951.	George Davidson	1,500	On the north side of Duck River.
2952.	James McQueston	2,627	On Duck River joining Thomas Polks lines.
2953.	James Huggins	1,000	On the north side of Duck River.
2954.	Samuel Maham?	2,000	On the northside Duck River on Cedar Creek.
2955.	Thomas Templeton & Armstrong	3,000	On the waters of Elk River on Lynn Creek.
2956.	Robert Irvin	2,600	On the main west fork of Stones River.
2957.	Nicholas Long	5,000	On the southside of Duck River.
2958.	John Armstrong	250	On the north fork of Duck River.
2959.	Jesse Maxwell	400	On the south fork of Richland Creek.
2960.	William Polk	5,000	On the southside of Duck River.
2961.	William Dobbins	1,500	On the southside of Duck River near the head of small creek.
2962.	Robert Beak & William McLean	5,000	On the northside of Knob Creek.
2963.	Ephraim McLean	5,000	On the northside on Knob Creek.
2964.	Stokeley Donelson	5,000	On the westside of Richland Creek on Elk River.
2965.	Richard Dallam	5,000	On the southside of Duck River on Fountain Creek.
2966.	Stokeley Donelson	5,000	On the southside of Duck River on a small fork of Fountain Creek.
2967.	Stokeley Donelson	5,000	On Richland Creek.

2968.	James Grant	5,000	On the westside of Tenessee River on Harbins Creek.
2969.	William Polk	5,000	On both sides Beaver Creek.
2970.	Robert Irwin	3,200	On Richland Creek of Elk River.
2971.	John Bigham	3,200	On Richland Creek of Elk River.

Middle District 1790

2972.	John Cooper	400	On both sides Cowpers Creek waters of Clear Fork.
2973.	Gilbert Christian	450	On a branch of Mill Creek waters of Cumberland River.
2974.	Henry Conway	640	Joining a place called the barrens.
2975.	John Porterfield	5,000	On Globe Creek a branch of Fountain Creek.
2976.	Landon Carter	1,280	On the westside of Cumberland Mountain on Brimstone Creek.
2977.	Caleb Tate	5,000	On a branch the waters of Elk River.
2978.	Caleb Tate	5,000	On the westside of Richland Creek.
2979.	James Cooper	640	On a branch of Clear fork of Cumberland River.
2980.	James Cooper	600	On Cowpers Creek the waters of Cumberland River.
2981.	Edward Armstrong	500	On the northside of Duck River.
2982.	Elias Langham	1,000	On the Clear Fork of Cumberland river.
2983.	John Haywood	5,000	On the waters of Richland Creek.
2984.	Martha Shepherd	2,000	On Richland Creek of Elk River.
2985.	Thomas Routledge	1,100	On the southside of Duck River.
2986.	William Shepherd & Joseph Phillips	5,000	On Richland Creek of Elk River.

Western District 1788

2987.	Edward Harris	1,000	On both sides of Clover Creek.
2988.	Edward Harris	1,000	On both sides Richland Creek.
2989.	Edward Harris	1,000	On both sides Richland Creek on a branch.
2990.	Edward Harris	1,000	On Clear Lick Creek of Richland Creek above Memphis right north of Wolf River.
2991.	Edward Harris	1,000	On both sides of Clover Lick Creek.

2992.	Edward Harris	1,000	On both sides of Clover Lick Creek.
2993.	Edward Harris	1,000	On the waters of Long Fork.
2994.	Edward Harris	1,000	On Clover Lick Creek on Obion River.
2995.	Edward Harris	1,000	On Clover Lick Creek on Obion River.
2996.	Edward Harris	1,000	On Clover Lick Creek on Obion River.
2997.	Edward Harris	1,000	On Clover Lick Creek of Obion River.
2998.	Edward Harris	1,000	On both sides of Clover Lick Creek on Obion River.
2999.	Edward Harris	1,000	On Obion River below big Clover Lick Creek.
3000.	Edward Harris	1,000	On the waters of Reelfoot River.
3001.	Samuel Harris	5,000	On the north fork of Loosahatchee River.
3002.	William Sharpe	5,000	On the southside of Obion River.
3003.	Abner Sharpe	2,000	On the northside of Looshatcher River.
3004.	Thomas Rice Sharpe	1,000	On the waters of Cany fork.
3005.	John McNitt Alexander	3,660	On the north fork of Loupshalcher River.
3006.	James Purveyance	1,000	On the waters of Long Fork.
3007.	James Patterson	1,000	On the waters of Long Fork.
3008.	James Patterson	1,000	On the waters of Long Fork.
3009.	John Sitgreaves	5,000	On the No th Fork of Looshatchon River.
3010.	William Hughlett	500	On the south fork of Doe River.
3011.	Martin Armstrong Jun.	5,000	On the Forked Deer River.
3012.	Elijah Patten	1,000	On the waters of the South Fork of Obion Riber.
3013.	Martin Armstrong	5,000	On the head of a branch of Richland Creek.
3014.	Alexander Reed	600	On the waters of the South Fork of Obion River.
3015.	Benjamin Smith	3,000	On the waters of Forked Deer river.
3016.	George Daugherty	2,000	On both sides Indian Creek on Big Halcher River.
3017.	Robert Weakley	2,000	On the waters of Obion River.
3018.	Henry Rutherford	2,000	On the South side of Forked Deer River.

3019.	George Daughterty	3,000	On Reelfoot River below the mouth of the second Bays.
3020.	John Stokes	2,500	On the Southside of North Fork of Forked Deer river.
3021.	Griffith Ruthford	3,000	On the southside of Forked Deer.
3022.	Martin Armstrong	5,000	On the Obion River.
3023.	James Martin	5,000	On the Obion River including the second main fork.
3024.	George McLean	1,000	On the waters of Flatt Creek.
3025.	Alexander McCullock	3,000	On the mouth of Looshalter river.
3026.	Alexander McCullock	2,000	On both sides of Looshalter river.
3027.	James Hall	2,000	On the southside of Indian Creek of Big Hatchers River.
3028.	Thomas Davidson	3,000	On the Obion River.
3029.	Augustus Harvey	2,500	On Reelfoot River including the mouth of Cane Creek.
3030.	Thomas Rice Sharpe	1,000	On the waters of Long Creek.
3031.	Thomas Polk	5,000	On the northside of Looshalter River.
3032.	William Polk	5,000	On Indian Creek of Big Hatcher River.
3033.	William Polk	2,000	On the South Fork of Forked Deer River.
3034.	George Houser	5,000	On or about one mile above the mouth of Hauson Creek.
3035.	George Daugherty	4,000	On Reelfoot River.
3036.	Jane Davidson	2,000	On both sides of Obion River.
3037.	Augustus Harvey	2,500	On Cove Creek of Reelfoot river.
3038.	Wikoff & Clarke	1,000	On Reelfoot River.
3039.	John Rights	5,000	On Housers Creek.
3040.	William Polk	3,000	On Mississippi below the mouth of Forked Deer River.
3041.	Wikoff & Clarke	400	On Reelfoot River.
3042.	John Stokes	2,500	On the northside of Forked Deer river.
3043.	Edward Sharpe	5,000	On the northside of Forked Deer River.
3044.	unreadable		
3045.	Richard Blackledys	5,000	On Wolf River below the mouth of Looshatcher River.
3046.	John Dugan	2,165	On both sides Obion River.
3047.	Robert Patton	1,000	On Rutherfords Fork of Obion River.

3048.	Jonathan Drake	1,600	On both sides Long Fork of Spring Creek.
3049.	Ephraim Davidson	2,000	On the northside of Forked Deer river.
3050.	Robert Goodlo	1,500	On the fork of Looshalcher and Wolf River.
3051.	Alexander McKee	1,500	On the east side of Grove Creek of Obion River.
3052.	Martin Armstrong	5,000	On the waters of Reelfoot and Grove Creek.
3053.	George Daugherty	2,500	On the northside Looshalter river.
3054.	George Daugherty	1,000	On the northside Looshalter river.
3055.	James Robertson	2,000	On both sides Looshalter river.
3056.	James Coor	1,000	On the southside Obion River.
3057.	William Davidson	2,000	On the southside Rutherfords fork of Obion.
3058.	Griffith Rutherford	3,000	On the southside of Forked Deer river.
3059.	Robert Martin	5,000	On the Obion River.
3060.	James Robertson	1,000	On the Obion River.
3061.	Richard Fenner	5,000	On the North Fork of Wolf River.
3062.	Benjamin McCulloch	5,000	On the northside of Forked Deer river.
3063.	Edward Cox	1,000	On the waters of Forked Deer river.
3064.	John Rice	5,000	On the southside of Big Hatcher River.
3065.	Micajah Greene Lewis	1,000	On the South Fork of Forked Deer river.
3066.	Wikoff & Clarke	390	On Reelfoot Creek.
3067.	Anthony Sharpe	3,500	On the North Fork of Forked Deer river.
3068.	Benjamin Smith	4,000	On the waters of Forked Deer river.
3069.	James Coor	1,000	On the waters of Obion River.
3070.	Richard Cross	5,000	On the north fork Looshatcher River.
3071.	James Coor	1,000	On the waters of the North Fork of Forked Deer river.
3072.	Snior? McCoy	1,000	On the waters of the North Fork of Forked Deer river.
3073.	Benjamin Smith	5,000	On the waters of forked Deer river.
3074.	William Terrill Lewis	1,000	On the south fork of Forked Deer river.

3075.	Robert Goodlor	3,000	On the northside Looshatcher River.
3076.	Adam Boyd	5,000	On the northside Looshatcher River.
3077.	George Cathey	1,130	On the waters of Rutherford's fork of Obion River.
3078.	George Daugherty	2,500	On the northside of Looshalter.
3079.	Henry Clarke	5,000	On the southside of Obion River.
3080.	Martin Armstrong	5,000	On the Obion River about 1 mile above the mouth.
3081.	James Dever	1,000	On Rutherfords Creek in Obion River.
3082.	George Daugherty	3,000	On Reelfoot River.
3083.	James Coor	1,000	On the waters of the north fork of Forked Deer river.
3084.	James Coor	1,000	On the waters of the north fork of Forked Deer river.
3085.	James Coor	1,000	On the waters of the north fork of Forked Deer river.
3086.	James Coor	1,000	On the waters of the north fork of Forked Deer river.
3087.	James Coor	1,000	On the waters of the north fork of Forked Deer river.
3088.	James Coor	1,000	On the waters of the north fork of Forked Deer river.
3089.	James Coor	1,000	On the waters of the north fork of Forked Deer river.
3090.	Thomas Tolbott	1,000	On both sides Looshalther river.
3091.	William Allston	2,000	On the southside Looshalther river.
3092.	James Martin	5,000	On both sides Obion River including Big Clover Lick.
3093.	Downham Clarke	5,000	On the Obion River.
3094.	George Daugherty	3,500	On the northside Wolf River.
3095.	Henry Rutherford	250	On the southside of Forked Deer river.
3096.	John Carter	1,000	In the fork of the Forked Deer River.
3097.	William Hughlett	500	On the north fork of Forked Deer River.
3098.	Henry Rutherford	250	On the southside of forked Deer River.
3099.	Mary Davidson	2,000	On the northside of Obion River.
3100.	John Brown	4,000	On the south fork of forked Deer river.
3101.	William Hawkins	3,510	On the south fork of forked Deer river.

3102.	Ephraim Davidson	2,000	On the south fork of Forked Deer river.
3103.	George Davidson	2,500	On the south fork of Forked Deer river.
3104.	Shadrach Hargess	2,100	On both sides Looshatchers river.
3105.	Martin Armstrong	5,000	On a south branch of Mississippi.
3106.	Benjamin Smith	3,000	On the north fork of Forked Deer River.
3107.	Ephraim McLean	1,000	On the southside Duck River near the mouth of Falling Creek.
3108.	James Templeton	920	On the waters of Rutherfords fork of Obion River.
3109.	Archibald Murphy	3,210	On Obion River and Forked Deer River.
3110.	Richard Blackledge	2,000	On Caney Creek.
3111.	James Dugin	3,000	On the southside of Obion River.
3112.	David Shelton	3,000	On Beaver Dam Creek on the waters of Forked Deer River.
3113.	James Davidson	1,000	On Rutherford's Creek of Obion River.
3114.	Abner Nash	1,000	On both sides the North Fork of Obion River.
3115.	Abner Nash	1,000	On the east side of the Obion River.
3116.	Abner Nash	1,000	On the waters of the north fork of Obion River.
3117.	Abner Nash	1,000	On the waters of the north fork of Obion River.
3118.	Abner Nash	1,000	On the waters of the north fork of Obion River.
3119.	Abner Nash	1,000	On the waters of the north fork of Obion River.
3120.	Abner Nash	1,000	On the north fork of Obion River.
3121.	Abner Nash	1,000	On the north fork of Obion River.
3122.	Abner Nash	1,000	On Grove Creek of Obion River.
3123.	Abner Nash	1,000	On the north fork of Obion River.
3124.	Abner Nash	1,000	On the north fork of Obion River.
3125.	Abner Nash	1,000	On the north fork of Obion River.
3126.	Abner Nash	1,000	On the north fork of Obion River.
3127.	Abner Nash	1,000	On both sides the north fork of Obion River.
3128.	Abner Nash	1,000	On both sides the north fork of Obion River.

3129.	Abner Nash	1,000	On both sides the north fork of Obion River.
3130.	Abner Nash	1,000	On both sides the north fork of Obion River.
3131.	Abner Nash	1,000	On both sides Grove Creek of Obion River.
3132.	Abner Nash	1,000	On the waters of the south fork of Obion River.
3133.	Abner Nash	1,000	On both sides the north fork of Obion River.
3134.	Abner Nash	100	On both sides the north fork of Obion River.
3135.	Abner Nash	1,000	On both sides the north fork of Obion River.
3136.	Abner Nash	1,000	On the east side of the North fork of Obion River.
3137.	Abner Nash	1,000	On the north fork of Obion River.
3138.	Stokeley Donelson	400	On the Eastside Grove Creek.
3139.	William Tyrell Lewis	1,000	On the waters of the North fork of Forked Deer River.
3140.	William Tyrell Lewis	1,490	On the south fork of forked Deer River.
3141.	Benjamin Smith	1,500	On Spring Creek branch of the Long Fork.
3142.	Frederick Miller	4,000	On Reelfoot River.
3143.	Joseph Sitgreaves	5,000	On the north fork of Looshalther river.
3144.	George Daugherty	2,000	On the west side of Reelfoot River.
3145.	Martin Armstrong	5,000	On the north fork of Forked Deer River.
3146.	William Terrill Lewis	1,500	On both sides of the South Fork of Forked Deer River.
3147.	Martin Armstrong	5,000	On Forked Deer River.
3148.	Benjamin Smith	5,000	On Forked Deer River.
3149.	William Terrell Lewis	1,000	On the waters of Reelfoot River.
3150.	Jesse Steed	1,500	On the southside Looshatchers river.
3151.	John Gray Blount & Thomas Blount	1,000	On the waters of Obion River.
3152.	John Gray Blount & Thomas Blount	1,000	On the south fork of Obion River.
3153.	John Gray Blount & Thomas Blount	1,000	On the south fork of Obion River.

3154.	John Gray Blount & Thomas Blount	1,000	On the waters of Reelfoot River.
3155.	John Gray Blount & Thomas Blount	1,000	On Rutherford's fork of Obion.
3156.	John Gray Blount & Thomas Blount.	1,000	On the southside of Obion River.
3157.	John Gray Blount & Thomas Blount	1,000	On the southside of Obion River.
3158.	John Gray Blount & Thomas Blount	1,000	On the waters of Obion River.
3159.	John Gray Blount & Thomas Blount	1,000	On the south fork of Obion River.
3160.	John Gray Blount & Thomas Blount	1,000	On both sides Looshatcher River.
3161.	John Gray Blount & Thomas Blount	1,000	On both sides Looshatcher River.
3162.	John Gray Blount & Thomas Blount	1,000	On the southside Looshatcher River.
3163.	John Gray Blount & Thomas Blount	1,000	On the waters of Reelfoot river.
3164.	John Gray Blount & Thomas Blount	1,000	On the southside of Looshatchers river.
3165.	John Gray Blount & Thomas Blount	1,000	On the head of Indian Creek of Big Hatcher River.
3166.	John Gray Blount & Thomas Blount	1,000	On the south fork of Obion River.
3167.	John Gray Blount & Thomas Blount	1,000	On the waters of Reelfoot River.
3168.	John Gray Blount & Thomas Blount	1,000	On a south branch of Indian Creek.
3169.	John Gray Blount & Thomas Blount	1,000	On the waters of Obion River.
3170.	John Gray Blount & Thomas Blount	1,000	On the south fork of Obion River.
3171.	John Gray Blount & Thomas Blount	1,000	On the south fork of Obion River.
3172.	John Gray Blount & Thomas Blount	1,000	On the north fork of Obion River.
3173.	John Gray Blount & Thomas Blount	1,000	On both sides Looshatchan river.
3174.	John Gray Blount & Thomas Blount	1,000	On the southside of Obion.
3175.	John Gray Blount & Thomas Blount	1,000	On the southside of Indian Creek.
3176.	John Gray Blount & Thomas Blount	1,000	On the southside of Obion River

3177.	John Gray Blount & Thomas Blount	1,000	On the southside of Obion River.
3178.	John Gray Blount & Thomas Blount	1,000	On both sides Loushatchan River.
3179.	John Gray Blount & Thomas Blount	1,000	On both sides Obion River.
3180.	John Gray Blount & Thomas Blount	1,000	On Indian Creek of Big Hatcher River.
3181.	John Gray Blount & Thomas Blount	1,000	On the south fork of Obion River.
3182.	John Gray Blount & Thomas Blount	1,000	On the southside Looshalther river.
3183.	John Gray Blount & Thomas Blount	1,000	On the southside Looshalther river.
3184.	John Gray Blount & Thomas Blount	1,000	On the south fork of Obion River.
3185.	John Gray Blount & Thomas Blount	1,000	On the south fork of Indian Creek.
3186.	John Gray Blount & Thomas Blount	1,000	On the waters of Reelfoot and Obion River.
3187.	John Gray Blount & Thomas Blount	1,000	On the waters of Reelfoot and Obion River.
3188.	John Gray Blount & Thomas Blount	1,000	On the northside of Obion River.
3189.	John Gray Blount & Thomas Blount	1,000	On the south fork of Indian Creek.
3190.	John Gray Blount & Thomas Blount	1,000	On the south fork of Indian Creek.
3191.	John Gray Blount & Thomas Blount	1,000	On the south fork of Obion River.
3192.	John Gray Blount & Thomas Blount	1,000	On the south fork of Obion River.
3193.	John Gray Blount & Thomas Blount	1,000	On the waters of Reelfoot river.
3194.	John Gray Blount & Thomas Blount	1,000	On the waters of Reelfoot river.
3195.	John Gray Blount & Thomas Blount	1,000	On both sides Indian Creek.
3196.	John Gray Blount & Thomas Blount	1,000	On the south fork of Obion River.
3197.	John Gray Blount & Thomas Blount	1,000	On Grove Creek.
3198.	John Gray Blount & Thomas Blount	1,000	On the waters of Reelfoot river.
3199.	John Gray Blount & Thomas Blount	1,000	On both sides of South Fork of Obion River.

3200.	John Gray Blount & Thomas Blount	1,000	On Obion River.
3201.	John Gray Blount & Thomas Blount	1,000	On both sides Spring Creek waters of the Long Fork.
3202.	John Gray Blount & Thomas Blount	1,000	On Looshatchen River.
3203.	John Gray Blount & Thomas Blount	1,000	On the waters of Reelfoot River.
3204.	John Gray Blount & Thomas Blount	1,000	On the waters of Reelfoot river.
3205.	John Gray Blount & Thomas Blount	1,000	On the waters of Reelfoot river.
3206.	John Gray Blount & Thomas Blount	1,000	On the southfork of Obion River.
3207.	John Gray Blount & Thomas Blount	1,000	On both sides Looshatcher River.
3208.	John Gray Blount & Thomas Blount	1,000	On both sides Looshatcher river.
3209.	John Gray Blount & Thomas Blount	1,000	On the waters of Indian Creek.
3210.	John Gray Blount & Thomas Blount	1,000	On the Obion River.
3211.	John Gray Blount & Thomas Blount	1,000	On the waters of Reelfoot River.
3212.	John Gray Blount & Thomas Blount	1,000	On the waters of Reelfoot River.
3213.	John Gray Blount & Thomas Blount	1,000	On Lick Fork of Obion River.
3214.	John Gray Blount & Thomas Blount	1,000	On both sides Lick Fork of Obion River.
3215.	John Gray Blount & Thomas Blount	1,000	On both sides Obion River.
3216.	John Gray Blount & Thomas Blount	1,000	On the south fork of Obion River.
3217.	John Gray Blount & Thomas Blount	3,000	On Rutherfords fork of Obion River.
3218.	John Gray Blount & Thomas Blount	1,000	On the head of Grove Creek.
3219.	John Gray Blount & Thomas Blount	1,000	On the southside of Obion River.
3220.	John Gray Blount & Thomas Blount	2,000	On Rutherfords fork of Obion River.
3221.	John Gray Blount & Thomas Blount	1,000	On the south fork of Obion River.
3222.	John Gray Blount & Thomas Blount	1,000	On the head of Looshatchee river.

3223.	John Gray Blount & Thomas Blount	1,000	On the southside Obion River.
3224.	John Gray Blount & Thomas Blount	1,000	On the south fork of Obion River.
3225.	John Gray Blount & Thomas Blount	1,000	On the southside Looshatchee river.
3226.	John Gray Blount & Thomas Blount	1,000	On the waters of Reelfoot River.
3227.	John Gray Blount & Thomas Blount	1,000	On the waters of Obion River.
3228.	John Gray Blount & Thomas Blount	1,000	On the southside Looshatchee river.
3229.	John Gray Blount & Thomas Blount	2,000	On both sides Obion River above Big Clover Lick.
3230.	John Gray Blount & Thomas Blount	1,000	On the North Fork of Forked Deer river.
3231.	John Gray Blount & Thomas Blount	1,000	On a south branch of Indian Creek.
3232.	John Gray Blount & Thomas Blount	1,000	On the south fork of Obion River.
3233.	John Gray Blount & Thomas Blount	1,000	On the waters of Obion River.
3234.	John Gray Blount & Thomas Blount	1,000	On the waters of Obion River.
3235.	John Gray Blount & Thomas Blount	1,000	On Rutherford's fork of Obion River.
3236.	John Gray Blount & Thomas Blount	1,000	On Indian Creek of Big Hatchee River.
3237.	John Gray Blount & Thomas Blount	2,000	On Rutherfords fork of Obion River.
3238.	John Gray Blount & Thomas Blount	3,000	On the waters of Obion River.
3239.	John Gray Blount & Thomas Blount	1,000	On Rutherford Fork of Obion River.
3240.	John Gray Blount & Thomas Blount	1,000	On the south fork of Obion River.
3241.	John Gray Blount & Thomas Blount	1,000	On Lick Fork of Obion River.
3242.	John Gray Blount & Thomas Blount	1,000	On the waters of Reelfoot River.
3243.	John Gray Blount & Thomas Blount	1,000	On the south fork of Obion River.
3244.	John Gray Blount & Thomas Blount	1,000	On the north fork of Forked Deer river.
3245.	John Gray Blount & Thomas Blount	1,000	On the north waters of Obion River.

3246.	John Gray Blount & Thomas Blount	1,000	On the waters of Obion River.
3247.	John Gray Blount & Thomas Blount	1,000	On the waters of Obion River.
3248.	John Gray Blount & Thomas Blount	1,000	On the waters of Reelfoot River.
3249.	John Gray Blount & Thomas Blount	1,000	On Grove Creek.
3250.	John Gray Blount & Thomas Blount	1,000	On Rutherfords fork of Obion River.
3251.	John Gray Blount & Thomas Blount	2,000	On the north fork of Forked Deer river.
3252.	Amelia Johnston	1,000	On the waters of Big Hatchee River.
3253.	William Barry Groves	1,500	On the waters of Big Hatchee River.
3254.	William Moore	1,300	On the waters of Big Hatchee River.
3255.	Daniel Mallett	5,000	On the waters of Big Hatchee River.

Western District 1789

3256.	James Porterfield	5,000	On the eastside of Mississippi.
3257.	David Hart	2,250	On the northside of Big Hatchee River.
3258.	John Windsor	1,000	On the waters of Big Hatchee.
3259.	Solomon Keith?	5,000	On both sides Big Hatchee.
3260.	not readable (on a fold)		
3261.	John Rice?	5,000	On the waters of Big Hatchee.
3262.	John Rice	5,000	On the Chickasaw Bluff.
3263.	John Rice	5,000	On Big Hatchee River.
3264.	John Rice	5,000	On Big Hatchee River.
3265.	John Rice	5,000	On both sides Big Hatchee River.
3266.	John Rice	5,000	On the north side of Big Hatchee.
3267.	John Rice	5,000	On the southside of Big Hatchee.
3268.	John Rice	5,000	On the southside of Big Hatchee.
3269.	John Rice	2,500	On the waters of Big Hatchee river.
3270.	John Rice	5,000	On the waters of Big Hatchee river.
3271.	John Rice	5,000	On the southside of Big Hatchee river.

3272.	John Rice	5,000	On the northside of Big Hatchee river.
3273.	John Rice	5,000	On both sides Big Hatchee river.
3274.	John Rice	5,000	On the waters of Big Hatchee.
3275.	John Rice	5,000	On both sides of Big Hatchee.
3276.	John Rice	5,000	On Big Hatchee River above fifteen miles from the mouth.
3277.	David Flowers	2,500	On the waters of Big Hatchee river.
3278.	John Brown	1,000	On the waters of Big Hatchee river.
3279.	Thomas Brown	1,000	On the waters of Big Hatchee river.
3280.	John Brown	1,000	On the waters of Big Hatchee river.
3281.	Thomas Brown	1,000	On the waters of Big Hatchee river.
3282.	Joseph Greer	1,500	On the waters of Big Hatchee river.
3283.	Robinson Munford	5,000	On the southside of Big Hatchee river.
3284.	Joseph Greer	1,500	On the North side of Big Hatchee river.
3285.	Robinson Munford	5,000	On the east side of the Mississippi.
3286.	Joseph Greer	1,500	On the waters of Big Hatchee river.
3287.	Jacob Blount	5,000	On the southside of Big Hatchee river.
3288.	Adrian Valek	5,000	On both sides Big Hatchee River.
3289.	Robinson Mumford	5,000	On the waters of Big Hatchee River.
3290.	Abraham Phillips	1,500	On the waters of Big Hatchee River.
3291.	John McGee	1,035	On the northside of the water of Big Hatchee.
3292.	Landon Carter	200	On the northside of the North Fork of Obion River.
3293.	Landon Carter	300	On the northside of the North Fork of Obion River.
3294.	Landon Carter	500	On both sides Harris fork of Obion.
3295.	Landon Carter	300	On the east side of Harris fork on Obion.
3296.	Landon Carter	200	On the north side of Obion River.

3297.	Landon Carter	300	On the east side of Harris Fork of Obion.
3298.	Landon Carter	400	On the north side of the North Fork of Forked Deer River.
3299.	Landon Carter	640	On a head branch of Harris's fork of Forked Deer River.
3300.	Landon Carter	400	On the waters of Harris Fork of Obion River.
3301.	Landon Carter	300	On the Long Fork.
3302.	Landon Carter	600	On Harris Fork of Obion River.
3303.	Landon Carter	640	On the east side of Harris's Fork of Obion River.
3304.	Landon Carter		On the Harris Fork of Obion River.
3305.	Landon Carter	330	On the northside of Obion River.
3306.	on a fold - unreadable.		
3307.	Landon Carter	640	On both sides Harris Fork of Obion River.
3308.	Philemon Hawkens	4,000	On Indian Creek.
3309.	John Gray Blount & Thomas Blount	1,000	On the northside of the north fork of Obion River.
3310.	John Gray Blount & Thomas Blount	1,000	On the northside of the north fork of Obion River.
3311.	William Terrill Lewis	1,500	On the head of the Long Fork of the Mississippi.
3312.	William Haughlett	3,000	On the Obion River.
3313.	Edward Harris	640	On the northside of Obion River.
3314.	John Estes	5,000	On the southside of Big Hatchee River.
3315.	John Estes	5,000	On both sides of Big Hatchee River.
3316.	John Estes	5,000	On Big Hatcha River.
3317.	Elijah Robertson	100	On the northside of Wolf River.
3318.	Elijah Robertson	500	On the eastside of Harris Fork of Obion River.
3319.	Archibald Murphy	4,350	On the south fork of Forked Deer river.
3320.	William Terrill Lewis	4,000	On a branch of Big Hatchee River.
3321.	John Rice	5,000	On Big Hatchee River.
3322.	James Patterson	2,500	On the Mississippi River.
3323.	John Gray Blount & Thomas Blount	5,000	On the southside of Big Hatchee River.
3324.	David Crawford	2,000	On the southwest side of the South Fork of Forked Deer river.

3325.	Joseph Greer	2,500	On the Southside of the Obion River.
3326.	John Estes	2,500	On the southside of Big Hatchee River.
	Total	2,150,542	

An estimate of the lands for which Grants have issued to the Officers and soldiers in the Continental Line of this state or their assigns pursuant to Act of Assembly.

1782
Davidson County

1.	Frederick Stump	640	On Whites Creek of Cumberland River.
2.	Jacob Stump	640	On Whites Creek of Cumberland River.
3.	Daniel Williams	640	On the northside of Cumberland River.
4.	John Montgomery	640	On the northside of Cumberland River.
5.	John Rains	640	On Browns Creek of Cumberland River.

1783

6.	Daniel Hogon	640	On a branch of Mill Creek.
7.	Amos Heaton	640	On a small creek of Whites Creek.
8.	Benjamin Drake Jun.	640	On a small creek of Cumberland river.
9.	David Rounsivale	640	On Whites Creek of Cumberland river.
10.	Henry Ramsey	640	On the northside of Cumberland river.
11.	Robert Espy	640	On the southside of Cumberland river.
12.	The heirs of William Cooper	640	On the northside of Cumberland river.
13.	Jonas Munafee	640	On the southside of Cumberland river on Browns Creek.
14.	Benjamin Logan	640	On Dentons Lick.
15.	Daniel Dunkham	640	On the southside of Cumberland River on Richlands Creek.
16.	James Espey	640	On the northside of Cumberland River.
17.	Isaac Johnston	640	On Richland Creek.

18.	Isaac Johnston	640	On the southside of Cumberland river on Richland Creek.
19.	Haden Wells	640	On the northside of Cumberland river on McAdon Creek.
20.	Haden Wells	640	On the north fork of McAdon's Creek.
21.	William Loggins	640	On the northside of Cumberland river on Whites Creek.
22.	Jacob Jones	640	On the southside of Red River.
23.	Heirs of Nicholas Gentry	640	On the southside of Cumberland river on Browns Creek.
24.	John Brown	640	On a small branch that runs into Mill Creek.
25.	David Love	640	On both sides Bledsoe's Creek.
26.	Dennis Condry	640	On the south fork of Whites Creek.
27.	William Gowan	640	On a small branch of Mill Creek.
28.	Isaac Lindsay	640	Below the mouth of Station Camp Creek.
29.	James Mayfield	640	On the headwaters of Mill Creek.
30.	Andrew (Killo or Mills?)	640	On the westside of Harpeth River.
31.	on a fold - blackened out		
32.	Richard Dodge	640	On the middle fork of Station Camp Creek.
33.	Ebenezer Tetus	640	On the southside of Cumberland River.
34.	Ephraim McLean	640	On Brown's Creek.
35.	James Bradley	640	On the north fork of Thompsons Creek.
36.	William Green	640	On Stewart's Creek a branch of Stones River.
37.	John Barrow	640	On the northside of Red River.
38.	Henry Tierney	640	On the southside of Harpeth river.
39.	John Bohannon Junr.	640	On the southside Cumberland River on Mill Creek.
40.	Isaac Drake	640	Between Big and Little Harpeth river.
41.	Zachariah White	640	On the southside Cumberland River and East side of Mill Creek.
42.	Samuel Barton	640	On the waters of Browns Creek.
43.	Samuel Wilson	640	On the west fork of Stone Creek.
44.	John Hamilton	640	On the eastfork of Station Camp Creek.

45.	Francis Hodge	640	On Cumberland River above the fork of Richland Creek.
46.	William Johnston	640	On the Southside Cumberland River on Mill Creek.
47.	John Evans	640	On the northside Cumberland River on Mill Creek.
48.	John Milner	640	On the northside Cumberland River on Milners Creek.
49.	Rowland Maddison	640	On the eastside Cumberland River on Bartons Creek.
50.	Michael Shaver	640	On the Northside Cumberland River on Station Camp Creek.
51.	John Thomas	640	On the northside of Cumberland river.
52.	Joseph Henderson	640	On the south road leading from Dentons Lick on Beavers Creek.
53.	Thomas Edmunson	640	On the Southside of Harpeth River.
54.	David Givin	640	On Farmers Creek of Stone River.
55.	William Campbell	640	On the West fork of Stewards Creek.
56.	Hugh McGary	640	On the east fork of Station Camp.
57.	James Ray	640	About 7 miles from the French lick.
58.	Samuel Walker	640	On the South Fork of Mill Creek.
59.	George Purtle	640	On the South side of Cumberland river west fork of Mill Creek.
60.	Moses Rentfro	640	On the West fork of Red River.
61.	Robert Dishe	640	On the West fork of Bledsoe's Creek.
62.	William Johnston	640	On the Northside Cumberland river.
63.	Samuel Scott	640	On the waters of Gibson's Creek.
64.	Daniel Johnston	640	On Heatons Trace near Gaspers Station.
65.	William Overall	640	On the east fork of Mill Creek.
66.	Benjamin Drake	640	On the South side Cumberland river waters of Mill Creek.
67.	Jonathen Drake	640	On the Hurricane Trace.
68.	William Gillaspie	640	On Red River near Rentfroe Station.
69.	William Bradshaw	640	On the Northside Cumberland river.
70.	Hugh McGary	640	On the east fork of Station Camp.
71.	George Daugherty	640	On Sycamore ___gh branch of Browns Creek of Gaspers Lick.

72.	Daniel Chambers	640	On the northside of the public.
73.	William Griffin	640	On Little Harpeth River.
74.	Roger Topp	640	On the northside Cumberland river on Bledsoes Creek.
75.	Charles McCartney	640	On the middle fork of Station Camp Creek.
76.	John Henderson	640	On the waters of Little Harpeth river.
77.	George Espy	640	On the northside Cumberland on Gaspers Lick Creek.
78.	James McAdon	640	On the northside Cumberland below the mouth of Red River.
79.	Arthur McAdon	640	On McAdons Creek.
80.	Philip Pushon	640	On Caney Branch waters of Bledsoes Creek.
81.	Hugh Henry Senr.	640	On Sulphur Creek south branch of Red River.
82.	David Henry	640	On Sulphur Creek south branch of Red River.
83.	John Crow	640	On the northside Cumberland River on the east fork of Whites Creek.
84.	John Dunham	640	On the east fork of Richland Creek.
85.	Bartelet Searsey	640	On Stones Creek Eastside of Stones River.
86.	Cornelius Riddle	640	On the southside Cumberland river.
87.	Peter Rentfroe	640	On a branch of Browns Creek.
88.	Samuel McCutchen	640	On both sides Little Harpeth.
89.	Samuel Ewing	640	On the northside Cumberland river.
90.	Patrick McCutchen	640	On the northfork Big Harpeth River.
91.	Lewis Davison	640	On the southside Red River above the Blue Spring.
92.	John Boyd	640	On the southside Cumberland River on Shimps? Creek.
93.	Joseph Daugherty	640	On Harpeth River on the west fork.
94.	John Holliday	640	On the waters of Mill Creek.
95.	William Leighton	640	On both sides Harpeth river.
96.	John Caffrey	640	On the south fork of Stones Creek.
97.	Isaac Rentfroe	640	On the fork of Millers Creek and Richland Creek.
98.	Thomas Davis	640	On the southside of Cumberland River.
99.	William Rentfroe	640	On Richland Creek.

100.	John Evans	640	On the eastside the main fork of Stone River.
101.	John Cowan	640	On Big Harpeth River.
102.	James Crutchfield	640	On the southside Cumberland river.
103.	Charles Campbell	640	On the lower fork of Station Camp Creek.
104.	John McVey	640	On Drakes Creek.
105.	William Stern	640	On the fork of Red River.
106.	James Robertson	640	On the southside Cumberland river.
107.	John Robertson	640	On the southside Cumberland river.
108.	William Russell	640	On the first west fork of Big Harpeth River.
109.	William Renfroe	640	On Richland Creek.
110.	Joseph Hay	640	On Arrington Creek eastside Harpeth.
111.	James Moore	640	On the ____ fork of
112.	inelligible		
113.	John Condry	640	On the Middle Fork of Station Camp Creek.
114.	Solomon Whole	640	On the sulphur fork of Red river.
115.	John Drake	640	On White's Creek.
116.	Charles Metcalfe	640	On a branch of Brown's Creek.
117.	Samuel Hays	640	On the waters of Stone's Creek.
118.	Archibald McNeal	640	On the southside Cumberland river.
119.	John Searsey	640	Near Auhers Station.
120.	Phillip Trammell	640	On the northside Cumberland river.
121.	Martin Molden	640	On the sulphur fork of Red River.
122.	William Nealy	640	On the northside Cumberland river.
123.	John Donelson	640	Between Stone's River and Cumberland river in the fork.
124.	Samuel Deeson	640	On the east fork of Station Camp Creek.
125.	Samuel McMurry	640	On the waters of Mill Creek.
126.	William Purnell	640	On the northside of Big Harpeth River.
127.	Robert Daugherty	640	On a large creek above Stone River.
128.	Richard Simms	640	On Sinking Creek.
129.	Richard Gross	640	On the northside of Little Harpeth River.

130.	John Phack	640	On the southside the east Fork of Big Harpeth.
131.	Edward Hogan	640	On Drakes Creek.
132.	Isaac Lucas	640	On the southside of Big Harpeth.
133.	Joseph Reed	640	On the waters of Mill Creek.
134.	Julius Landers	640	On the waters of Mill Creek.
135.	Samuel Morrow	640	On the northside Cumberland river.
136.	Abel Gower	640	On John Fletchers Lick Creek.
137.	Samuel Price	640	On the first large fork of Bledsoe's Creek.
138.	Moses Winters	640	On the waters of Caleb's Creek.
139.	James Farris	640	On the fork of Big Harpeth.
140.	Hugh Hays	640	On Jones Bent of Cumberland river.
141.	Nathaniel Hays	640	Joining Hugh Hays lines.
142.	John Cayswood	640	On the westside of Mill Creek.
143.	Willard Grimes	640	On the Sulphur Fork of Red River.
144.	James Foster	640	On the fork of Mill Creek.
145.	Elijah Gower	640	On the southside Cumberland River.
146.	James Harwood	640	On the northside Cumberland River.
147.	Meredith Rains	640	On Brown's Creek.
148.	John Hamilton	640	On the westfork of Station Camp Creek.
149.	Thomas Jones Given	640	On a branch of the east fork of Mill Creek.
150.	John Donelson Sen.	640	On a branch of Big Harpeth.
151.	William McMerry	640	On the Big fork of Gaspers Creek.
152.	Philips Mason	640	On the northside Cumberland River.
153.	Nicholas Trammell	640	On Station Camp Creek.
154.	James Freeland	640	On the westside of Mill Creek.
155.	Thomas Hamilton	640	On the Big Fork of Harpeth River.
156.	Zachariah Green	640	On the west fork of Station Camp Creek.
157.	James Franklin	640	On the west fork of Station Camp Creek.
158.	Samuel Shelton	640	On Station Camp Creek.
159.	Jesse Maxfield	640	On the westside of Mill Creek.
160.	Evan Evans	640	On the second fork of Bledsoe's Creek.
161.	David Maxfield	640	On the west fork of Mill Creek.

162.	John Turner	640	On the waters of Mill Creek.
163.	Peter Looney	640	On the southside Cumberland River.
164.	Patrick Quigby	640	On Turneys Creek.
165.	David Looney	640	On the west fork of Station Camp Creek.
166.	Robert Cartright	640	On the west side of Station Camp Creek.
167.	George Nealey	640	On the south fork of Gibson's Creek.
168.	Jacob Himberlin	640	On the waters of Bledsoes Creek.
169.	Thomas Gillaspie	640	Joining James Towles lines.
170.	David Mitchell Junr.	640	On Browns Creek.
171.	Michael Himberlin	640	On the west side of Bledsoes Creek.
172.	Jacob Steel	640	On the north side Cumberland river.
173.	John Galloway	640	On the middle fork of Bledsoes Creek.
174.	Dennis Clark	640	On the north side Cumberland river.
175.	Ephraim Drak & Daniel Dunham	640	On Little Harpeth River.
176.	Hugh Simpson	640	On the head of a branch of little Harpeth.
177.	Samuel Landers	640	On the eastside of the middle fork of Bledsoes Creek.
178.	Martin King	640	On Overalls Creek.
179.	Daniel Turner	640	On the southwest side of Station Camp Creek.
180.	William Overall	640	On the waters of the west fork of Mill Creek.
181.	Henry Houdishall	640	On the northside Cumberland river.
182.	Daniel Garrett	640	On Indian Creek.
183.	William Moor	640	On the southside Cumberland river.
184.	James McKean	640	On the west fork of Station Camp Creek.
185.	Joseph Milligan	640	On the west side of Stones River.
186.	James Green	640	On the southside Cumberland river.
187.	Andrew Thomas	640	On Richland Creek.
188.	Alexander Thompson	640	On the southside Big Harpeth.
189.	William Collinsworth	640	On the westside of Little Harpeth.
190.	Abraham Jones	640	On Stones River.

191.	John Withers		
192.	Benjamin Parker	640	Joining John Withers lines.
193.	John Blackemore	640	On the westside Cumberland River above Bledsoes Creek.
194.	Nathan Turpin	640	On Red River.
195.	Daniel Chambers	640	On the southside Cumberland River.
196.	James Crockett	640	On the head of the middle fork of Station Camp Creek.
197.	Archilles Holloway	640	On the northside Cumberland River.
198.	Thomas Pharris	640	On the northside Cumberland River.
199.	William Summers	640	On the southside Cumberland River.
200.	George Newell	640	On the mouth of Little Creek.
201.	James Clendenning	640	On the northside of Cumberland river.
202.	William Hood	640	On the northside Richland Creek.
203.	William Henry	640	On the Eastside of Stone River.
204.	William Taylor	640	On Richland Creek.
205.	Philip Catron	640	On the southside Cumberland river.
206.	Pater Catron	640	On the southside Cumberland river.
207.	Jonathan & John Drake	640	On the waters of Cumberland river.
208.	Andrew Rule	640	On the middle fork of Bledsoe's Creek northside Cumberland.
209.	Edward Sarreymore	640	On the southside Cumberland river.
210.	Jonathan Green	640	On the southside Cumberland river.
211.	David Shannon	640	On the northeast branch of White's Creek.
212.	Henry Watkins	640	On Drakes Creek.
213.	John Higgison	640	Joining McMurtry's lines.
214.	Berry Caywood	640	On the west fork of Brown's Creek.
215.	William Ellis	640	On a branch of Brown's Creek.
216.	John Cockrell	640	On Little Harpeth Creek.
217.	John Kissinger	640	On the northside of Big Harpeth river.
218.	Mark Robinson	640	On the northside of Cumberland.
219.	Nathan Taris	640	On the fork of Mill Creek.
220.	Joshua Pinnick	640	On the southside Cumberland river.
221.	Isaac Neely	640	On the northside Cumberland river.
222.	Roger Topp	640	On the northside of Red River.

223.	William Snoddy	640	On the middle fork of Station Camp Creek.
224.	Edward Tomlinson	640	Near Neilys lick.
225.	Michael Stones	640	On Stones Creek.
226.	William Morris	640	On the second creek above Stones River.
227.	William Galloway	640	On the first fork of Gaspers Creek.
228.	James Cunningham	640	On the southside Cumberland river.
229.	Henry Highland	640	On the southside Cumberland river.
230.	Thomas Jones	640	On Cedar Creek south branch of Cumberland River.
231.	James Rentfro	640	On both sides of Red River.
232.	John Donelson	640	On the westside of Big Harpeth River.
233.	Robert Neely	640	On the northside Cumberland river.
234.	William Fletcher	640	On Spring Creek
235.	James Hollis	640	On Red River at the mouth of Sturgeon Creek.
236.	Benjamin Drake	640	On the Sulphur fork of Red River.
237.	Robert Russell	640	On the southside Stone River a branch of Stewart's Creek.
238.	Andrew Steel	640	On the first big creek that runs in Cumberland river.
239.	Thomas Thompson	640	On the east fork of Station Camp Creek.
240.	Abraham Chefsom	640	On the southside of Richland Creek.
241.	Magnessa McDonald	640	On the lefthand fork of Richland Creek.
242.	Lawrence Stephens	640	On the northside of Harpeth river.
243.	Jacob Stevens	640	On the westside of Stone River.
244.	William Simpson	640	On the southside Cumberland river.
245.	Jonathan Jennings	640	On Stones Creek.
246.	William Cocke	640	On the northside Cumberland river.
247.	Michael Sarrick	640	On Richland Creek.
248.	John Wilson	640	On the northside Cumberland on the middle fork of Red River.
249.	Thomas Kilgore	640	On the south fork of red river.
250.	Alexander Bohannon	640	On the northside Cumberland river.
251.	John Fulkinson	640	On Stewarts Creek a branch of Stones Creek.

252.	Rowland Maddison	640	On the northside Red River.
253.	Robert Givans	640	On Mill Creek southside Cumberland.
254.	Edward Carvin	640	On the northside Cumberland river.
255.	Samuel Habbard	640	On a south branch of Richland Creek.
256.	Hugh Henry	640	On the east side of Cedar Creek.
257.	George Muncher	640	On the westside of Station Camp Creek.
258.	William Donehoe	640	On the Sulphur Fork.
259.	Andrew Ewing	640	On the westfork of Mill Creek.
260.	David Gowan	640	On the southside Cumberland river.
261.	John Mulherrin	640	On Richland Creek southside Cumberland river.
262.	Jesse Boilstone	640	On the west fork of Bledsoe's Creek.
263.	James Robinson	640	On the southside Cumberland river.
264.	Will Price	640	On Goose Creek above Bledsoe's Creek.
265.	Maurice Shane	640	On the northside Cumberland River.
266.	John Sawyer	640	On the middle fork of Bledsoe's Creek.
267.	John Kennady	640	On Little Harpeth River.
268.	Solomon Turpin	640	On Red River below Rentfroes Station.
269.	Christopher Funkhouser	640	On Little Harpeth River.
270.	George Carlisle	640	On a creek of Big Harpeth River.
271.	James Harris	640	On the headwaters of Stoners Lick Creek.
272.	Joseph Rentfroe	640	On both sides Richland Creek.
273.	John Hobson	640	On Big Harpeth River.
274.	James Hollice	640	On the east fork of White's Creek.
275.	John Wilson	640	On Stones River.
276.	John Cockrill	640	On Stewarts Creek a branch of Stones River.
277.	John King	640	On Big Harpeth River.
278.	George Leeper	640	On the head branch of Station Camp Creek.
279.	Andrew Kincannon	640	On Big Harpeth River.
280.	William McCormack	640	On the west fork of Mill Creek.
281.	Robert Lucas	640	On east fork of Richland Creek.

282.	Isaac Shelby	640	On the waters of Browns Creek.
283.	Lewis Crane	640	On the northside Cumberland river.
284.	William Stewart	640	On the eastside of Stone's River.
285.	Peter Looney	640	On Sinking Creek.
286.	Absalom Thompson	640	On Stone's River.
287.	Jesse Benton	640	On the northside Cumberland river.
288.	John Hughes	640	On Crockett's Creek southside Cumberland.
289.	David Looney	640	On the west fork of Station Camp Creek.
290.	John Deeson	640	On the northside Cumberland River west fork of Station Camp.
291.	Thomas Woodard	640	On the northside Cumberland River.
292.	Simon Woodard	640	On the northside Cumberland River on Bledsoes Creek.
293.	Edward Swanson	640	On the eastside of the west fork of Big Harpeth.
294.	John Phillips	640	On Bledsoes Creek.
295.	Frederick Edwards	640	On the west fork of Cedar Creek.
296.	William Frame	640	On the Sulphur Fork of Red River.
297.	Christopher Beeley	640	On Stones Lick Creek.
298.	Nicholas Conrad	640	On Spring Creek southside of Cumberland.
299.	Philip Conrad	640	On Bartons Creek southside of Cumberland.
300.	Jennitt John	640	On the southside Cumberland.
301.	Ezekiel Douglass	640	On the southside Cumberland and on the northside of Big Harpeth.
302.	William McMurry	640	On a north branch of Big Harpeth.
303.	Edward Bradley	640	On the waters of Stones River.
304.	Abraham Simaster	640	On Dry Creek northside Cumberland river.
305.	Ephraim Pratt	640	On the northside Cumberland river.
306.	Morgan Osborne	640	On the southside Cumberland river.
307.	Henry Hicory	640	On Maiden Creek northside of Cumberland River.
308.	William Gossney	640	On Bartons Creek southside Cumberland.
309.	William Purnell	640	On Richland Creek a branch of Red River.

310.	Charles Thompson	640	On Richland Creek a branch of Red River.
311.	John Miller	640	On the forks of Bledsoe's Creek.
312.	Timothy Terrill	640	On the middle fork of Stones River on Farmers Creek.
313.	James Robinson	640	On the middle fork of Stones River.
314.	John Barnard	640	On the southside of Cumberland.
315.	Evan Baker	640	On dry branch near Nashbro.
316.	John Gibson	640	On the northside Cumberland river.
317.	Joseph Hannah	640	On the westside of Harpeth River.
318.	Joel Hobbles	640	On a branch of Harpeth River.
319.	James Cook	640	On Drake's Creek.
320.	Elijah Tarriss	640	On the first creek below the mouth of Red River.
321.	Nathaniel Henderson	640	On the southside Cumberland river.
322.	John Sevill	640	On Overalls Mill Creek a branch of Stones River.
323.	Pleasant Henderson	640	Joining the lands reserved for the French Lick.
324.	Titus Murry	640	On the northside Cumberland River.
325.	George Kannady	640	On the westside Cedar Creek.
326.	Jonathan Anthony	640	On Stewarts Creek a branch of Stones River.
327.	Hugh Leeper	640	On Leepers fork of Harpeth River.
328.	Michael Cashitts	640	On the head of Skeggs Creek a branch of Big Barren River.
329.	Barrah Bryant	640	On the fork of Bledsoes Creek.
330.	James Anthony	640	On the west fork of Stones River.
331.	Isaac Henry	640	On Stuart's Creek of Stones River.
332.	John Estis	640	On the southside Cumberland at the mouth of a small creek.
333.	Daniel Frazier	640	On the east fork of White's Creek.
334.	Edmund Jennings	640	On the west fork of Mill Creek.
335.	John Lamsden	640	On Heatons Station Creek.
336.	Moses Webb	640	On the eastside Mill Creek.
337.	Moses Pharrus	640	On the waters of Drakes Creek.
338.	John White	640	On Haltpone Creek northside Cumberland.
339.	John Cotter	640	On a branch of Station Camp Creek.

340.	Gasper Mansker	640	On Mansker's Creek.
341.	David Fain	640	On the east fork of Mill Creek.
342.	John Anderson	640	On the westside of Bledsoes Creek.
343.	Jesse Maxey	640	On the east fork of Station Camp Creek.
344.	John Gilkey	640	On the east fork of Mill Creek.
345.	Solomon Phelps	640	On the eastside of Mill Creek.
346.	Francis Armstrong	640	On the west fork of Richland Creek.
347.	William Hinson	640	On the west fork of Goose Creek.
348.	Isaac Kittrell	640	On the northside of Cumberland River.
349.	Isaac Lefeaver	640	On the southside of Cumberland River.
350.	unreadable		
351.	Thomas Sharpe	640	On Stuart's Creek a branch of Stones River.
352.	Daniel Smith	640	On both sides Drakes Creek near the mouth.
353.	James Shaw	640	On the northside Cumberland opposite Nashbro.
354.	James Shaw	640	On the fork between Cumberland and Red River.
355.	Henry Lovell	640	Near Ash's Station.
356.	Elmore Douglass	640	On the east fork of the middle fork of Station Camp Creek.
357.	John Poe	640	On the northside Cumberland River.
358.	James Freeland	640	On the southside Cumberland River.
359.	James Leeper	640	On the waters of Little Harpeth.
360.	Mark Robenson	640	On the southside Cumberland on Richland Creek.
361.	James Freeland	640	On the southside Cumberland.
362.	Isham Clayton	640	On the southside Cumberland and eastside Browns Creek.
363.	Elias Mires	640	On the southside Big Harpeth River.
364.	Thomas Hainey	640	On the east fork of Station Camp Creek.
365.	Henry Ohara	640	On the southside Cumberland waters of Stuarts Creek.
366.	George Green	640	On the east fork of Bledsoes Lick Creek.

367.	Ephraim Payton	640	On the west fork of Station Camp Creek.
368.	Burgess White	640	On the northside Big Harpeth mouth of Buffalo Creek.
369.	Daniel Mungle	640	On the Middle fork of Goose Creek.
370.	Stephen Rhea	640	On a branch of Mill Creek.
371.	Sampson Wilson	640	On the westfork of Goose Creek.
372.	Jarrott Manifee	640	On the southside Big Harpeth.
373.	John Morgan	640	On Bledsoe Creek.
374.	John Dunkan	640	On Spencers Creek southside Cumberland.
375.	John Craig	640	On the waters of Harpeth river.
376.	William Craig	640	On the waters of Harpeth river.
377.	Henry Rule	640	On the eastside of Gaspers Creek.
378.	John Blackamore	640	At the mouth of Dry Creek northside Cumberland.
379.	William Ashert	640	On the northside Cumberland river.
380.	William McGouch	640	On Arrington Creek east side of Harpeth.
381.	Charles Robinson	640	On the northside of Great Harpeth River.
382.	James Todd	640	On the westside of Stones River.
383.	John Herd	640	On the waters of Harpeth River.
384.	Roger Topp	640	On the southside of Cumberland.
385.	Evan Baker	640	Joining his own and Samuel Conns lines.
386.	Nathaniel Hart	640	On a branch of Stuart Creek.
387.	Charles Brantley	640	On the westfork of Red River.
388.	Alexander Allison	640	On the headwaters of middle fork of Station Camp Creek.
389.	Charles Brown	640	On the first creek of Stones River above the Clover Bottom.
390.	William Bailey	640	On the west fork of Station Camp Creek.
391.	William Bowen	640	On the southside Cumberland river.
392.	William Stewart	640	On Spring Creek.
393.	Matthew Pain	640	On the northside Cumberland and mouth of Gaspers Creek.
394.	Benjamin Pettitt	640	On the southside Cumberland.
395.	George Paine	640	On the southside Cumberland above the mouth of Cedar Creek.

#	Name	Acres	Location
396.	Roger Topp	640	On the east fork of Little Harpeth.
397.	Sampson Sawyers	640	On Little Harpeth.
398.	William Parker	640	On Station Camp Creek.
399.	John Blackemoore	640	On the westside of Drake's Creek.
400.	Elmore Douglass	640	On the middle fork of Station Camp Creek.
401.	Martin Harden	640	On Stones Creek.
402.	David Craig	640	On the waters of Great Harpeth river.
403.	Murthy Mcaboy	640	On the second creek above Goose Creek.
404.	Matthew Neely	640	On the northside Cumberland between Gibsons and Dry Creek.
405.	William White	640	Joining Charles Bowen's lines.
406.	John Hendricks	640	On Indian Creek.
407.	James Turpin	640	On Red River.
408.	James McGavock	640	On Big Harpeth River.
409.	William Burgess	640	On the second Big Creek above Stones River.
410.	Thomas Burgess	640	On the southside Cumberland river.
411.	Elijah Robinson	640	On the eastfork of Mill Creek.
412.	Andrew Crockett	640	On Little Harpeth Creek.
413.	James Toler	640	On the first creek of Stone's River above the Station.
414.	Archibald Bohannon	640	On the west side of Stone's River including the Clover Bottom.
415.	Henry Harden	640	On the northside Cumberland river.
416.	Abraham Price	640	About 2 miles from Bledsoe's Lick.
417.	James Mulherrin	640	On the southside Cumberland river.
418.	Thomas Denton	640	On the middle fork of Red River.
419.	Spilly Coleman	640	On the southside Cumberland river.
420.	David Shelton	640	On the southside Cumberland river on the Caney Fork.
421.	Nicholas Baker	640	On the east fork of Stones River.
422.	Richard Cox	640	On Indian Creek.
423.	Matthew Anderson	640	On the eastside of the west fork of Station Camp.
424.	James Malding	640	On the middle fork of Red River.
425.	William Newing	640	On the head spring of Little Harpeth.

426.	Robert Roseberry	640	On an east bank of Richland Creek.
427.	William McWherter	640	On the fork of Sinking Creek.
428.	William Montgomery	640	On Drakes Creek.
429.	John McMurtry	640	On the middle fork of Gasper's Creek.
430.	James Givens	640	On the westside Little Harpeth.
431.			
432.	Henry Daughterty	640	On the Dry Fork of Bledsoe's Creek.
433.	William Mitchell	640	Joining William Loggans lines.
434.	William Moore	640	On the southside Stones River.
435.	James Thompson	640	On the headwaters of Lick Creek.
436.	Joseph Jackson	640	On the second creek above Stones river.
437.	James Brown	640	On the southside Cumberland east fork Mill Creek.
438.	Ebenezer Titus	640	On a branch of Little Harpeth river.
439.	John Holt	640	On a branch of Stones River.
440.	James Crockett	640	On the southside Little Harpeth.
441.	James Hays	640	On the southside Cumberland above Drake's Creek.
442.	James Lawless	640	On the southside Cumberland opposite the mouth of Drake's Creek.
443.	Thomas Kilgore	640	On the southside Manskers lick.
444.	Thomas Miggerson	640	On a fork of Overalls Creek.
445.	Hugh Logan	640	On the second creek above Goose Creek.
446.	James Shanklin	640	On the southside Cumberland.
447.	William Moore	640	On the southside Cumberland 6 miles below Harpeth.
448.	John Shockley	640	On Goose Creek northside Cumberland.
449.	Elijah Robinson	640	On the French Lick Branch.
450.	Edward Cox	640	On the eastfork of Station Camp.
451.	Joseph Blackford	640	In the fork between Cumberland and Red River.
452.	Joseph Bean	640	On the northside Red River.
453.	Isaac Bledsoe	640	On the waters of Bledsoe's Lick Creek.

#	Name	Acres	Location
454.	Isaac Bledsoe	640	On the waters of Bledsoe's Lick Creek.
455.	Perry Graves	640	On the southside Cumberland River.
456.	Ebenezer Mann	640	On a small branch below Sinking Creek.
457.	James Smith	640	On Bledsoe's Creek.
458.	James Ray	640	Below the mouth of Mairsobone Creek.
459.	Lewis Reeland	640	On the waters of Drakes Creek.
460.	Ralph Wilson	640	On Stones River above the Station.
461.	William Ray	640	About 7 miles from Bledsoes Creek.
462.	William Collier	640	On the southside Red River.
463.	James Robinson	640	Joining McGavocks claim on Harpeth.
464.	Richard Henderson	640	On the southside Cumberland river.
465.	Robert Looney	640	On Knife Creek northside Cumberland river.
466.	Thomas Spencer	640	On both sides Drake Creek.
467.	Charles Deneth	640	On the west fork of Mill Creek.
468.	William Lucas	640	On a branch of Richland Creek.
469.	John Phillips	640	On the northside Cumberland river.
470.	Thomas Manphall?	640	On the waters of Harpeth River.
471.	John Crockett	640	?
472.	Richard Hogan	640	On a small fork of Bledsoes Creek.
473.	John Owen	640	On the third big creek above Stones River.
474.	Samuel Newell	640	On the westside of the west fork of Station Camp Creek.
475.	Anthony Bledsoe	640	On the waters of Bledsoe's Creek.
476.	Horatio Rolls	640	On the west fork of Bledsoe's Creek.
477.	John Fletcher	640	On Norris Spring Branch.
478.	Jordan Gibson	640	On the northside Bledsoes Lick Creek.
479.	George Freeland	640	Between the public lands of Dentons Lick and French Lick.
480.	John Calloway	640	On the upper fork of Station Camp Creek.
481.	Anthony Bledsoe	640	On the southside Cumberland 3 miles above Drakes Lick.
482.	Archibald Taylor	640	On the waters of Bledsoes Creek.

483.	Robert Montgomery	640	On the west fork of Bledsoes Creek.
484.	Joseph Moseley	640	On Stewarts Creek.

Total Preemptions 309,760 Acres

Major General Nathaniel Green

1786
Davidson County

1.	Archibald Lytle	7,200	On the west fork of Stones River.
2.	Alexander Martin	2,314	On Big Harpeth River.
3.	George Daugherty	4,800	On both sides of Walnut Creek.
4.	Matthew McCawley	640	On both sides Spring Creek.
5.	Matthew McCawley	761	On both sides of a small creek near Brushy.
6.	James Bosley	274	On both sides Cumberland River.
7.	Lazaras Floren	274	On Little Harpeth.
8.	Thomas Mulloy	228	On the southside of Harpeth on Cumberland River.
9.	Richard Floren	274	On the southside of Harpeth.
10.	William Hargrove	2,560	On the northside of Harpeth on Wells? Creek
11.	Samuel Budd	3,840	On both sides of lick at Bird Creek.
12.	Samuel Jones	3,840	On Spring and Cedar Creek.
13.	William Mebane	7,200	On both sides the westfork of Big Harpeth.
14.	Reading Blount	4,800	On the waters of Stones River.
15.	William Blount	1,240	On Marks Creek northside Tenessee.
16.	John Blount	274	On Big Harpeth River.
17.	William Blount	1,240	On the waters of Big Harpeth River.
18.	John Gray Blount	1,097	On the waters of Big Harpeth River.
19.	John Gray Blount	640	On Marks Creek east side of _?_ .
20.	Tilghman Dixon	3,840	On Dixon's Creek.
21.	Robert Tenner	2,057	On both sides Sulphur Fork of Red River.
22.	William Lenton	1,417	On Parsons Creek of Red River.

23.	Selly Hamey	7,200	On the northside of Cumberland.
24.	Rebecca Parkison	2,560	On the head of the first creek below Harpeth.
25.	William Armstrong	3,840	On the southside Cumberland river.
26.	Thomas Dudley	2,560	On the waters of Wells Creek.
27.	Samuel Ashe	1,500	On both sides the east and west fork of Thompsons Creek.
28.	William Bushe	2,560	On both sides the east and west fork of Thompsons Creek.
29.	Thomas Clarke	2,560	On the southside Cumberland river.
30.	Elijah Moore	3,840	On both sides Duck River.
31.	George Davidson	5,760	On the northside Tennessee River.
32.	Charles Gerrard	2,560	On the southside Cumberland river.
33.	Joseph McDowald	1,737	On Pleasant Creek waters of Cumberland.
34.	James McRoy	3,840	On the northside Cumberland River.
35.	James Armstrong	7,200	On the westside of Stones River.
36.	Anthony Sharpe	3,840	On Big Harpeth River.
37.	Thomas Tinney	2,560	On Richland Creek.
38.	Benjamin Bayley	4,480	On the northside Cumberland.
39.	Hardy Murfree	5,760	On the west fork of Big Harpeth river.
40.	James Thackstone	4,352	On the west fork of Big Harpeth river.
41.	Charles Dean	2,560	On both sides west fork of Goose Creek.
42.	Frederick Hargett	1,508	On Willow Creek.
43.	Hardy Murfree	1,168	On the waters of Stones Creek.
44.	Nathaniel Williams	2,560	On the northside Cumberland river.
45.	Curtis Ivey	2,560	On both sides Harpeth River.
46.	Peater Beacote	3,840	On both sides Duck River.
47.	Clement Hall	3,840	On the waters of Overall Creek a branch of Stones River.
48.	Thomas Armstrong	3,840	On the main westfork of Stones River.
49.	Thomas Callendar	3,840	On the northside Cumberland river.
50.	Joseph Terrible	1,371	On the waters of Mill Creek.
51.	Alexander Nelson	763	On the eastside Big Harpeth River.
52.	Nehemiah Long	1,783	On the waters of Halfpone Creek.
53.	Robert Brownfield	1,000	On the eastfork of Buffaloe Creek.

54.	James Mills	3,840	On a large creek northside Tenessee.
55.	Samuel Hogan	12,000	On the southside Cumberland river at mouth of Caney Fork.
56.	John Kingsbury	4,800	On Beaver Creek waters of Cany Fork.
57.	John Armstrong	5,760	Joining the Officers and Soldiers south boundry line.
58.	Nathaniel Jones	2,560	On the southside Cumberland river.
59.	Jonathan Loomas	3,940	On Cedar Creek southside Cumberland.
60.	James Tate	1,553	On the southside Tennessee.
61.	John Macon	1,097	On the eastside Buffaloe Creek.
62.	Walter Allen	912	On Spring Creek southside Cumberland river.
63.	Dixon Marshall	2,560	On the northside Cumberland river.
64.	William Terrible	3,062	On Beaver Creek.
65.			
66.	Samuel Ashe	2,560	On Wolf Creek.
67.	William Facon? (Bacon)	3,840	On the Fork of Elk Creek.
68.	Hardy Murfree	2,560	On both sides Cedar Creek.
69.	Joshua Hadley	3,840	On the northside of Duck River.
70.	Joseph Blythe	4,800	On the head of Duck River.
71.	Benjamin Carter	3,840	On both sides Carter's Creek.
72.	Nathaniel Alexander	1,000	On the northside of Tennessee river.
73.	Thomas Donohoe	4,800	On Goose Creek northside Cumberland River.
74.	Joseph Muntford	3,840	On the east fork of Stones River.
75.	James Fergus	4,000	On the waters of Mill Creek.
76.	William Sanders	2,560	On the mouth of Dixon's Creek.
77.	Francis Child	3,840	On Canee Fork waters of Cumberland River.
78.	James Cole Mentflorence	1,420	On both sides Red River.
79.	James Bradley	1,280	On the waters of the east fork of Mill Creek.
80.	Martin Phifer Jun.	1,143	At the mouth of Goose Creek.
81.	Nathaniel Dixon	944	On the southside Cumberland river.
82.	Jesse Steed	2,560	On Leepers Fork waters of Harpeth River.

83.	Robert Tenner	3,840	On Blue Creek.
84.	William Polk	1,888	On both sides the main west fork of Harpeth River.
85.	Nathaniel Laurens	2,560	On Spring Creek southside Cumberland River.
86.	John Campbell	2,560	On the West fork of Lick Creek on Cumberland River.
87.	James Tatom	2,560	Joining the Virginia Line.
88.	John Williams	1,144	On the northside Cumberland river.
89.	Robert Douglass	2,560	On Mill Creek a branch of Caney Fork.
90.	Christopher William Brocke	1,000	On the southside Cumberland river.
91.	Absalom Burgess	1,000	On the southside of Cumberland river.
92.	Lardner Clark	228	On the west fork of Harpeth river.
93.	John Nicholls	1,000	On both sides Big Harpeth River.
94.	Thomas Brooks	429	On the southside Cumberland River.
95.	Archibald Henderson	773	On Beaver Creek.
96.	Philip Burgess	640	On Camp Creek.
97.	Christopher Owens	640	On the southside Big Harpeth river.
98.	James Jamison	640	On Camp Creek.
99.	Hardy Murphree	640	On both sides Spring Creek.
100.	Christopher Guice?	640	On Guices Creek.
101.	David Edwards	640	On Sycamore Creek.
102.	Nathaniel Hughs	316	On Sinking Creek a branch of Red River.
103.	Sutherland Mayfield	640	On Mill Creek.
104.	John Allen	640	On the east fork of Buffaloe Creek.
105.	Lardner Clarke & Wykoff	228	On the northside Cumberland river.
106.	John Drury	640	On Yellow Creek.
107.	James Hamilton	274	On Stones River.
108.	Elisha Davis	274	On the southside Cumberland river.
109.	Robert King	640	On Caleb's Creek of Richland Creek.
110.	Mourning Wheeler & Elizabeth Underwood	640	On the waters of Mill Creek.
111.	William Baxton	640	On the eastfork of Yellow Creek.
112.	Anthony Gavin?	640	On the main westfork of Stones River.

113.	David Edwards	640	On Station Camp Creek.
114.	John Jennings	365	On Spencers Creek.
115.	Joshua Howard	274	On both sides of Whites and Heatons Creek.
116.	James Peel	640	On a large creek running into Tenessee River.
117.	William Parr	274	On the northside of Cumberland river.
118.	Thomas Jaunt	640	On Blount's Creek of Tennessee River.
119.	John Hick	1,000	On Persons Creek.
120.	Benjamin Reed	640	On the waters of Little Harpeth river.
121.	John McNees	640	On the westside of Harpeth River.
122.	Michael Bullen	640	On Camp Creek.
123.	John Nilson	274	On the northside Cumberland River.
124.	James Brown	640	On the Sulphur Fork of Red River.
125.	Hancock Nicholls	640	On the eastfork of Camp Creek.
126.	William Beck	640	On the southside Cumberland River.
127.	Josiah McDonald	274	On the southside Cumberland River.
128.	George Daugherty	640	On the eastfork of Buffaloe Creek.
129.	Mason Williams	228	On the waters of Stones Creek.
130.	Marmaduke Scott	640	On the eastfork of Yellow Creek.
131.	Memicum Hunt	1,000	On the westfork of Harpeth River.
132.	Jacob Matthews	640	On Willis's Creek.
133.	Richard Thomas	228	On Parsons Creek a branch of Red River.
134.	Hardy Murphree	640	On the waters of Wolf Creek.
135.	John Buckannon	640	On the waters of Mill Creek.
136.	Thomas Taylor	640	On the westside of the west fork of Harpeth river.
137.	John Donelson	640	On the waters of Big Harpeth river.
138.	Robert Bradley	640	On Camp Creek.
139.	John Nicholls	773	On both sides Yellow Creek.
140.	James Ross	274	On Sinking Creek.
141.	Elisha Hunt	640	On the headwaters of Whites Creek.
142.	Philip Cate	640	On Camp Creek northside Duck River.

143.	William Anderson	274	On the eastside Big Harpeth River.
144.	William Lomas	274	On the northside Cumberland River.
145.	Hardy Murphree	228	On Eaton's Creek North side of Cumberland River.
146.	David Bizzell	640	On both sides Bartons Creek.
147.	Hardy Murphree	440	On the waters of Wolf Creek.
148.	Thomas Davis	640	On both sides Blue Creek.
149.	Peter Dunnock	640	On the east fork of Yellow Creek.
150.	Stephen Lynn	1,000	On Thompson's Creek.
151.	Michael Smith	640	On a small branch of Cumberland River.
152.	Green Hill	640	On the northside of Tenessee River.
153.	Ransom Savage	560	Joining Peter Clouds lines.
154.	Hardy Murphree	640	On both sides Spring Creek.
155.	Adam Boyd	7,200	On the northside Cumberland River.
156.	Benjamin Flood	640	On the southside Cumberland River.
157.	Seivis Brown	640	On the waters of Station Camp Creek.
158.	Peter Cloud	274	On Gaspers Creek.
159.	Nancy & Elizabeth Reardon	640	On the waters of Stones River.
160.	William Davis	640	On the southside Stones? River.
161.	Peter Paynor	274	On the southside of Cumberland River.
162.	John Butler	228	On the waters of Stones River.
163.	Abner Lamb	2,560	On the northside Cumberland River.
164.	Thomas Armstrong	640	On the southside Stones River.
165.	John White	228	On the westfork of Big Harpeth River.
166.	Green Hill	640	On Mill Creek waters of Little Harpeth.
167.	James Purdie	281	On the southside Cumberland River.
168.	Lardner Clark	640	On the fork of Mill Creek.
169.	Hardy Murphree	640	On some branches of Murphress Fork.
170.	Hardy Murphree	274	On both sides the east fork of Whites Creek.
171.	William Sexton	640	On the waters of Cedar Creek.
172.	John Richardson	274	On the waters of Boones Creek.
173.	George Nevill	350	On Red River.

174.	Thomas Spencer	1,000	On the northside Cumberland river.
175.	Robert Thompson	274	On the westside Big Harpeth River.
176.	James Robinson	428	On the east side of the west fork of Harpeth.
177.	James Brickell	228	On the waters of Richland Creek.
178.	Tedzik Williams	280	On the waters of Richland Creek.
179.	Timothy Acuff	640	Between Stewart and Farmers Creek.
180.	Jonathan Drake	640	On Cumberland River.
181.	Green Hill	1,000	On the southside Duck River.
182.	James Robertson	274	On the southside Cumberland river.
183.	Thomas Jennings	365	On a branch of Kaspers Creek.
184.	Green Hill	640	On the northside of Tenesee river.
185.	James Hollis	640	On a branch of Halfpone Creek.
186.	William Johnston	428	On Red River.
187.	Humphrey Hogan	640	On both sides of Sulphur fork of Red River.
188.	John Pierce	640	On the southside Cumberland river.
189.	William White	274	On the waters of Whites Creek.
190.	Thomas Fletcher	580	On the East fork of Mill Creek.
191.	James Robertson	274	On the waters of Big Harpeth.
192.	William Holderness	640	On the waters of Goose Creek.
193.	James Summers	857	On Red River.
194.	Henry Winborne	389	On the waters of Stones River.
195.	John Wells	640	On the waters of Stones River.
196.	Silas Senton	640	On the southside Cumberland river.
197.	Joseph Mitchell	274	On the waters of Stones River.
198.	William Washington	1,000	On Parsons Creek.
199.	David Edwards	640	On a branch of Sycamore Creek.
200.	Ezekiel White	274	On the waters of Stones River.
201.	Thomas Powell	320	On the waters of Stones River.
202.	Daniel McMahan	228	On the waters of Big Harpeth.
203.	William Ponder	318	On the waters of Stones River.
204.	Abraham Spyers	360	On the northside of Cumberland river.
205.	James Launders	640	On Rock Creek.
206.	Ezekiel Polk	640	On Richland Creek.

No.	Name	Acres	Location
207.	John Williams	657	On the middle fork of Goose Creek.
208.	Green Hill	274	On the northside Cumberland river.
209.	James Robertson	274	On the bent of Cumberland above the mouth of Richland Creek.
210.			
211.	Badger Asker?	640	On Hawk Creek south of Cumberland River.
212.	Jason Thompson	640	On the waters of Mill Creek.
213.	Hardy Murphree	228	On the waters of west Harpeth river.
214.	James Robertson	274	On the bent of Cumberland river above Richland Creek.
215.	Hardy Murphree	228	On both sides the east fork of Station Camp Creek.
216.	Benjamin Hodges	640	On Spring Creek.
217.	Henry Johnston	640	On Blount's Creek northside Tenessee.
218.	Dempsey Jenkins	320	On the waters of Stones River.
219.	Benjamin Smith	420	On the waters of Stones River.
220.	William Bowman	640	On the waters of Stones River.
221.	Richard Phillips	274	On the southside of Richland Creek.
222.	John Gambier Scull	1,127	On a creek of Duck River.
223.	Bryant Smith	342	On the waters of Stones River.
224.	James Thompson	274	On the waters of Richland Creek.
225.	Abraham Hargiss	228	On Red River.
226.	Job Rotchell	640	Between Red River and Sulphur Fork.
227.	John Lewis Beard	640	On Harpeth River southside Cumberland River.
228.	John Lewis Beard	640	On Harpeth River southside Cumberland River.
229.	Green Hill	640	On Big Hurricane Creek waters of Stones River.
230.	Hardy Murfree	274	On the waters of Sycamore Creek.
231.	James Saunders	640	On the northside Cumberland River.
232.	Hardy Holmes	2,560	On Farmers Creek waters of Stones River.
233.	Hardy Jones	360	On Spring Creek.
234.	Hardy Murfree	640	On Spring Creek.
235.	James Emmett	1,600	On both sides the south fork of Meadow Creek.

236.	Isaac Pennington	266	On Red River.
237.	Thomas Dicky	1,000	On the waters of Harpeth River.
238.	James Colston	274	On the northside Cumberland river.
239.	Giles Carter	274	On both sides Maddefons Creek.
240.	Leticia Archer	640	On the southside Cumberland river.
241.	William Beck	640	On the eastside of Spring Creek.
242.	Sutherland Mayfield	640	On the east fork of Mill Creek.
243.	Joel Lewis	640	On the east fork of Yellow Creek.
244.	Robert Jordan	640	On the northside Tennessee river.
245.	Isaac Butler	228	At the mouth of McAdoes Creek.
246.	Thomas Cotten	640	On the waters of Stones River.
247.	Robert Nelson	357	Joining James Shaws preemption.
248.	Lardner Clark	420	On the waters of Stones River.
249.	Hardy Murfree	914	On both sides Cedar Creek.
250.	Caleb Phifer	640	On Pleasant Creek.
251.	William Mardery	357	On the waters of Hayes Creek a branch of Big Harpeth.
252.	Robert Nelson	429	On the westside of Big Harpeth river.
253.	James McCuestion	420	On the east fork of Mill Creek.
254.	Thomas Dicky	640	On the waters of Stones River.
255.	Thomas Sawyer	274	On the southside Cumberland River.
256.	David Adkens	640	On the east fork of Yellow Creek.
257.	John Baptist Ashe	445	On Ashes? Creek northside of Tennessee.
258.	John Nelson	4,800	On Nelson Creek a branch of Big Harpeth.
259.	John Walker	1,709	On a creek of Duck Creek.
260.	Alexander Brevard	3,840	On Brevards Creek northside Tenessee.
261.	James Martin	1,114	On West Harpeth River.
262.	William Walton	3,840	On the northside Cumberland river.
263.	Jacob Turner	3,840	On the main fork of Halfpone Creek.
264.	Joseph Brevard	2,560	On the northside Tennessee river.
265.	William Ross	1,000	On Sinking Creek a branch of red river.
266.	Griffith Rutherford	1,000	On the northside Tennessee river.
267.	Archibald Butts	1,000	On the northside Cumberland river.

268.	Gideon Lamb	6,171	On Thompson's Creek South side of Cumberland river.
		1787	
269.	Willoughby Williams	640	On the eastside of Blooming Grove.
270.	Willoughby Williams	640	On both sides Buzzard Creek eastside of Blooming Grove.
271.	James Glasgow	640	On both sides Buzzard Creek eastside of Blooming Grove.
272.	James Glasgow	640	On the War Trace Creek.
273.	James Glasgow	228	On the northside of Cumberland river.
274.	Richard Fenner	2,560	On the waters of Station Camp Creek.
275.	Richard Fenner	640	On the Sulphur Fork of red river.
276.	Richard Fenner	640	On the southside Cumberland river.
277.	Richard Fenner	640	On the southside Cumberland river.
278.	Richard Fenner	640	On the southside Cumberland river.
279.	James Cole MonFlorence	640	On the northside Cumberland river.
280.	James Cole MonFlorence	640	On Collins River.
281.	James Cole MontFlorence	640	On the southside Cumberland river on Collins River.
282.	James Cole MontFlorence	640	On the southside Cumberland river.
283.	James Cole MontFlorence	640	On a branch of Cedar Creek.
284.	James Cole MontFlorence	640	On the southside Cumberland river and on Collins River.
285.	James Cole MontFlorence	640	On the northside Cumberland River.
286.	James Cole MontFlorence	640	On the southside Cumberland river.
287.	James Cole MontFlorence	640	On the southside Cumberland river.
288.	Andrew Breakey	640	On the waters of Sulphur Fork.
289.	Andrew Breakey	640	On the southside Red River.
290.	Andrew Breakey	640	On a branch of Sulphur fork.
291.	Andrew Breakey	640	On the southside of Red River.
292.	Andrew Breakey	640	On Millers Creek.
293.	Andrew Breakey	640	On the fork of Cumberland and Red River.
294.	John Rice, Abraham Reston & Elisha Rice	640	On the eastside of Stones River.
295.	John Rice, Abraham Reston & Elisha Rice	640	On a branch of Smith's Creek.

296.	John Rice, Abraham Reston & Elisha Rice	640	On the southside of Stones River.
297.	John Rice, Abraham Reston & Elisha Rice	1,000	On the middle fork of Drake's Creek.
298.	John Rice, Abraham Reston & Elisha Rice	640	On the northside of Tennessee river.
299.	John Rice, Abraham Reston & Elisha Rice	640	On the northside of Tennessee river.
300.	John Rice, Abraham Reston & Elisha Rice	640	On the northside of Tennessee river.
301.	John Rice, Abraham Reston & Elisha Rice	640	On the westside of Stones River.
302.	John Rice, Abraham Reston & Elisha Rice	640	On the northside Tennessee river.
303.	John Rice, Abraham Reston & Elisha Rice	640	On Smith's Creek on a fork of Cany Fork.
304.	John Reese & James Sappington	640	On Carrs Creek of Sulphur fork.
305.	John Reese & Compy	640	On the west fork of Jones Creek.
306.	Solomon Kett	640	On the southside Cumberland river.
307.	James Saunders	640	On Drakes Creek.
308.	Robert Burton	640	On a branch of Smith's Creek.
309.	James Lanier	640	On Long Creek waters of the Barren River.
310.	Richard Fenner	640	On the waters of Stones River.
311.	John Rice, Abraham Reston & Elisha Rice	640	On Smith Creek on a fork of Caney Fork.
312.	James Cole MontFlorence & Richard Fenner	640	On the northside Cumberland river.
313.	James Cole MontFlorence & Richard Fenner	640	On the southside Cumberland river.
314.	Richard Fenner	640	On the waters of Sulphur fork.
315.	Richard Fenner	640	On Mooney Fork Creek.
316.	Richard Fenner	640	On the waters of Second Creek a branch of Stones River.
317.	Richard Fenner	640	On the southside Cumberland river.
318.	Richard Fenner	640	On the southside Cumberland river.
319.	James Cole Mont Florence	640	On the southside of Sulphur fork.
320.	Andrew Armstrong	640	On the west fork of Goose Creek.
321.	Andrew Armstrong	1,000	On a branch of Sulphur fork.
322.	William Ross	640	On the waters of Red River.
323.	William Ross	640	On the waters of Red River.

324.	Samuel Buchannon	640	On the waters of Spring Creek.
325.	Samuel Buchannon	400	On the waters of Stones River.
326.	Robert Marley	640	On the waters of Spring Creek.
327.	Robert Marley	640	Joining his own and Blounts lines.
328.	Robert Marley	640	On the waters of Spring Creek.
329.	Eli Newland	220	On the waters of a west fork of Spring Creek.
330.	William Ross	640	On the ridge between Red River and Station Camp Creek.
331.	William Ross	640	On the ridge between Red River and Station Camp Creek.
332.	William Buxton	640	On the headwaters of Station Camp Creek.
333.	William Buxton	640	On the northside Cumberland river.
334.	Oliver Tuton	640	On the northside Cumberland River.
335.	Oliver Tuton	640	On the northside Cumberland River.
336.	William Tuton	274	On the eastside Cany Fork River.
337.	William Tuton	640	On the southside Cumberland River.
338.	William Tuton	274	On the northside Cumberland River.
339.	William Tuton	274	On the southside Cumberland River.
340.	Robert Weakley	640	On the northside Cumberland River.
341.	Robert Weakley	640	On the northside Cumberland river on the north waters of Sycamore Creek.
342.	Robert Weakley	640	On the north waters of Sycamore Creek.
343.	Robert Weakley	640	On the westside of Sycamore Creek.
344.	James Donnelly	274	On the clear branch of Richland Creek.
345.	William Faitte	640	On the waters of Half pone Creek.
346.	William Gubbins	640	On the southside the Sulphur fork of Red River.
347.	William Saunders	640	On Maney Fork a branch of Stones River.
348.	John Thompson	640	On the west fork of Red river.
349.	John Boyd	640	On the waters of Spring Creek.
350.	Mary? Allen	?	On the southside Big Harpeth.
351.	Martin Armstrong	640	On Sturgeon Creek the northside of Sulphur Fork.
352.	Benjamin Sheppard	640	On both sides the middle fork of Drakes Creek.

353.	Benjamin Sheppard	640	On the westside of the east fork of Drakes Creek.
354.	Benjamin Sheppard	640	On both sides of large creek of Big Barron River.
355.	Benjamin Sheppard	640	On the east fork of Drakes Creek.
356.	Benjamin Sheppard	640	On the east fork of Drakes Creek.
357.	Benjamin Sheppard	640	On both sides the third creek of Big Beaver River.
358.	Benjamin Sheppard	640	On both sides the east fork of Drakes Creek.
359.	Benjamin Sheppard	640	On the west fork of Drakes Creek.
360.	Benjamin Sheppard	640	On the southside of Big Barron River.
361.	Benjamin Sheppard	640	On both sides the west fork of Drakes Creek.
362.	Benjamin Sheppard	640	On the main fork of Big Barren.
363.	Benjamin Sheppard	640	On the westside of the east fork of Drakes Creek.
364.	Benjamin Sheppard	640	On the northside Cumberland river.
365.	Benjamin Sheppard	640	On the eastfork of Drakes Creek.
366.	Benjamin Sheppard	640	On both sides the east fork of Drakes Creek.
367.	Benjamin Sheppard	640	On the westside the middle fork of Drakes Creek.
368.	Benjamin Sheppard	640	On both sides the east fork of Drakes Creek.
369.	Robert Nelson	640	On the sulphur fork of Red River.
370.	Robert Nelson	640	On the northside Cumberland river.
371.	Robert Nelson	640	On Red River.
372.	William Lytle	3,840	On the northside Cumberland river.
373.	John Buchannon	640	On Stones River.
374.	James Lanier	640	On Punchen Camp branch of Barren River.
375.	John Blair	640	On the east fork of Spring Creek.
376.	Robert Nelson	640	On the northside Cumberland River.
377.	Robert Nelson	640	On the southside of Red River.
378.	John Nicholls	1,000	On the waters of Station Camp Creek.
379.	John Nicholls	640	On the northside Cumberland river.
380.	Joseph Fleming	640	On the northside Cumberland river on Brushy Creek.
381.	John Barns	640	On the southside Cumberland river.

382.	Richard Dauge	640	On a north branch of Sycamore.
383.	Benjamin Sheppard	640	On the northside Cumberland river.
384.	Benjamin Sheppard	640	On both sides Drakes Creek.
385.	Benjamin Sheppard	640	On both sides the eastfork of Drakes Creek.
386.	John Allison	228	Joining his other claim.
387.	Robert Nelson	640	On Goose Creek.
388.	Robert Nelson	640	On both sides Red River.
389.	Robert Nelson	1,000	On Big Harpeth River.
390.	John Blair	1,000	On the waters of Spring Creek.
391.	James Lanair	640	On the southside of Big Barron River.
392.	Thomas McCrory	640	On the waters of Big Harpeth.
393.	John Nicholls	640	On the westside of Sycamore Creek.
394.	John Nicholls	640	On the waters of Sulphur Fork of Red River.
395.	Archibald Lytle	640	On Second Creek.
396.	John Allison	220	On the northside Cumberland river.
397.	Robert Nelson	640	On Groves Creek.
398.	Robert Nelson	640	On the northside Cumberland river.
399.	John Nicholls	640	On the northside Cumberland river.
400.	John Nicholls	457	On the northside Cumberland river.
401.	John Nicholls	1,000	On the westside Caney Fork.
402.	John Nicholls	1,000	On Spring Creek.
403.	John Nicholls	640	On the waters of Red River.
404.	John Nicholls	640	On the eastside of Caney Fork.
405.	Reading Blount	640	On the south branch of Sycamore Creek.
406.	Reading Blount	640	On the south branch of Sycamore Creek.
407.	Reading Blount	640	On the northside Cumberland river.
408.	Reading Blount	640	On the north branches of Marrow Bone Creek.
409.	Reading Blount	640	On the south branches of Sycamore Creek.
410.	Reading Blount	640	Between Sycamore and Marrow Bone Creek.
411.	Reading Blount	640	On Sycamore Creek.
412.	Reading Blount	640	On the south branches of Sycamore Creek.

413.	Reading Blount	640	On the south branches of Sycamore Creek.
414.	John Gray Blount	7,200	On the east fork of Stones River.
415.	Miller Sawyer	1,000	On the east side of Caney fork.
416.	John Ingles	3,840	On the waters of Bledsoes Creek.
417.	William Hughlett	640	On the southside Cumberland river.
418.	Moses Hazard	640	On meat camp of Barton's Creek.
419.	William Cole	274	On the northside of Sulphur fork of Red River.
420.	Melone Mullen	228	On the southside of Big Harpeth river.
421.	Ennis Ward	274	On meat camp or Bartons Creek.
422.	John Barbey	274	On the southside Cumberland river.
423.	John Koin	571	On Spencers Creek.
424.	James Douge	428	On the southside Cumberland river.
425.	William Thompson	428	On the North Cross Creek.
426.	Willoughby Williams	640	On the southside Richland Creek.
427.	Willoughby Williams	640	Near Turnball's near Clay Lick.
428.	Martin Armstrong	640	On the southside Richland Creek.
429.	Martin Armstrong	1,000	On the southside Cumberland river.
430.	Martin Armstrong & Anthony Crouthers	2,560	On Thompsons Creek.
431.	John Wilson	640	On Sulphur Fork.
432.	William McClure	4,840	On the northside Cumberland river.
433.	James Bryant	274	On Mill Creek.
434.	John Nicholls	640	On the northside Cumberland river.
435.	Jesse Reed	274	On the southside Big Barren river.
436.	James Bradley	640	On a branch of Stones River.
437.	Missendon Matthews	274	On Station Camp Creek.
438.	Matthew Kincannon	640	On the waters of Second Creek.
439.	Joshua Hadley	274	On the northside Cumberland river.
440.	Joshua Davis	640	On Fifth Creek.
441.	Henry Hannaws	274	On the northside Cumberland river.
442.	Anthony Hart	2,194	On the Caney Fork northside Cumberland river.
443.	Thomas Buncomb	7,200	On the westside of Richland Creek.
444.	Jesse Shute	640	On Spring Creek.
445.	David Shelton	640	On the southside Cumberland.

446.	James Glasgow	228	On Blooming Grove Creek.
447.	John Marshall	640	On Maney Fork Creek a branch of Stones River.
448.	John Marshall	640	On Maney Fork Creek a branch of Stones River.
449.	John Marshall	228	On Station Camp Creek.
450.	John Marshall	640	On Maney Fork Creek.
451.	John Marshall	640	On Maney Fork Creek.
452.	John Marshall	357	On Maney Fork Creek.
453.	John Marshall	640	On Hurricane Creek of Maney Fork Creek.
454.	John Marshall	228	On Maney Fork Creek of Stones River.
455.	John Marshall	640	On Maney Fork Creek of Stones River.
456.	John Marshall	640	On Maney Fork Creek of Stones River.
457.	John Marshall	640	On Maney Fork Creek of Stones River.
458.	John Marshall	297	On Maney Fork Creek.
459.	John Marshall	640	On Maney Fork Creek.
460.	John Marshall	640	On Maney Fork Creek.
461.	John Marshall	220	On Maney Fork Creek.
462.	John Marshall	274	On Maney Fork Creek.
463.	William Saunders	640	On Maney Fork Creek of Stones River.
464.	Archibald Marlen	297	On both sides of Stone's Creek.
465.	Dempsy Campbell	640	Between Blooming Grove and Cross Creek.
466.	Henry Hughs	640	On the middle fork of Station Camp Creek.
467.	James Bradley	228	On the head of Crane's Creek.
468.	Thomas Scuydon	274	On Third Creek southside Cumberland River.
469.	William Saunders	640	On Maney Fork Creek.
470.	David Kannady	640	On the waters of Station Camp Creek.
471.	Thomas Evans	640	On the southside Cumberland river.
472.	James Bradley	428	On the waters of Second Creek.
473.	William Saunders	640	On Maney Fork Creek.
474.	Thomas Campbell	274	On the northside Cumberland river.

475.	Jesse Harrison	274	On the southside Cumberland river.
476.	John Garrold	440	On the northside Cumberland river.
477.	Thomas Montcriefe	274	On the southside Cumberland river.
478.	Charles Gilmore	640	On Spring Creek.
479.	Thomas Barrott Jun.	3,840	On the southside Cumberland river.
480.	Martin Armstrong	640	On the southside Cumberland river.
481.	William Sheppard	357	On the northside Cumberland river.
482.	William Sheppard	274	On the northside Cumberland river.
483.	John McCoy Alston	640	On Red River.
484.	Stephen Cantrell	640	On the Sulphur Fork of Red River.
485.	Thomas Barker	220	On the south fork of Red River.
486.	Thomas Isbell	640	On Long Creek of Barren River.
487.	Peggy Allen	640	On the Sulphur Fork of Red River.
488.	Martin Armstrong	640	On the head waters of Marrowbone Creek.
489.	Willoughby Williams	404	On the northside Spencer Creek.
490.	Elijah Robertson	640	On the northside Cumberland river.
491.	James Hoggett	228	On Sulphur Creek on northside Cumberland river.
492.	Richard Fanner	640	On Sulphur Creek of Red River.
493.	Hardy Murfree	274	On the first branch of Sulphur fork.
494.	John Taylor	430	On Manson Creek.
495.	William McNeily	640	On the southside Cumberland river.
496.	John & James Bonner	1,097	On the northside Cumberland river.
497.	Reubin Douglass	640	On the waters of Station Camp Creek.
498.	James Saunders	640	On the southside Cumberland river.
499.	Samuel Lockhart	5,760	On the northside Tennessee at the mouth of Indian Creek.
500.	Nicholas Coonrod?	640	On the northside Cumberland river.
501.	James Snell	274	On the westside Wartrace Creek.
502.	Thomas Hamilton	640	On the northside Cumberland river.
503.	Thomas Pashire	2,560	On the eastside of Big Harpeth River.
504.	Joshua Davis	640	On both sides Third Creek.
505.	Thomas Evans	640	On the waters of Big Harpeth.
506.	George _____	640	On Third Creek.

No.	Name	Acres	Location
507.	Joshua Davis	640	On Third Creek.
508.	Joshua Davis	640	On the eastside of the Caney fork.
509.	Edwin Hickman	640	On the northside of Cumberland river.
510.	Samuel Allen	640	On the head of Gilkerson's Creek.
511.	Thomas Hamilton	640	On the westside of Caney fork.
512.	Evan Shelby	640	On the northside Cumberland river.
513.	William Tate	420	On Red River.
514.	Willoughby Williams	365	On the southside of Cumberland river.
515.	Charlie Griggs	274	On the southside of Cumberland river.
516.	Mark Richman	640	On the southside Cumberland river.
517.	Jacob Mussick	2,560	On the southside Cumberland river.
518.	William Stolop	357	On the waters of Goose Creek.
519.	Edward Douglass	640	On the waters of Station Camp Creek.
520.	Joseph Forbes	420	On the waters of Mill Creek.
521.	Arthur Tyner	274	On the southside Cumberland river.
522.	Richard Andrews	2,200	On the northside Cumberland river.
523.	William Mitchell	1,000	On the waters of Stones River.
524.	Thomas Fornes	640	On the southside Cumberland river.
525.	William Wykoff & Lardner Clark	274	On the waters of North Cross Creek.
526.	William Wykoff & Lardner Clark	274	On the southside Cumberland river.
527.	Joseph Cartwright	640	On Halfpone Creek.
528.	John Standley	228	On Beaver Dam Creek.
529.	Nathaniel McCann	2,560	On the southside Cumberland river.
530.	William Waters	2,011	On both sides Roaring river southside Cumberland.
531.	Jonathan Guess	640	On the southside Cumberland river.
532.	John McPherson	640	On the southside Red River.
533.	John Williamson	228	On the waters of Mill Creek.
534.	James West Green	4,800	On the first creek below Harpeth River.
535.	Benjamin Sheppard	640	On both sides the middle fork of Drake's Creek.
536.	Benjamin Sheppard	640	On the southside Big Barren River.
537.	Charles Gilmore	640	On the northside Cumberland river.

No.	Name	Acres	Location
538.	Charles Gilmore	640	On the northside Cumberland river.
539.	John Harden	228	On Blooming Grove Creek.
540.	William Fletcher	1,000	On the southside Cumberland River.
541.	John Larkin	1,000	On Jones Creek.
542.	Thomas Smith	640	On the northside Cumberland River.
543.	Barnard Tatum	640	On Spring Creek.
544.	John Bowers	228	On Sulphur Fork.
545.	Stephen Mennett	640	On Barton's Creek.
546.	James Lancer	640	On Puncheon Camp Creek.
547.	Zebulon Hubbart	228	On Red River.
548.	John Bush	914	On the waters of Stewart's Creek.
549.	Thomas Berry	429	On the north fork of Main Harpeth river.
550.	James Lamb	640	On Long Creek.
551.	Robert Calss?	274	On southside Cumberland River.
552.	Edwin Hickman	1,000	On southside Cumberland River.
553.	William Hughlett	640	On southside Richland Creek.
554.	Martin Armstrong	640	On both sides east fork of Yellow Creek.
555.	Hezekiah Senton	1,000	On the northside Cumberland River.
556.	John Marshall	640	On Maney Fork Creek.
557.	Levi Coller	640	On the waters of Goose Creek.
558.	William Saunders	640	On Maney Fork Creek.
559.	William Saunders	640	On Maney Fork Creek.
560.	Daniel Smith	640	On the northside Cumberland River.
561.	Spencer Donelson	428	On the middle fork of Red River.
562.	James Glasgow	640	On the southside Cumberland River.
563.	Thomas Woodward	640	On the north fork of Red River.
564.	Marmaduke Scott	640	On the dry fork of Bledsoe's Creek.
565.	Jesse Reid	640	On the southside Big Barren river.
566.	Isaac Colson	640	On the northside Cumberland river.
567.	William Saunders	640	On a north branch of Maney Fork Creek.
568.	Abraham Denny	365	On Caleb Creek.
569.	John Wilson	274	At the mouth of Drake's Creek.
570.	Edwin Hickman	640	On Hickman's Creek.

571.	Isaac Moore	3,840	On Taylor's Creek.
572.	Jesse Reid	640	On Long Creek.
573.	James Roberts	274	On the southside Cumberland river.
574.	Anthony Hart	640	Near the head of Gilkerson's Creek.
575.	Anthony Hart	640	On Long Creek.
576.	Anthony Hart	640	On the west fork of Little Bush Creek.
577.	Thomas Clarke	7,200	On the southside Cumberland river.
578.	Jacob Castlemain	640	On both sides Stones Lick Creek.
579.	George Bradley	3,840	On the southside Cumberland river.
580.	John & James Bonner	228	On the southside Cumberland river.
581.	Anthony Croutcher	640	On the northside Sycamore Creek.
582.	James Robertson	335	On the southside Cumberland river.
583.	Willoughby Williams	274	On the southside Cumberland river.
584.	John Collins	274	On Pleasant Creek.
585.	Daniel Swigg	240	On the waters of Station Camp Creek.
586.	Robert Callihan	640	On Bartons Creek.
587.	Lardner Clarke	640	On the northside Cumberland river.
588.	John Vance	3,840	On the northside Cumberland river at the mouth of Brushy Creek.
589.	John Potter	228	On the southside Big Harpeth River.
590.	David Phillips	228	On the southside Big Harpeth River.
591.	Frederick Blount	640	On the Sulphur Fork of Red River.
592.	Noah Woodard	640	On the north fork of Cumberland river.
593.	John Ford	640	On the southside of Cumberland river.
594.	Daniel Thompson	274	On the southside of Cumberland river.
595.	Wikoff & Clarke	640	On the southside Cumberland river.
596.	William Jimmerson	640	On the southside Cumberland river on Bartons Creek.
597.	John Marshall	640	On the north fork of Maney Fork Creek.
598.	John Davis	3,840	On the mouth of Beaver Creek.
599.	Elijah Robertson	640	On the northside Cumberland river.

600.	Thomas Norris	357	On the east boundary of Brown's Survey.
601.	William Gubbins	274	On the Sulphur Fork of Red River.
602.	William Jenkins	274	On the northside Cumberland river.
603.	John & James Bonner	738	On the northside Cumberland river.
604.	George Wells	428	On the Sulphur Fork of Red River.
605.	John Billips	274	On the eastside of Stones River.
606.	David Denny	274	On Calebs Creek.
607.	Benjamin Thomas	640	On the Lick Fork of Jones Creek.
608.	Timothy Demunroe	1,000	On the northside Cumberland River.
609.	Benjamin Jones	640	On the northside Cumberland River.
610.	Mann Phillips	640	On the southside of Big Barren river.
611.	Charles Gilmore	640	On the waters of Stones Creek.
612.	Dennis Reardon	1,000	On the southside Cumberland river.
613.	Samuel Macon	357	On the southside Cumberland river.
614.	James Campen	2,560	On the southside Cumberland river at the mouth of Elk Creek.
615.	Sarah Routledge	2,560	On the waters of Stones River.
616.	William Walker	1,000	On the Sulphur Fork of Red River.
617.	Blount Whittmill	824	At the mouth of Big Harpeth river.
618.	John Eborne	1,445	On the westfork of Stones river.
619.	William Terrill Lewis	3,840	On the southside Cumberland River.
620.	Richard William Caswell	640	On the Sulphur Fork of Red River.
621.	Richard William Caswell	640	On the Sulphur Fork of Red River.
622.	Archibald Murphy	274	On the waters of Drake's Creek.
623.	Alexander Allen	640	On the eastside of Sulphur Fork of Red River.
624.	Eusebius Bushell & William Dobbins	640	On the waters of Stones River.
625.	Eusebius Bushell & William Dobbins	1,000	On the waters of Stones River.
626.	Eusebius Bushell & William Dobbins.	640	On the waters of Stewart's Creek.
627.	Eusebius Bushell & William Dobbins	640	Joining Moses Shelby's lines.
628.	Eusebius Bushell & William Dobbins	1,000	On the west fork of Stones River.
629.	Eusebius Bushell & William Dobbins	640	On the southside Cumberland river.

630.	Eusebius Bushell & William Dobbins	1,000	On the westfork of Stone's River.
631.	Eusebius Bushell & William Dobbins	1,000	On the waters of Stones River.
632.	Eusebius Bushell & William Dobbins	228	On the waters of Stones River.
633.	Eusebius Bushell & William Dobbins	1,000	On the waters of Stones River.
634.	Eusebius Bushell & William Dobbins	1,000	On the southside Cumberland river.
635.	Eusebius Bushell & William Dobbins	640	On the southside Cumberland river.
636.	Eusebius Bushell & William Dobbins	640	On the southside Cumberland river.
637.	Eusebius Bushell & William Dobbins	1,000	On the waters of Stones River.
638.	Jesse Roberts	640	On the northside Cumberland river.
639.	Thomas Berry	274	On Indian Creek northside Tenessee River.
640.	Thomas Berry	274	On Indian Creek northside Tenessee River.
641.	Thomas Berry	640	On Indian Creek northside Tenessee River.
642.	Lardner Clarke	1,000	On Bissells Saleen the waters of Clarke Creek.
643.	Lardner Clarke	640	On Bissells Saleen the waters of Clarke Creek.
644.	Lardner Clarke	640	On Bissells Saleen the waters of Clarke Creek.
645.	Robert Hayes	1,000	On Bissells Saleen the waters of Clarke Creek.
646.	Robert Hayes	640	At the mouth of Gibson's Creek.
647.	Robert Nelson	640	On the eastside of Big Harpeth river.
648.	Samuel Budd	640	On the northside Millers Creek.
649.	Lardner Clarke	640	On the waters of Hurricane Creek.
650.	William Turnball	640	On the headwaters of Spring Creek.
651.	James Tatom	640	On the head draught of Sycamore Creek.
652.	William Clarke	640	On the middle fork of Red River.
653.	Wikoff & Clarke	640	On Elk Creek.
654.	William Jackson	274	On the eastside of Big Harpeth River.
655.	Samuel Budd	640	Between Millers and Brush Creek.

656.	John McRory	640	On the south waters of Big Harpeth.
657.	James Bradley	274	On the eastfork of White's Creek.
658.	James Lanier	640	Joining Nicholas Conrods survey.
659.	John Rice	274	On the east fork of Mill Creek.
660.	Alexander Irving	640	On both sides Big Harpeth River.
661.	Samuel McCraid	640	On the head draught of Sycamore.
662.	Joshua Davis	640	On the waters of the Saleen.
663.	Joshua Davis	640	On the waters of the Saleen.
664.	William Turnbull	640	On the head waters of Spring Creek.
665.	Jesse Cook	274	On Brush Creek.
666.	John Wilson	640	At the mouth of War Trace Creek.
667.	Nancy Sheppard	640	On the northside Tenessee.
668.	Nancy Sheppard	640	On the northside of Tenessee.
669.	Nancy Sheppard	640	On the northside of Tenessee.
670.	Benjamin Sheppard	1,000	On Indian Creek northside Tenessee.
671.	Benjamin Sheppard	1,000	On Bizzells Saleen.
672.	Benjamin Sheppard	1,000	On Bizzells Saleen.
673.	Benjamin Sheppard	1,000	On Haysi Creek northside Tenessee.
674.	Benjamin Sheppard	1,000	On Indian Creek northside Tenessee.
675.	Robert Johnston	640	On the northside Cumberland river.
676.	Anthony Hart	640	On the head of Milners Creek.
677.	Hayden Wills	274	On the northside Cumberland river.
678.	James Lanier	640	On Brush Creek.
679.	Anthony Hart	640	On Elk Creek.
680.	Andrew Carnahan	640	On the waters of Big Harpeth River.
681.	Reading Blount	640	On the waters of Long Creek.
682.	Reading Blount	640	On Sycamore Creek.
683.	Thomas Taylor	320	On the waters of Whites Creek.
684.	Mann Phillips	640	On the waters of the Saleen.
685.	Mann Phillips	640	Joining his own lines.
686.	Phillip Trammy	640	On the middle fork of Red River.
687.	Joseph Carr	274	On Big Harpeth River.
688.	Thomas Thompson	640	On the westfork of Jones Creek.
689.	Samuel Budd	640	On the westfork of Milners Creek.

690.	James Glasgow	640	On Sinking Creek a branch below Harpeth River.
		1788	
691.	Sarah Nash	1,200	On the first big creek below Harpeth River.
692.	Nancy Sheppard	640	On the waters of Sycamore Creek.
693.	Nancy Sheppard	640	On the waters of Gaspers Creek.
694.	Nancy Sheppard	640	On the waters of Sulphur Fork of Red River.
695.	Nancy Sheppard	640	On Sycamore Creek.
696.	Nancy Sheppard	640	On the waters of Sulphur Fork.
697.	Nancy Sheppard	640	On the waters of Sulphur Fork.
698.	Nancy Sheppard	640	On the waters of Gaspers Creek.
699.	Thomas Love	640	On both sides Sycamore Creek.
700.	Tobias Goodman	640	On the north branch of Sycamore.
701.	Robert Kerr	274	On the Sulphur Fork of Red River.
702.	William McEadon	274	On the southside of Red River.
703.	William Reason	412	On Millers Creek.
704.	James Lanier	640	On the southside Kerrs Creek.
705.	Matthew Kincannon	640	On Second Creek.
706.	Alexander Flood	304	Near Blooming Grove Creek.
707.	Thomas McCrory	640	On the waters of Big Harpeth river.
708.	Joseph Hendricks	640	On the eastfork of Stones River.
709.	John Nicholls	640	On the head of a branch.
710.	Nehemiah Pearcy	640	On Millers Creek.
711.	Charles Robeson	640	On the head of Calebs Creek.
712.	William Cox	228	On the head of Millers Creek.
713.	Anthony Hart	640	On the northside Cumberland river.
714.	Thomas Hogg	640	On the waters of Sycamore Creek.
715.	Micajah Thomas	640	On the waters of Sycamore Creek.
716.	Micajah Thomas	640	On the southside Beavers Creek.
717.	William Holderness	640	On the head of Nelsons and Kerrs Creek.
718.	Anthony Hart	640	On the head of Nelsons and Kerrs Creek.
719.	Anthony Hart	640	On the waters of Sycamore Creek.

720.	Morgan Bryan	274	On Beaver Dam Creek a branch of Red River.
721.	William Dobbins	640	On a branch of Kerrs Creek.
722.	Joseph Brock	640	On Pearson's Creek.
723.	Thomas Farmer	640	On the head of Calebs Creek.
724.	James Locke	274	On Tenessee River.
725.	Joseph Dixon	640	On Brushy Creek northside Cumberland River.
726.	John Nicholls	640	On the Sulphur Fork of Red River.
727.	James Lanier	640	On Winters Creek.
728.	Valentine Lewis	228	On Spring Creek.
729.	Charles Gilmore	640	On the north waters of Sycamore Creek.
730.	Thomas Thompson	640	On the eastside of Stones River.
731.	Wykoff & Clarke	640	On the northside Cumberland river.
732.	Thomas Isbell	640	On the southside Big Barren River.
733.	William Nash	640	On the eastside Stones river.
734.	Thomas McCrory	640	On the westside of Stones River.
735.	William Bowman	640	On the north fork of Red River
736.	Thomas Isbell	640	On the southside Big Barren River.
737.	James Lanier	640	On the main salt lick fork of Big Barren River.
738.	James Lanier	640	On the main salt lick fork of Big Barren River.
739.	Joseph Howard	274	On Big Harpeth River.
740.	Thomas Hickman	640	On the waters of Stones river.
741.	Andrew Hampton	640	On Elk Fork of Red River.
742.	Isaac Bledsoe	640	On Bledsoe Creek.
743.	Thomas Hickman	640	On the waters of Stones River.
744.	Thomas Hickman	640	On the waters of Stones River.
745.	William Donohoe	640	On Second Creek an east branch of Stones River.
746.	John Clendenning	2,560	On the southside Big Harpeth river.
747.	Richard Fenner	640	On the northside Sycamore Creek.
748.	Wykoff & Clarke	228	On Guesses Creek.
749.	James Taylor	535	On the waters of Mill Creek.
750.	David Jones	1,000	On the west fork of Red River
751.	James Cole Montflorence	1,000	On the eastside of the west fork of Station Camp Creek.

752.	Martin Gardner Sheppard	640	On the waters of the Sulphur Fork of Red River.
753.	James Lanier	640	On the eastfork of Big Barren River.
754.	Richard Tenner	640	On the waters of Sycamore Creek.
755.	James & George Win?	228	On the eastside Bledsoe's Creek.
756.	Robert Hayes	640	On the head of Wartrace Creek.
757.	John Cordery	274	On Sulphur's Creek.
758.	William Stewart	640	On the northside Cumberland river.
759.	Thomas Hickman	640	On the eastfork of Stones River.
760.	William Tate	640	On the westside of Samuel Hepleys claim.
761.	Daniel Smith	274	On the waters of Drakes Creek.

Sumner County 1788

762.	Michael Montgomery	228	On the waters of Collins River.
763.	William Bowman	640	On the north fork of Red River.
764.	William Bowman	640	On the north fork of Red River.
765.	William Bowman	640	On the north fork of Red River.
766.	Philemon Thomas	640	On Bradley's Lick Creek.
767.	Philemon Thomas	640	On Bradley's Lick Creek.
768.	Thomas Hickman	278	On the waters of Caney Fork.
769.	James Saunders	640	On the head of the south fork of Bradleys Creek.
770.	James Saunders	640	On the head of the south fork of Bradleys Creek.
771.	Joseph Ellison	274	On the head of the south fork of Bradleys Creek.
772.	James Saunders	640	On the northside Cumberland river.
773.	James Saunders	228	On the waters of Goose Creek.
774.	James Saunders	464	On the westfork of Station Camp Creek.
775.	James Saunders	640	On the northside Bradleys Lick Creek.
776.	James Saunders	228	On the waters of Cumberland river.
777.	James Saunders	640	On the fork of Bradley's lick Creek.
778.	Michael Montgomery	640	On the waters of Collins river.
779.	Daniel Smith	640	On Drake's Creek.
780.	John Rice	228	On the waters of Caney Fork.

781.	David Looney	357	On the waters of Caney Fork.
782.	William Bowman	640	On both sides of the Long branch of north fork of Red River.
783.	William Bowman	640	On both sides of the Long branch of north fork of Red River.
784.	William Bowman	640	On both sides of the Long branch of north fork of Red River.
785.	Daniel Jones	1,234	On the head of a creek of Big Barren River.
786.	David Hart	274	On the west fork of Goose Creek.
787.	William Bowman	640	On the north fork of Red River.
788.	James Lee	228	On the west fork of Goose Creek.
789.	William Saunders	640	On the waters of Collins river.
790.	Wykoff & Clarke	640	On the southside Cumberland river.
791.	Ambrose Jones	640	On middle fork of Drakes Creek.
792.	Ambrose Jones	640	On the eastside of Stones River.
793.	John Sitgreaves	640	On the eastside of Buffalo Creek.

Davidson County 1788

794.	John McNees	1,000	On the northside Cumberland river.
795.	John McNees	1,000	On the northside Cumberland river.
796.	John McNees	1,000	On the northside Cumberland river.
797.	John McNees	640	On the northside Cumberland river on bear Creek.
798.	John McNees	640	On the northside Cumberland river on Bear Creek.
799.	Elijah Robertson	640	On the eastfork of Stones River.
800.	Elijah Robertson	640	On the waters of Caney Fork.
801.	Elijah Robertson	640	On Hickmans Creek a branch of ?.
802.	Elijah Robertson	640	On Hickman Creek a branch of ?.
803.	Elijah Robertson	640	On Hickmans Creek a branch of ?.
804.	Elijah Robertson	1,000	On the waters of Cany Fork.
805.	Elijah Robertson	640	On the waters of Cany Fork.
806.	Elijah Robertson	640	On the waters of Cany Fork.
807.	Elijah Robertson	640	On the waters of Cany Fork.
808.	Elijah Robertson	640	On the waters of Cany Fork.
809.	Elijah Robertson	640	On the waters of Cany Fork.
810.	Elijah Robertson	640	On the waters of Cany Fork.
811.	Elijah Robertson	640	On the waters of Cany Fork.

812.	Elijah Robertson	640	On the waters of Cany Fork.
813.	Elijah Robertson	640	On the waters of Cany Fork.
814.	Elijah Robertson	640	On the waters of Cany Fork.
815.	Elijah Robertson	640	On the waters of Cany Fork.
816.	Elijah Robertson	640	On the waters of Cany Fork.
817.	Elijah Robertson	640	On the waters of Cany Fork.
818.	Elijah Robertson	640	On the waters of Cany Fork.
819.	Elijah Robertson	640	On the waters of Cany Fork.
820.	Elijah Robertson	640	On the waters of Cany Fork.
821.	Peter Robertson	640	On the waters of Cany Fork.
822.	Peter Robertson	1,000	On the waters of Cany Fork.
823.	Peter Robertson	1,000	On the waters of Cany Fork.
824.	Lardner Clark	1,000	On the waters of West Harpeth.
825.	Howell Taleena	3,560	On the southside Cumberland.
826.	Wikoff & Clarke	1,000	On the southside of Cumberland.
827.	Joseph Brock	640	On the southside of Cumberland.
828.	Joseph Brock	640	On the southside of Cumberland.
829.	Andrew Armstrong	640	On the northside of Red River.
830.	Daniel Anderson	640	On the waters of Cany Fork.
831.	William Tuton	640	On the northside Red River.
832.	Jason Thompson	640	On Mill Creek.
833.	Joseph Brock	640	On the northside Cumberland.
834.	Joseph Brock	640	On the northside Cumberland.
835.	Andrew Armstrong	640	On the northside Cumberland.
836.	Andrew Armstrong	1,286	On the northside Cumberland.
837.	Daniel Anderson	640	On the waters of Caney Fork.
838.	Daniel Anderson	640	On the northside Cumberland.
839.	Daniel Anderson	640	On the northside Cumberland.
840.	Robert Norris	640	On the waters of Caney Fork.
841.	Richard Fenner	640	On the waters of Caney Fork.
842.	Richard Fenner	640	On the waters of Red River.
843.	Anthony Croutcher	640	On the northside of Red River.
844.	Anthony Hart	640	On the head of Brown's Creek.
845.	Joseph Brock	640	On the waters of Red River.
846.	Joseph Brock	640	On the waters of Red River.

847.	Joseph Brock	640	On Bear Creek northside
848.	Joseph Brock	640	On the northside Cumberland.
849.	Anthony Hart	640	On Halfpone Creek.
850.	William Tuton	640	On the northside Cumberland.
851.	Joseph Brock	640	On the northside Cumberland.
852.	Richard Fenner	640	On the northside Cumberland on Folley.
853.	Eusebius Bushell & William Dobbins	640	On the southside of Cumberland.
854.	Daniel Anderson	640	On the northside of Cumberland.
855.	John Jones	640	On the waters of Cany Fork.
856.	Andrew Armstrong	640	On the northside Red River.
857.	Edward Douglass	274	On the waters of Station Camp Creek.
858.	James Cole Montflorence	640	On the southside of Cumberland.
859.	James Cole Montflorence	640	On the southside of Cumberland.
860.	Joseph Brock	640	On the waters of Red River.
861.	Joseph Brock	640	On the waters of Red River.
862.	Daniel Anderson	640	On the waters of Caney Fork.
863.	Isaclore Sherratt	640	On the east fork of Stones River.
864.	Robert Carteright	366	On the waters of Station Camp Creek.
865.	Joseph Brock	640	On the northside Cumberland.
866.	Joseph Brock	640	On the northside Cumberland.
867.	Joseph McClammy	2,560	On the Caney Fork.
868.	Andrew Armstrong	640	On the northside of Red River.
869.	Daniel Anderson	640	On the waters of Red River.
870.	James Cole Montflorence	1,000	On Weakley's Creek on the
871.	Andrew Armstrong	640	On the first fork Big Barren.
872.	Richard Fenner	640	On the waters of Sulphur Fork.

Sumner County 1788

873.	James Cole Montflorence	640	On the northside Cumberland.
874.	James Cole Montflorence	640	On the waters of Red River.
875.	James Cole Montflorence	1,000	On the westfork of Barton.
876.	John Ford	274	On the northside Cumberland.
877.	Richard Fenner	640	On the waters of Red River.
878.	Wikoff & Clarke	640	On the southside Cumberland.

879.	Anthony Hart	640	On the westfork of Spring.
880.	William Futon	640	On the northside Cumberland.
881.	William Futon	640	On the northside Cumberland.
882.	Isedore Sherrett	640	On the eastfork of Stones River.
883.	Samuel Shannon	228	On the waters of Whites.
884.	Ambrose Jones	640	On the eastside of Cedar Creek.
885.	John Rice	640	Joining his own lines.
886.	John Rice	428	Joining his own lines.
887.	John Ford	640	On the northside Cumberland.
888.	Acquilla Sugg	640	On the first creek above
889.	Sampson Williams	640	On the southside Cumberland.
890.	Acquilla Sugg	1,000	On the eastfork of Stones River.
891.	Acquilla Sugg	1,000	On the eastfork of Stones River.
892.	Acquilla Sugg	640	On Stones Lick Creek.
893.	George Augustus Sugg	640	On a small creek above
894.	George Augustus Sugg	640	On Stones Lick Creek.

Sumner County 1789

895.	Robert Nelson	640	On the northside Cumberland.
896.	John Ford	640	On the southside Cumberland.
897.	John Ford	640	On the southside Cumberland.
898.	John Ford	640	On the northside Cumberland.
899.	John Ford	640	On the northside Cumberland.
900.	John Ford	640	On the northside Cumberland.
901.	Joshua Hadley	640	On the waters of Cumberland river.
902.	Joshua Hadley	640	On the eastfork of big Barren river.
903.	George Augustus Sugg	640	On the main fork of Stones river.
904.	Samuel Marson	640	On Spring Creek.
905.	John Ford	640	On the northside Cumberland river.
906.	Stephen Brooks	640	On the waters of Stones River.
907.	Samuel Marson	640	On Spring Creek waters of Sycamore Creek.
908.	Acquilla Sugg	640	On the eastside Stones River.
909.	Daniel James	640	On the northside Cumberland river.
910.	Alexander Ewing	640	On both sides Caney Fork.
911.	Stephen Brooks	640	On the eastside Stones River.

No.	Name	Acres	Location
912.	Stephen Brooks	640	On the eastside Stones River.
913.	James Scurlock	2,560	On both sides Harpeth River.
914.	David Ambrose	1,000	On Sycamore Creek.
915.	Reading Blount	640	On the eastfork of Stones River.
916.	Reading Blount	640	On the northside Cumberland river.
917.	Reading Blount	640	On the eastfork of Stones River.
918.	James Todd	640	On the waters of Caney Fork.
919.	Acquilla Sugg	640	On the eastside Stones River.
920.	Thomas Sams	640	On the southside Cumberland river.
921.	Thomas Sams	640	On the southside Cumberland river.
922.	George A. Sugg	640	On the main eastfork of Stones River.
923.	James Glasgow	1,000	On the northside Cumberland river.
924.	James Glasgow	640	On the waters of Cedar Lick Creek.
925.	Willoughby Williams	640	On the southside Cumberland.
926.	Willoughby Williams	1,000	On the waters of Caney Fork on Cumberland.
927.	Acquilla Scugg	640	On the waters of Stones Lick Creek.
928.	Acquilla Scugg	640	On the East Fork of Stones River.
929.	James Milherrin	640	On Caney Fork.
930.	James Milherrin	640	On Caney Fork.
931.	Eli West	420	On the southside Cumberland river.
932.	Acquilla Scugg	640	On the waters of Stones Lick Creek.
933.	Acquilla Scugg	640	On the eastside of Stones River.
934.	Acquilla Scugg	640	On the eastside of Stones River.
935.	Daniel Anderson	640	On the northside Cumberland river.
936.	James Glosler Brehon	2,560	On the southside Cumberland river.
937.	William Nash	640	On the eastside of Stones river.
938.	William Nash	640	On the eastside of Stones river.
939.	William Nash	640	On the eastside of Stones river.
940.	William Nash	640	On the eastside Cumberland river.
941.	William Nash	640	On the northside Cumberland river.
942.	William Hughlett	640	On Sulphur Fork of Red River.
943.	James Mulkerrin	640	On Hickman's Creek.
944.	John Reed	640	On the southside Cumberland river.

Davidson County 1789

945.	John Buchanan	640	On Cedar Lick Creek.
946.	James Milkerrin	640	On Hickman's Creek.
947.	Richard Gains	640	On the westfork of Cedar Lick Creek.
948.	David Poor	640	On the northside Cumberland river.
949.	John Nicholls	640	On the eastfork of Stones river.
950.	James Milherrin	640	On the eastfork of Stones river.
951.	James G. Brehen	640	On the Caney Fork.
952.	James G. Brehen	640	On the waters of Mulherrons Creek.
953.	Reading Blount	640	On the waters of Caspey Fork.
954.	Reading Blount	640	On the eastfork of Stones River.
955.	Reading Blount	640	On the waters of Campy Fork.
956.	Reading Blount	640	On Halfpone Creek.
957.	Reading Blount	640	On the east fork of Stones river.
958.	Elias Ford	640	Joining John Harrils survey.
959.	Stephen Cantwell	1,000	On the northside Cumberland river.
960.	Stokeley Donelson	640	On the southside of Cumberland.
961.	John McCutchen	228	On the eastside Stones river.
962.	John Anderson	1,000	On the waters of Caney Fork.
963.	John Clendenning	429	On head of Brown's Creek.
964.	Abraham Kannady	·640	On the headwaters of Cedar Lick Creek.
965.	James Locke	274	On the eastfork of Stones River.
966.	John Ford	640	On Puncheon Camp Creek.
967.	John Whitsell	640	On a branch of the Caney Fork.
968.	Joseph Kerr	640	On the northside Cumberland river.
969.	Jesse Taunt	1,000	On the eastfork of Cedar Lick Creek.
970.	unintelligible		
971.	John Elliot	640	On the waters of Cedar Lick Creek.
972.	Charles Dixon	274	On the eastfork of Stones River.
973.	John Logue	1,000	On the southside Cumberland.
974.	Tilman Dixon	274	On the eastfork of Stones River.
975.	John B. Hammond	357	On the southside Cumberland river.
976.	John Welch	1,580	On the eastfork of Stones River.

977.	Stokeley Donelson	640	On a branch of Caney Fork.
978.	Stokeley Donelson	640	On a branch of Caney Fork.
979.	Stokley Donelson	640	On the southside Cumberland river.
980.	Stokeley Donelson	640	On a branch of the Caney Fork.
981.	Stokeley Donelson	640	On the waters of Stones River.
982.	Stokeley Donelson	640	On the eastfork of Stones River.
983.	Stokeley Donelson	640	On a branch of Caney Fork.
984.	Stokeley Donelson	640	On a branch of Caney Fork.
985.	James Rowland	640	On the waters of Grove Creek.
986.	John Donelson	640	On both sides Big Harpeth river.
987.	George A. Sugg	640	On the second creek above Stewarts Creek.
988.	George A. Sugg	640	On the eastside Stones River.
989.	Acquilla Sugg	640	On the eastside Stones River.
990.	George A. Sugg	640	On the eastside Stones River.
991.	George A. Sugg	640	On the eastside Stones River.
992.	George A. Sugg	640	On the eastside Stones River.
993.	James Glosler Bechen	1,000	On the northside Cumberland river waters of Red river.
994.	William Tuton	640	On Caney Fork.
995.	William Tuton	640	On the Caney Fork.
996.	Jarvis Williams	640	On Smith Fork of Caney Fork southside Cumberland river.
997.	Jonathan Drake	640	On Raccoon Creek waters of Halfpone Creek.
998.	James Saunders	640	On the east fork of Stones River.
999.	James G. Brehen	640	On the northside Cumberland river.
1000.	James G. Brehen	640	Joining David Henrys preemption.
1001.	Simon Bright	1,000	On the northside of Cumberland.
1002.	James Glosler Brehen	640	On the waters of Red River.
1003.	James Glosler Brehen	640	On the waters of Red River.
1004.	James Glosler Brehen	640	On the northside Cumberland river.
1005.	James Glosler Brehen	640	On the headwaters of Sulphur Fork and Gastons Creek.
1006.	William Sheppard	1,000	On the northside Cumberland river.
1007.	Matthew Locke	428	On the eastfork of Stone River.
1008.	Matthew Locke	236	On the eastfork of Stone River.
1009.	Griffith Rutherford	428	On the eastfork of Stone River.

1010.	Isaac Right	365	On the waters of Stones River.
1011.	Robert Weakley	640	On the eastfork of Stones River.
1012.	James White	3,840	On Cumberland river opposite the mouth of Richland Creek.
1013.	Robert Weakley	640	On the eastfork of Stones River.
1014.	Robert Weakley	640	On the waters of Halfpone Creek.
1015.	Jonathan Drake	640	On the waters of Halfpone Creek.
1016.	Robert Weakley	640	On the eastfork of Stones River.
1017.	Thomas Glooter	640	On the northside Cumberland River.
1018.	Richard Cathey	640	On the eastfork of Stones River.
1019.	John Nicholls	640	On Weakley Creek.
1020.	John Nicholls	640	On Barretts Creek.
1021.	Zophar? Crockett	274	On the waters of eastfork of Stones River.
1022.	Robert Greer	1,000	On the east branch of Halfpone Creek.
1023.	William Slade	1,607	On Cedar Lick Creek.
1024.	Philip Jones	2,560	On the headwaters of Cedar Lick Creek.
1025.	John Buchannon	640	On the waters of Bartows Creek.
1026.	John Cummens	1,000	On the dry fork of Halfpone Creek.
1027.	James Mulkerrin	640	On a branch of Caney Fork on Hickmans Creek.
1028.	William Shaw	640	On the waters of Red River.
1029.	William Cathey	640	On the east fork of Stones River.
1030.	James Lanier	640	On the middle fork of Red River.
1031.	John Buchannon	640	On Stones River.
1032.	James Anderson	640	On a branch of Caney Fork.
1033.	Barnabas Boiles	228	On the eastfork of Whites Creek.
1034.	Andrew Bartain	228	On the eastfork of Whites Creek.
1035.	Benjamin Rogers	357	On the northside of Red River.

Sumner County 1789

1036.	James Saunders	640	On the southfork of Bradley Creek.

Davidson County 1789

1037.	Micajah Thomas	640	On the eastfork of Stones River.
1038.	Robert Thompson	640	Between Cedar and Spencers Creek.
1039.	William Wallace	640	On Stones Lick Creek eastside of Stones River.

1040.	John Nicholls	640	On the first fork of Duck River.
1041.	Jonathan Drake	640	On the east fork of Halfpone Creek.
1042.	Griffith Rutherford	640	On the east fork of Stones River.
1043.	Abraham Riston	640	On Spencer Creek.
1044.	Thomas Mulloy	640	On the northside Cumberland river including White Creek.
1045.	Daniel Smith	228	On the southside Cumberland river.
1046.	John Donelson	428	On the southside Cumberland river.
1047.	James Hunter	640	On the waters of Spencer Creek.
1048.	John Armstrong	3,840	On the northside Cumberland river.
1049.	Martin Armstrong	274	On the east waters of Cedar Lick Creek.
1050.	Martin Armstrong	640	On the southside Cumberland river.
1051.	John Nichols	640	On the southfork of McAdow Creek.
1052.	Joseph Cossway	640	Between Gaspers and Kerrs Creek.
1053.	Peter Rhem	428	On the southside Cumberland river.
1054.	David Passmore	580	On the northside Cumberland river.
1055.	Robert McCullok	640	On the south fork of McAdow Creek.
1056.	James Cole Montflorence	640	On the northfork of Sycamore Creek.
1057.	James Cole Montflorence	640	On the northfork of Sycamore Creek.
1058.	James Cole Montflorence	640	On the northfork of Sycamore Creek.
1059.	William Clarke	640	On the east fork of the North Fork of Sycamore Creek.

Tennessee County 1789

1060.	Jacob McCarthy	228	On Sulphur Fork.

Davidson County 1789

1061.	James McQuistion	640	On Cripple Creek waters of Stones River.
1062.	Sampson Williams	428	On the northside Cumberland river.
1063.	Christian Lash	640	On both sides Halfpone Creek.
1064.	Anthony Hart	640	In the fork of McAdoe Creek.
1065.	Thomas Blair	640	On the southside Cumberland river.
1066.	Jeremiah Smith	274	On Overalls Creek.
1067.	William Ray	1,000	On the southside Cumberland river.
1068.	Joseph Ross	640	On the southside Cumberland river.
1069.	John Marshall	640	Joining the Virginia line.
1070.	Jasen Thompson	640	On Mill Creek.

1071.	John Eaton	640	On the waters of Parsons Creek.
1072.	Edward Douglass	228	On the west fork of Station Camp Creek.
1073.	Benjamin Drake	640	On the northfork of McAdoe Creek.
1074.	James Douglass	274	On the eastfork of Station Camp Creek.
1075.	Joseph McDonald	640	On the eastside Mill Creek.
1076.	Charles Gilmore	640	On the southside Sycamore Creek.
1077.	Phillip Phillips	640	On the waters of Mill Creek.
1078.	Reading Blount	640	On the south waters of Persons Creek.
1079.	Sampson Williams	640	On the northside Cumberland river.
1080.	John Thompson	640	On the eastwaters of Mill Creek.
1081.	Joseph Ross	640	On Sycamore Creek.
1082.	Jacob Boston	228	On the waters of Whites Creek.
1083.	George Frazier	640	On both sides Sycamore Creek.
1084.	John Craddock	274	On the dry fork of Red River.
1085.	Isaac Thomas	274	On the main east fork of Mill Creek.
1086.	Jason Thompson	640	On the waters of Spring Creek.
1087.	Joseph McDowell	640	On Mill Creek.
1088.	Minor Cannon	640	On the waters of Mill Creek.
1089.	Robert Thompson	640	On the waters of Hurricane Creek.
1090.	John McFarland	640	Between Cedar and Spencers Creek.
1091.	Daniel Anderson	640	On the waters of Murfrees Creek.
1092.	John Craddock	640	On the northside Red River.
1093.	Charles Gilmore	640	On the north branches Sycamore Creek.
1094.	Elijah Robertson	540	On the southfork of McAdoe Creek.
1095.	James Saunders	914	On the northside Cumberland river.
1096.	John Craddock	640	On the westfork of Station Camp Creek.
1097.	Charles Gilmore	640	On the northside Cumberland river.
1098.	Jason Thompson	640	On the waters of Mill Creek.

Tennessee County 1789

1099.	Howell Tatum	640	On the northside Cumberland river.

Sumner County 1789

1100.	Anthony Hart	640	On the northside Caney Fork river.

1101.	Anthony Hart	640	On the northside Caney Fork river.
1102.	Anthony Hart	434	On the waters of Collins River.
1103.	Anthony Hart	640	On the northside Caney Fork river.
1104.	Anthony Hart	640	On the head of Hickman's Creek.
1105.	Anthony Hart	640	On the waters of Hickman's Creek.
1106.	Richard Shaffer	640	On the northside of Caney Fork of Stones River.
1107.	John Marshall	640	On a branch of the west fork.
1108.	Josiah Love	640	On the northside Cumberland river.
1109.	John Marshall	640	On both sides the south fork of Big Barren River.
1110.	Jesse Reed	640	On the westside of Caney Fork river.
1111.	Jesse Reed	640	On the westside of Caney Fork river.
1112.	Jesse Reed	640	On the westside of Caney Fork river.
1113.	Jesse Reed	640	On the westside of Caney Fork river.
1114.	Jesse Reed	640	On the westside of Caney Fork river.
1115.	Jesse Reed	640	On the headwaters of Collins river.
1116.	Andrew Boyd	640	On the southside Cumberland river.
1117.	Daniel Anderson	640	On the northside Cumberland river.
1118.	William Sanders	640	On the waters of Caney Fork.
1119.	Isaac Bledsoe	640	On Bledsoe Creek.
1120.	Thomas Taylor	429	On the southside Cumberland river.
1121.	John Boyd	274	On the southside Cumberland river and waters of Caney Fork.
1122.	John Baker	640	On the southside Cumberland river and waters of Caney Fork.
1123.	John Marshall	640	On the waters of Big Barren River.
1124.	John Marshall	640	On the waters of Caney Fork.
1125.	John Marshall	220	On Manscoe Creek on Maney Fork Creek.
1126.	John Marshall	640	On the east fork of Stones River.
1127.	John Marshall	640	On the south fork of Big Barren river.
1128.	John Marshall	640	On Collins river a fork of the Caney Fork.

1129.	John Marshall	640	On the south fork of Big Barren river.
1130.	Alexander Kirkpatrick	640	On the northside Cumberland river.
1131.	Robert Weakley	640	On the head Maddisons Creek.
1132.	John Marshall	228	On Money Fork Creek.
1133.	John Marshall	640	On the east fork of Stones River.
1134.	Jesse Reed	640	On the waters of Hickmans Creek westside Caney Fork.
1135.	Jesse Reed	640	On the waters of Hickmans Creek.
1136.	Jesse Reed	640	On the waters of Hickmans Creek.
1137.	Jesse Reed	640	On the waters of Hickmans Creek.
1138.	Jesse Reed	640	On the waters of Hickmans Creek.
1139.	Jesse Reed	640	On the waters of Hickmans Creek.
1140.	Jesse Reed	640	On the waters of Hickmans Creek.
1141.	Alexander Reed	220	On Drakes Creek.
1142.	Andrew Armstrong	640	On the head of Drakes Creek.
1143.	John Baker	640	On the northside Cumberland river.
1144.	James Cole Montflorence & Richard Fenner	228	Between the middle and north fork of Red River.
1145.	James Cole Montflorence & Richard Fenner	274	On the northside of Cumberland.
1146.	John Boyd	274	On the waters of Caney Fork.
1147.	John Brown	640	On the waters of Hickory Creek.
1148.	John Haywood	1,000	On both sides Caney Fork.
1149.	Andrew Armstrong	640	On the head of Drakes Creek.
1150.	William Dix	640	On the waters of Bradleys Lick Creek.
1151.	Josiah Love	640	On the north fork of Red River.
1152.	John Clerer	620	On the northside of Tenessee.

Tenessee County 1789

1153.	James Cole Montflorence	1,000	On Spring Creek.
1154.	James Cole Montflorence	640	On the northside Sulphur Fork.
1155.	James Cole Montflorence	640	On the northside Sulphur Fork.
1156.	Richard Fenner	640	On the northside Cumberland river.
1157.	Richard Fenner	640	On Bear Creek.
1158.	Richard Fenner	640	On Spring Creek.
1159.	Richard Fenner	640	On Spring Creek.

1160.	William Ramsey	640	On the northside Cumberland river.
1161.	Jesse Rhymes	1,000	On the northside Cumberland river.
1162.	Jesse Rhymes	640	On the northside Cumberland river.
1163.	William Green	640	On the southside Sulphur Fork.
1164.	Robert Nelson	274	On Red River.
1165.	James Gloster Brehen	640	On the waters of Sulphur Fork.
1166.	Lewis Cannon	1,184	On Spring Creek.
1167.	Theodore Mullett	640	On Sulphur Fork of Red River.
1168.	Joseph & James Gray	3,840	On Spring Creek.
1169.	John Eaton	640	On the westside of Spring Creek waters of Sycamore Creek.
1170.	Goolleb Krouse	640	On the eastfork of Stones River.

Davidson County 1790

1171.	John Drew	640	On the northside Cumberland river.
1172.	John Drew	640	On the northside Cumberland river.

Sumner County 1790

1173.	John Drew	640	On the northside Cumberland river.

Davidson County 1790

1174.	Robert Nelson	640	On the northside Cumberland river.
1175.	Robert Weakley	640	On the southside Cumberland river.
1176.	John Buchannon	640	On the headwaters of Big Harpeth River.
1177.	Robert Nelson	640	On the eastside Big Harpeth River.
1178.	John Buchannon	640	On the waters of Mill Creek.
1179.	John Buchannon	640	On the southside Cumberland river.

Tenessee County 1790

1180.	John Dickson	640	On the southside Cumberland river.
1181.	Robert Nelson	274	On Blooming Grove Creek.
1182.	William Beek	1,096	On both sides of Upper Barton Creek.

Davidson County 1790

1183.	Owen Tyler	640	On the middle fork Barton Creek.
1184.	William Cochram	640	On the southside Cumberland river.
1185.	William Cochram	640	On Bartons Creek below Harpeth River.

Tenessee County 1790

1186.	William Cochram	640	On the southside Cumberland river.
1187.	William Cochram	640	On the southside Cumberland river.

Sumner County 1790

1188.	Joshua Hadley	640	On the southside Big Barren River.
1189.	Joshua Hadley	640	On the waters of the east fork of Big Barren River.
1190.	David Wilson	357	On the westfork Bledsoes Creek.

Davidson County 1790

1191.	John Buchannon	640	On the waters of Stones River.
1192.	David Jones	1,096	On the southside Red River.
1193.	Jason Thompson	640	On Mill Creek.
1194.	John Donelson	630	On the southside Cumberland river.

Tenessee County 1790

1195.	Willoughby Williams	640	On the northside Cumberland river.
1196.	Willoughby Williams	640	On the northside Cumberland river.
1197.	Willoughby Williams	640	On the northside Cumberland river.
1198.	Thomas McDaniel	640	On Harpeth River.

Davidson County 1790

	James Hunter	640	On the waters of Spencers.

Sumner County 1790

1200.	Alexander Mebane	640	On the waters of the south west fork of Caney Creek.
1201.	Alexander Mebane	640	Joining Phillips and Campbell lines.
1202.	Alexander Mebane	640	On the Caney Fork River.
1203.	Alexander Mebane	640	On the waters of Caney Fork river.
1204.	Alexander Mebane	640	On the waters of Caney Fork river.
1205.	Alexander Mebane	640	On the southside Cumberland river.
1206.	Alexander Mebane	640	On the waters of the Southwest fork _blotted_.
1207.	Alexander Mebane	640	On the waters of the Southwest fork.
1208.	Alexander Mebane	640	On the waters of the Southwest fork.
1209.	Alexander Mebane	640	On the waters of the Southwest fork.

1210.	Robert Bell	640	On the waters of Mill Creek.

Davidson County 1790

1211.	Frances Faulkner	428	On the southside Cumberland river.
1212.	Lardner Clark	640	On Big Harpeth River.
1213.	Seburn Jones	640	On the northside Cumberland River.

Tenessee County 1790

1214.	John Gray Blount	640	On the northside Cumberland river.
1215.	Philip Shackler	640	On the northside Cumberland river.
1216.	Philip Shackler	640	On the northside Cumberland river.
1217.	Daniel Anderson	640	On the northside Cumberland river and northside Blooming Grove Creek.
1218.	John Ramsey	640	On the southside Cumberland river.
1219.	Thomas Johnston	228	On the waters of Stones River.
1220.	John Motherell	228	On the northside Cumberland river.
1221.	Thomas Edmundson	258	On the west fork of Mill Creek.
1222.	Thomas Gloster	357	On the waters of Barton Creek.
1223.	James Gloster Brehen	1,000	On the soutnside Cumberland river.
1224.	Phillips & Campbell	640	On the east fork of Drakes River.
1225.	Adam Laurence	640	On the northside Cumberland river.
1226.	Samuel Kannon	640	On the waters of Stones River.
1227.	James Gloster Brehen	640	On the southside Cumberland river.
1228.	James Gloster Brehen	640	On the southside Cumberland river.
1229.	James Gloster Brehen	640	On the northside Cumberland river.
1230.	John Gray Blount	640	On the northside Cumberland river.
1231.	John Gray Blount	640	On the northside Cumberland river.

Sumner County 1790

1232.	James Briston	228	On the east fork of Goose Creek.
1233.	Daniel Anderson	640	On the northside Cumberland river.
1234.	Howell Tatum	274	On the southside Cumberland river.

Davidson County 1790

1235.	John Nicholls	640	On the fork of Red River and Cumberland River.
1236.	James Cole Montflorence	228	On the southwest side of Harpeth River.
1237.	Bradley Gambell	640	On Mill Creek.
1238.	Pleasant Lockett	640	On the northside Cumberland river.

1239.	John Elliott	640	On the westfork of Stones River.
1240.	Thomas Hogg	640	On the southside Cumberland westside Yellow Creek.
1241.	Daniel Anderson	640	On the northside Cumberland river.
1242.	Willoughby Williams	1,000	On Blooming Grove Creek northside Cumberland River.
1243.	John Rice	420	Joining William Ramseys lines.
1244.	Mann Phillips	228	In the fork of Red River.
1245.	Benjamin Casselman	640	Near the headwaters of Cedar Creek.
1246.	Robert Thompson	480	On the southside Cumberland river.
1247.	Elias Fort?	688	On the northside Cumberland river.
1248.	Wikoff & Clarke	274	On the southside Cumberland river.

Sumner County 1790

1249.	Daniel Anderson	640	On the northside Cumberland river.
1250.	Richard Fenner	640	On the eastside of Yellow Creek southside of Cumberland River.
1251.	Thomas Hammelton	640	On both sides of Cumberland river.

Davidson County 1790

1252.	Charles Braidon	1,000	On the waters of Spring Creek.
1253.	David Shelton	640	On the waters of Round Lick Creek.
1254.	Robert Russell	640	On the waters of Round Lick Creek.
1255.	John Trousdale	640	On the northside Cumberland River.
1256.	John McNees	640	On a branch of Duck Spring Creek.
1257.	Martin Armstrong & Anthony Croutcher	2,560	On the waters of White's Creek northside Cumberland River.
1258.	John McNees	640	On the northside Cumberland river.
1259.	John Lancaster	2,560	On the westside of Caney Fork.
1260.	John Rice	640	Joining his own lines on a former claim.
1261.	Phillips & Campbell	640	On the eastside Caney Fork.
1262.	David Shelley	640	On the northside Drakes Creek.
1263.	James Brown	640	On the northside Cumberland river.
1264.	John Brown	640	On the southside Cumberland river.
1265.	Thomas Hogg	640	On the southside Cumberland river.
1266.	Philip Phillips	640	Opposite the mouth of Folley Creek.
1267.	Bradley Gambill	640	On the waters of Barton Creek.

Tenessee County 1790

1268.	John Gray Blount	640	On the waters of Red River.
1269.	John Hays	640	On the southside Cumberland river.
1270.	John McNees	640	On Bear Branch waters of Duck Spring Creek.

Sumner County 1790

1271.	Phillips & Campbell	640	On the waters of Bartons Creek.
1272.	William Ray	640	On the southside Cumberland river.

Davidson County 1790

1273.	David McRea	640	On the waters of battleground Creek.
1274.	John & James Brown	523	On the headwaters of Goose Creek.
1275.	John Dever	228	On the middle fork of Station Camp Creek.
1276.	Howell Tatum	640	On Yellow Creek.
1277.	John & James Brown	523	On Peyton's Creek.
1278.	Robert Caper	1,000	On a westfork of Jones Creek.
1279.	Chloe Goodman	640	On Big Harpeth River.
1280.	James Gloster Brehen	640	On the southside Cumberland river.
1281.	Jacob Cassalman	640	On the waters of Bartons Creek.
1282.	Joseph Martin	640	On the westside of Stones River.
1283.	John Elliott	640	On the westfork of Stones River.
1284.	James Cole Montflorence	1,000	On the northside Cumberland river.
1285.	Laurence O'Brien	640	On the northside Cumberland river.
1286.	?	640	On the waters of Mill Creek and Stones River.
1287.	Thomas Malloy	228	On the northside Cumberland river.
1288.	Lardner Clarke	640	On the southside Cumberland river.
1289.	Sara O'Bryan	640	On the northside Cumberland river.
1290.	Daniel Anderson	640	On the northside Cumberland river.
1291.	James Gloster Brehen	640	On the southside Cumberland river.
1292.	Henry Ross	274	On waters of Spencers Creek.
1293.	William Blount	228	On the west fork of Cedar Lick Creek.
1294.	Phillips & Campbell	640	On the west fork of Round Lick Creek.
1295.	Daniel Anderson	640	On the northside Cumberland river.
1296.	Adam Laurence	1,000	On the waters of Cumberland river.

1297.	Thomas Gloster	640	On the southside of Sulphur Fork of Red river.
1298.	Seburn Jones	1,000	On the northside Cumberland river.
1299.	Daniel Jones	1,000	On the northside Cumberland river on the eastside Blooming Grove Creek.
1300.	Lardner Clark	1,000	On the waters of Hurricane Creek.
1301.	Charles Gerrard	640	On the northside Cumberland river.
1302.	Crafford Johnston	640	On the northside Cumberland river on Blooming Grove Creek.
1303.	Anthony Hart	640	On the northside Cumberland river.
1304.	Daniel Anderson	640	On the northside Cumberland river on Blooming Grove Creek.

Sumner County 1790

1305.	Samuel Barton	640	On Cedar Fork and Round Lick.
1306.	Elias Fort	389	On the headwaters of Goose Creek.
1307.	Mann Phillips	274	On the northside of Red River.
1308.	Phillips & Campbell	1,000	On McNeeley's Creek a branch of the Caney Fork.
1309.	Phillips & Campbell	640	On Round Lick Creek.
1310.	Phillips & Campbell	640	On the southside Cumberland.
1311.	Daniel Anderson	640	On the southside Cumberland river.

Davidson County 1790

1312.	John Rice	640	On the northside Cumberland river.
1313.	John Rice	640	On the northside Cumberland river below the mouth of Red River.
1314.	John Brown	228	On the southside Cumberland river.
1315.	Laurence O'Brian	640	On Brush Creek of Yellow Creek.
1316.	John Granberry	792	On the southside Cumberland river.
1317.	Jacob Robinson	428	On the southside Cumberland river.
1318.	Thomas Hogg	640	On both sides Yellow Creek.
1319.	John Rice	640	On the northside Cumberland river.
1320.	Phillip Shackler	640	Opposite the head of Peytons Creek.
1321.	Howell Tatum	640	On Yellow Creek southside Cumberland river.
1322.	Robert Bell	228	On the waters of Mill Creek.
1323.	Curtis Williams	100	On the northside Cumberland river.
1324.	Wykoff & Clarke	357	On the westfork of the North Cross Creek.

1325.	Joziah Payne	640	On the southside Cumberland river.
1326.	Thomas Lovell	100	On the northside Cumberland river.
1327.	David Rolston	220	On the northside Cumberland river.
1328.	John Rice	640	On the waters of Richland Creek.
1329.	Thomas Harp	640	On the waters of Yellow Creek.
1330.	Phillips & Campbell	640	On the middle fork of Bartons Creek.
1331.	Howell Tatum	640	On Yellow Creek.

Tenessee County 1790

1332.	Howell Tatum	640	On Yellow Creek.
1333.	James Robertson	640	Opposite Neily's Island southside Cumberland River.
1334.	Bennett Hell	428	On the North Cross Creek.
1335.	John Blair	640	On the waters of Stones River.
1336.	David Douglass	640	On the waters of Bartons Creek.

Sumner County 1790

1337.	Phillips & Campbell	640	On the headwaters of Peyton's Creek.
1338.	Phillips & Campbell	640	On the Middle Fork of Peyton's Creek.
1339.	Evan Shelby	420	On the northside Cumberland river.
1340.	Joseph Hopkins	640	On Duck Spring Creek.
1341.	Phillips & Campbell	640	On the eastside of Stones River.
1342.	Bradley Gambill	640	On the waters of Bartons Creek.
1343.	John Hays	640	On the waters of Yellow Creek.
1344.	James Gloster Brehen	640	On the waters of Yellow Creek.
1345.	John Gray Blount	640	On the eastfork of Blooming Grove Creek.

Davidson County 1790

1346.	James Mebane	1,000	On Meat Camp on Barton Creek.

Tenessee County 1790

1347.	James Gloster Brehen	640	On the southside Cumberland river.
1348.	Samuel Barton	640	On the waters of Cedar Creek.
1349.	Thomas Jeffrys	520	On the waters of Station Camp Creek.
1350.	Harrison Parsons	640	On the waters of Stones River.
1351.	Andrew Bay	357	On the waters of Spencers Creek.

1352.	Phillips & Campbell	640	On the middle fork of Bartons Creek.

Sumner County 1790

1353.	Phillips & Campbell	1,000	On McNeeley's Creek.
1354.	Abraham Rogers	640	On both sides of the Caney Fork.
1355.	Thomas Massey	640	On a small fork of Stewart Creek.
1356.	William Stewart	365	On the lower side of White's Creek.
1357.	Samuel Ross	640	On the waters of Spencers Creek.
1358.	Robert Irven	640	On the waters of Little Harpeth river.
1359.	Robert Irven	640	On the waters of Little Harpeth river.
1360.	Frederick Hargett	640	On the northside Cumberland river.

Davidson County 1790

1361.	Thomas Morrison	640	On the waters of Cedar Lick Creek.
1362.	Thomas Evans	220	On the waters of Gaspers Creek.

Sumner County 1790

1363.	Sherrard Barrow	640	On the waters of Collins River.
1364.	Sherrard Barrow	640	On the southside Cumberland river.

Davidson County 1790

1365.	Henry Barrow	640	On the southside Cumberland river.

Sumner County 1790

1366.	James Barrow	640	On the waters of Round Lick Creek.
1367.	Betsy Barrow	640	On the waters of Round Lick Creek.
1368.	Matthew Barrow	640	On the waters of Round Lick Creek.
1369.	James & George Winchester	640	On the northside Cumberland river.
1370.	James Mabane	640	On the waters of Battle Ground Creek.
1371.	James McCain	640	On the east branch of Drakes Creek.

Tenessee County 1790

1372.	James Lee	228	On Ramseys Fork of Sycamore Creek.

Sumner County 1790

1373.	James Lee	640	On Jennings Fork of Round Lick Creek.

1374.	John Lee	640	On Jennings Fork of Round Lick Creek.
1375.	Edward Douglas	182	On the waters of Station Camp Creek.
1376.	John Baker	462	On waters of Round Lick Creek and Cedar Creek.
1377.	Archibald Lytle	640	On the southside Cumberland River.
1378.	Samuel Motherell	640	On the southside Cumberland River.
1379.	Thomas Brown	640	On the southside Cumberland River on Spencer Creek.
1380.	Morgan McFarlon	640	On the southside Red River.

Davidson County 1790

1381.	William Rowan	640	On the waters of Little Harpeth River.
1382.	Cornelius Drake	640	On the waters of Little Harpeth River.
1383.	John White	640	On the waters of Little Harpeth River.
1384.	Archibald Lytle	1,000	On the southside Cumberland river.
1385.	John Smith	640	On the southside Beaver Creek southside Cumberland River.
1386.	Samuel McMurrey	320	On the northside Cumberland river.
1387.	John Overton	274	On the northside Cumberland river.
1388.	Abraham Young	274	On the waters of Red River.
1389.	Howell Tatum	640	On the Sulphur Fork of Red River.
1390.	William Wickoff	274	On the east fork of North Cross Creek.

Sumner County 1790

1391.	Samuel Barton	640	Between the head of Round Licks branch and Cedar Creek.
1392.	John & James Bonners	640	On the northside Cumberland River waters of Big Barron.
1393.	Samuel Barton	640	Between the head of Round Lick Branch and Cedar Creek.

Davidson County 1790

1394.	John & James Bonner	1,600	On the head of the western most branch of Spring Creek.

Tenessee County 1790

1395.	John Gray Blount	640	On the southside Red River.
1396.	John Gray Blount	640	On the southside Spring Creek.

1397.	John Gray Blount	640	On the southside Spring Creek.
1398.	John Gray Blount	1,000	On the southside Spring Creek.
1399.	John Gray Blount	1,000	On the southside Spring Creek.
1400.	John Gray Blount	1,000	On a draught of Spring Creek.
1401.	Charles Homer	640	About 2 miles from Turnbulls Horse Camp.

Davidson County 1790

1402.	Abraham Jones	640	On the waters of Big Harpeth river.
1403.	John Buckannon	640	On Jennings Fork of Round Lick Creek.
1404.	John Devers	274	Including the main fork of Marrowbone Creek.

Sumner County 1790

1405.	Michael Robertson	640	On Smith Fork of the Caney Fork.
1406.	James Robertson	274	On the waters of Big Harpeth river.
1407.	James Sisk	640	On the waters of The First Creek below the Cross Creek.

Davidson County 1790

1408.	John Eaton	4,800	On the waters of Big Harpeth River.
1409.	Samuel Gainer	640	On Sycamore Creek northside of Big Harpeth River.
1410.	James Dean	640	On Big and Little Harpeth River.
1411.	John Nicholls	640	On the waters of Harpeth River.
1412.	John Rice Compy	1,000	On the first creek below Bartons Camp Creek.

Davidson County 1791

1413.	Elijah Robertson	640	About 2 miles south from Nashville.
1414.	Joseph Holland	640	On the first creek below Cross Creek.

Sumner County 1791

1415.	Samuel Barton	640	On Jennings Fork of Round Lick Creek.
1416.	John Franks	640	On the northside Cumberland river.

Tennessee County 1791

1417.	Anthony Foster	640	On a branch of Blooming Grove Creek.
1418.	John Devers	228	On Sycamore Creek.

Sumner County 1791

1419.	John Buchannon	640	On Jehnings Fork of Round Lick Creek.
1420.	Philip Shackler	640	At the three fork of Paytons Creek.

Davidson County 1791

1421.	David McEwen	274	On the waters of Big Harpeth River.
1422.	Archibald Lytle	640	On the waters of Spencers Creek southside Cumberland.
1423.	John Hamilton	1,000	On Marrow Bone Creek north of Cumberland.
1424.	Frederick Fisher	640	On the headwaters of Whites Creek.
1425.	George A. Sugg	640	Between the waters of Marrowbone and Whites Creek.
1426.	George A. Sugg	640	Between the waters of Marrowbone and Whites Creek.
1427.	George A. Sugg	640	Between the waters of Marrowbone and Whites Creek.
1428.	George A. Sugg	640	Between the waters of Marrowbone and Whites Creek.
1429.	George A. Sugg	640	Between the waters of Marrowbone and Whites Creek.

Tenessee County 1791

1430.	Thomas Blount	640	On Tenessee River below the mouth of Duck River.
1431.	Thomas Blount	640	On Tenessee River below the mouth of Duck River.

Sumner County 1791

1432.	Samson Williams & John Boyd	642	On Dixon's Creek southside Cumberland river.
1433.	Thomas Taylor	640	On Dixon's Creek southside Cumberland river.
1434.	William Dillon	336	On Dixon's Creek southside Cumberland river.
1435.	Ephraim Peyton	640	On a creek called William Camp.
1436.	Adam Miller	640	On Round Lick Creek southside Cumberland.

Tenessee County 1791

1437.	Cornelius Calingham	274	On Deers Creek southside Cumberland river.

Davidson County 1791

1438.	Phenix Cox	640	On waters of Marrowbone Creek.

Tenessee County 1791

1439.	William Alford	640	On the waters of Tenessee above the mouth of Duck River.
1440.	William Alford	640	On the waters of Tenessee.
1441.	William Alford	640	On the waters of Tenessee.
1442.	William Alford	640	On the waters of Tenessee.
1443.	John Darden	274	On Round Lick Creek.

Sumner County 1791

1444.	Philip Shackler	640	On the southside Cumberland River.
1445.	John Hamilton	640	On Sams Creek on southside Cumberland River.
1446.	James Mulherrin	333	On the southside Cumberland River.
1447.	Isaac Bledsoe	457	At the mouth of Bledsoes Creek.

Tenessee County 1791

1448.	Willoughby Williams	274	On Dyers Creek southside Cumberland river.

1,239,498

2275 Warrants to Sundry Officers and Soldiers for which grants have not yet issued;
1,549,726

3723 Total Warrants
2,789,224 Total number of acres.

An estimate of lands granted to Colonel Martin Armstrong surveyor of the land allotted to the officers and soldiers of the Continental line and his assigns for his services.

Davidson County 1786

#	Name	Acres	Location
1.	Martin Armstrong	3,840	On both sides of Sugar Creek.
2.	James Robertson	100	In the bent of Cumberland River above Richland Creek.
3.	Robert Thompson	100	On the waters of Fletchers Lick Creek.
4.	James Bosley	21	On the southside Cumberland River near Stone Lick.
5.	James Bosley	107	On the waters of French Lick Branch.
6.	Robert Kerr	228	On Sulphur Lick Creek of Red River.
7.	James Bosley	139	On the southside Cumberland river.
8.	James Bosley	34	On the southside Cumberland river.
9.	Lardner Clark	560	On Indian Camp Creek.

Davidson County 1787

#	Name	Acres	Location
10.	Obed Roberts	640	On Camp Creek the North waters of Duck River.
11.	William Moore	100	On the northside Cumberland river.
12.	Henry Rutherford	378	On Sycamore Creek.
13.	Robert Nelson	250	On the southside Cumberland river.
14.	Robert Nelson	150	On the North of Cumberland River about 3 miles from Nashville.
15.	Robert Nelson	250	On the South of Cumberland River.
16.	Robert Nelson	60	On the northside Cumberland River.
17.	Robert Nelson	200	On the northside Cumberland River.
18.	Robert Nelson	100	On the eastside Calebs Creek.
19.	Samuel Handley	100	On Cobbs Creek waters of Richland Creek running in Stones River.
20.	William Murray	100	On the waters of Hurricane Creek.
21.	Lardner Clark	640	On the northside Cumberland River.
22.	Frederick Stamp	150	On the waters of White's Creek.
23.	Frederick Stamp	150	On the Dry Fork of Browns Creek.
24.	Frederick Stamp	150	On the waters of Whites Creek.
25.	Thomas Crumpstock	100	On the northside Cumberland river.
26.	John Drake	26	On the westside Milners Creek of the Sulphur Fork of Red River.

27.	Lardner Clark	96	On the westfork of Mills Creek.
28.	John Grammer	40	On the Wartrace Creek.
29.	Joseph Brock	640	On the southside of Red River.
30.	James Hoggett	60	On the northside Cumberland river at the mouth of Sulphur Fork.
31.	Lardner Clark	200	In the Big Bent below the mouth of Stones River.
32.	Joseph Brock	640	On the southside Red River.
33.	Thomas Malloy	160	On the southside Red River.
34.	James Hoggott	160	On Sulphur Creek.
35.	John Cox	100	On the westside Whites Creek.
36.	James Sanders	200	On Rocky Creek the westside Cumberland River.
37.	James Russell	100	On the southside Cumberland river.
38.	Absalom Hooper	238	On both sides Whites Creek.
39.	Abraham Miller	46	On the Sulphur Fork of Red River.
40.	William Murry	163	Joining John Thomas's lines.
41.	Andrew Crockett	106	Joining William Collingsworth preemptions.
42.	John Mulherrin	396	On both sides of Mill Creek.
43.	Jacob Moyers	400	On the eastside of Stones River.
44.	Clarke & Wekoff	228	On the eastfork of Blooming Grove Creek.
45.	Mark Noble	100	On Sycamore Creek below the lower path that crosses said creek.
46.	John Buchannon	200	On the westside of Stones River.
47.	Christopher Grice	100	On the waters of Grices Creek.
48.	Solomon White	150	On the waters of Red River.
49.	Curtice Williams	100	On the waters of Blooming Grove Creek.
50.	Thomas Crumstock	100	On the northside Cumberland river.
51.	Robert Thompson	100	On the waters of Richland Creek.
52.	Martin Armstrong	400	On the northside Cumberland river.
53.	Martin Armstrong	274	On the waters of Sinking Creek.
54.	Martin Armstrong	425	On the southside Cumberland river.
55.	Martin Armstrong	306	Joining James Shaw's preemption.
56.	Martin Armstrong	640	On the northside Cumberland river 2 miles below Yellow Creek.
57.	Martin Armstrong	640	On both sides Red River.

58.	James Glasgow	1,428	On Goose Creek northside Cumberland river.
59.	John Rice	168	On the east bank Mill Creek.
60.	John Rice	640	On the head Milners Creek waters of Richland Creek.
61.	Martin Armstrong	1,000	On the long branch of Drakes Creek.
62.	Isaac Drake	50	On the road leading to Red River.

Davidson County 1789

63.	Robert Campbell	50	On Mauldens trace on a branch of Lick Fork.
64.	Jesse Caen	100	On the waters of Sulphur Fork.
65.	Daniel Smith	50	On the east branch of Drakes Creek.
66.	James Lanier	180	Joining the east boundary of Capt. Vances claim.
67.	James Hoggett	60	At the mouth of Sulphur Fork.
68.	Samuel Shannon	82	On the waters of Whites Creek.
69.	Lardner Clark	150	On the waters of Whites Creek.
70.	Martin Armstrong	228	On the waters of Station Camp Creek.

Sumner County 1789

71.	James Douglass	236	On Bradley's Lick Creek.

Davidson County 1789

72.	Martin Armstrong & Anthony Croutcher	500	On the southside Cumberland river.

Sumner County 1789

73.	Thomas Jones	50	On the waters of Drakes Creek.

Davidson County 1789

74.	James McKaen	50	On the waters of Drakes Creek.
75.	Samuel Lewis	100	On the westside Sulphur Creek.
76.	James Saunders	228	On the waters of Rocky Creek.

Sumner County 1789

77.	James Saunders	50	On Station Camp Creek.

Davidson County 1789

78.	Samuel Lewis	100	On Sulphur Creek.
79.	Samuel McGown	60	On White's Creek.

80.	Robert Ervin	50	On the waters of Drakes Creek.
81.	Robert Ervin	50	On the middle fork of Red River.
82.	Robert Ervin	50	On the waters of Red River.
83.	Martin Armstrong	640	On the northside Cumberland river.
84.	Martin Armstrong	400	On the northside Cumberland river.

Tennessee County 1789

85.	Thomas Clark	128	On the northside Red River.

Davidson County 1789

86.	Christopher Guin	100	On Heaton's Lick Branch.
87.	Alexander Reed	100	On the waters of Mansion Creek.
88.	Alexander Reed	50	On a branch of Whites Creek.
89.	Alexander Reed	50	On a branch of Whites Creek.
90.	Alexander Reed	50	On a branch of Whites Creek.
91.	Alexander Reed	200	On a branch of Whites Creek.
92.	Wikoff & Clarke	228	On the waters of Puzzle Creek.
93.	Hugh Lewis	100	On Brush Creek.
94.	Lardner Clark	228	On the waters of Mill Creek.
95.	John Buchannon	138	On the waters of Mill Creek.
96.	Morgan Bryant	100	On the Sulphur Fork of Red River.
97.	John Buchannon	20	On the waters of Little Harpeth River.
98.	John Buchannon	200	On the westside of Mill Creek.

Tennessee County 1790

99.	John Dixon & James Russell	62	On the east branch of Yellow Creek.

Davidson County 1790

100.	Jason Thompson	104	On Mill Creek.
101.	Robert Nelson	3	On the first island above the mouth of Red River.
102.	James Hoggett	70	On Sulphur Creek.
103.	John Walker	21	On the northside Cumberland river.
104.	Christopher Griel	90	On the waters of Grices Creek.
105.	James Ireson	100	On the waters of Whites Creek.
106.	James Ireson	100	On the waters of Whites Creek.
107.	John Rice	168	On the eastside Mill Creek.
108.	Martin Armstrong	200	Joining Neeley's Lick.

109.	Samuel Barton	100	On the headwaters of Haynes Creek.

Tenessee County 1790

110.	Thomas McIntosh	100	On the westside of Upper trace Creek.

Davidson County 1790

111.	James Bailey	75	On the southside Cumberland river.

Tenessee County 1790

112.	Robert McCray	23	On the Sulphur Fork of Red River.
113.	Benjamin McIntosh	50	In the Barrens called the Walnut Flatt.
114.	Joshua Baker	8	On the northside Cumberland river.
115.	William Wikoff	228	On the northside Cumberland river.
116.	Robert Weakley	38	On the north waters of Little Harpeth.
117.	Adam Lynn	50	On a fork of Gaspers Creek.
118.	Adam Lynn	50	On a fork of Gaspers Creek.
119.	John Shelby	2,500	On the first big creek below the mouth of Red River.
120.	Martin Armstrong	1,260	Including the Goose Ponds.

Total Service Rights 30,203

An estimate of the lands granted to the Commissioners, Surveyors, Officers and Guard for assertaining the Bounds of the lands allotted to the officers and soldiers of the Continental Line.

Davidson County 1787

1.	George Maxwell	320	On Kaspers Creek.
2.	Daniel Flanery	320	On Red River.
3.	Turner Williams	320	On the northside Cumberland river.
4.	John Rice	320	Below the mouth of Red River on Cumberland River.
5.	James Bailey	320	Joining James Robertsons pre-emption.
6.	Samuel McCutcheon	320	On Little Harpeth river.
7.	Thomas Malloy	320	Above the first timbered island below the Cross Creek.

8.	Thomas Murray	320	On the southside Cumberland river.
9.	Nathaniel McClure	320	On Whites Creek.
10.	Nathaniel Holley	320	On the waters of Sulphur Fork.
11.	Adam Hampton	320	On Sulphur Fork of Red River.
12.	Jesse Maxey	640	Joining Thomas Sharps lines.
13.	Robert Branks	320	On the westside Stones River.
14.	George Nevill	320	On Mill Creek.
15.	Ephraim McCan	320	On the northside Cumberland river.
16.	Thomas McFarlan	320	On the northside Cumberland river.
17.	Ephraim McCan	320	On the northside Cumberland river.
18.	Isaac Bledsoe	1,196	On the fork between Bledsoes Creek and Bledsoes Lick.
19.	James McGavock	640	On the southside Cumberland river.
20.	Ebenezer Peters?	320	On the north waters of Little Harpeth.
21.	William Fraser	320	On the waters of Drake's Creek.
22.	Samuel McMurry	320	On Indian Camp Creek.
23.	Mark Robertson	640	On the waters of Spencers Creek.
24.	John Rice	320	In the fork of Red River and Cumberland.
25.	John Harris	320	At the mouth of West Fork.
26.	Faukner Elliott & Isaac Peterson	480	On the northside of Red River.
27.	Thomas Molloy	320	On Cumberland River.
28.	Robert Nelson	320	On the northside Cumberland river.
29.	Jacob Pennington	320	On Spring Creek.
30.	Samuel Varner	640	On the waters of Whites Creek.
31.	Adam Hampton	320	On the Sulphur Fork of Red River.
32.	Gasper Manier	640	On Gaspers Creek.
33.	Gasper Manier	320	On the headwaters of Red River.
34.	Gasper Manier	640	On Gaspers Creek.
35.	Moses Wilkison	320	Joining his own and John Elliott's lines.
36.	Jonathan Drake	640	On the waters of Little Harpeth.
37.	James Robertson	2,000	On Richland Creek.
38.	John Sawyer	320	On a branch of Harrington.
39.	John Aylett	640	On the Cumberland river.
40.	James Cary	480	On Rocky Creek.

41.	Robert Heaton	320	On Buzzard Creek.
42.	Thomas Cox	320	Joining his own lines.
43.	Evan Shelby	1,200	On Stewart's Creek.
44.	William Marshall	320	On the waters of Big Harpeth.
45.	William Edmiston	320	On both sides Harringtons Creek.
46.	Isaac Lindsey	320	At the mouth of Wells Creek.
47.	Thomas Kilgore	800	On Bartons Creek.
48.	John Stewart	640	On Milners Creek waters of Sulphur Fork.
49.	John McMurry	320	On the northside of Big Harpeth.
50.	Anthony Bledsoe	6,280	On both sides Bledsoes Creek.
51.	Moses Wilkison	286	On Cumberland River joining John Ayteth.
52.	James Byrns	320	On the waters of Gaspers Creek.
53.	Isaac Shelby	5,000	On Stones River.
54.	David Brigham	320	On Station Camp Creek.
55.	Daniel Smith	3,140	At the mouth of Drake's Creek.
56.	Lardner Clark	320	On the eastfork of Mill Creek.
57.	Benjamin Drake	320	On the waters of Whites Creek.
58.	William Borem	320	On Stewards Creek.
59.	James Robertson	320	In the bent of Cumberland river.
60.	Ebenezer Titus	320	On a branch of dry creek.
61.	James Mears	320	On the waters of Whites Creek.
62.	John Henderson	320	On Little Harpeth.
63.	Stephen Cantrell	640	On Stewarts Creek a branch of Stones River.
64.	John Bowen	320	On Stewarts Creek a branch of Stones River.
65.	Isaac Johnston	190	On the waters of Richland Creek.
66.	Moses Shelby	1,200	On both sides Stewarts Creek.
67.	Anthony Sharpe	320	On the middle fork of Goose Creek.
68.	James McFadden	320	On Red River.
69.	William Head	640	On the middle fork of Goose Creek.
70.	Isaac Bledsoe	320	On Bledsoe's Creek.
71.	William Collinsworth	640	On the waters of Little Harpeth.
72.	John Greenaway	640	On the waters of Little Harpeth.
73.	Edward Cox	640	On the waters of Mill Creek.

74.	Benjamin Pettitt	640	On Whites Creek.
75.	Jesse Thomas	320	On Big Harpeth River.
76.	William McGarick	320	On both sides Harringtons Creek.
77.	Samuel Buchannon	320	On the head of Whites Branch.
78.	Jonah Ramsey	640	On the waters of Halfpone Creek.
79.	Henry Ramsey	960	On the east fork of Bledsoes Creek.
80.	Thomas Cox	640	On the waters of Stones River.
81.	George Freeland	320	On the bank of Cumberland river.

Davidson County 1788

82.	James Shaw	320	On the southside of the Cross Creeks.
83.	William Bowen	320	At the mouth of Gaspers Creek.
84.	John Barron	320	On the northside Cumberland river.
85.	Samuel Barton	320	On the waters of Big Harpeth.
86.	James Shaw	320	On the bank of the South Cross Creek.
87.	Jesse Maxwell	320	On the northside Cumberland River.
88.	John Rice	320	On the waters of Caney Fork.
89.	Elisha Robertson	320	Joining James Robertson's lines.
90.	James Clendenning	320	On the northside Cumberland river.
91.	John Stewart	320	On Red River.
92.	John Elliott	640	On the southside Cumberland river.
93.	Thomas Sharp	320	On the waters of Big Harpeth River.
94.	Peter Turney	640	On the waters of Indian Camp Creek.
95.	Robert Looney	640	On Station Camp Creek.
96.	James Espy	320	On the northside Cumberland river.
97.	John Stewart	320	On Sulphur Fork of Richland Creek.
98.	William Gibbons	720	Joining Lucas and Fioneys lines.

Davidson County 1790

99.	Mark Noble	320	On the waters of Sycamore Creek.
100.	Jeremiah Pierce	320	On the waters of Harpeth River.
101.	James Menees	320	On the westside of Mill Creek.
102.	Elmore Douglass	320	On a branch of Station Camp Creek.

Davidson County 1791

103.	Howell Tatum	960	On Yellow Creek.
104.	John Buchannon	320	On the waters of Stones River.
105.	William Medlock	320	On the waters of Stones River.
106.	Robert Heaton	320	On Main Yellow Creek.
107.	Absalom Tatum	5,000	On Duck River.
108.	Dempsey Jenkins	320	On the southside Cumberland river.
	Total	65,932	

General accounts of lands apporpriated by the State of North Carolina within the Western Territory Ceded by the said State to the United States of America as p the foregoing Estimate.

To the claimants of the Counties of Sullivan, Washington, Greene and Hawkens:	879,262	2,150,542
To ditto in the Eastern, Middle and Western Districts:	1,271,250	
To the settlers on Cumberland preemptions:		309,760
To Major General Greene:		25,000
To the Officers and Soldiers in the Continental Line:	1,239,490	2,789,224
To ditto for which warrants have been granted and for which grants have not yet been issued:	1,549,726	
To the surveyor of the military land for his services:		30,203
To the commissioners, Surveyors, Officers and Guard for ascertaining the bounds of the military land:		65,932
	Total	5,370,661 acres

State of North Carolina
    I James Glasgow Secretary of the said State hereto set my Hand this 20th day of July 1791.

End

INDEX

NORTH CAROLINA LAND GRANTS
IN TENNESSEE

Prepared by
Colleen Morse Elliott
Fort Worth, Texas

ACUFF, Timothy 38,144
ADAIR, David 100
  John 40,63,95,97,98,100
ADAMS, David 50
  John 16,38
  Philip 8
ADARE, David 50
ADCOCK, Leonard 10,11,12,27
ADKENS, David 146
AKE, Joseph 94
ALEXANDER, Ebenezer 102
  George 104
  John 26
  John McNitt 108
  Nathaniel 140
ALFORD, William 187
ALISON, James 29
ALLEN, Alexander 158
  Benjamin 86
  John 72,141
  Mary 149
  Peggy 154
  Samuel 155
  Walter 140
ALLISON...10,21,35
  Alexander 134
  Charles 8
  Francis 12
  James 12,57,86
  John 31,32,151
  John, Sr. 12,18
  Robert 2,14,23
  Thomas 104
ALLSTON, William 111
ALSTON, John McCoy 154
AMBROSE...35
  David 168
AMES, Thomas 44
AMESS, Thomas 99
AMIS, Thomas 53
ANDERSON...2
  Benjamin 70
  Daniel 165,166,168,173,174,178,179,180,181
  James 171
  John 31,53,133,169
  Matthew 135
  William 45,46,47,93,143
ANDREWS, Richard 155
ANNESLEY, William 60
ANSLY, William 57
ANTHONY, Abraham 34,35
  James 132
  Jonathan 132
  William 45
ARCHER, Leticia 146
ARENTON...14
ARMSTRONG, Andrew 28,148,165,166,175
  Edward 107
  Francis 133
  James 66,139
  John 105,106,140,172
  Lanty 3,89
  Martin 76,82,83,91,98,99,102,103,104,105,108,109,110,111,112,113,149,152,154,156,172,179,188,189,190,191,192
  Martin, Jr. 108
  Mary Ann Elizabeth 101
  Robert 22,58
  Thomas 139,143
  Thomas Temple 102

ARMSTRONG, cont'd:
  William 42,94,95,139
ARNOLD, John 23
ARNTON...23
ARNWINE, John 91
ARONWARE, John 48
ARUNTON...2
ASHE, John Baptist 146
  Samuel 139,140
ASHER, Charles 32
  Charles, Sr. 32
ASHERT, William 134
ASHMORE, James 58,59
ASHORT, William 65
ASKER, Badger 145
ATHENSON, Benjamin 79
ATHENSON/ATHANSON, Nathan 79,80
ATKINSON, Nathen 79
AYLETT, John 193
AYTETH, John 194

BABB, Philip 73
BACON, William 140
BAGS, John 64
BAILEY, Claudius 63,64,67
  Cothriel 30
  James 192
  John 39,48
  Robert 14,22
  Walter 52
  William 40,134
BAKER...21
  Elisha 72
  Evan 132,134
  Francis 35
  John 174,175,184
  Joshua 192
  Nicholas 135
  Thomas 4
BALCH, Amos 60,87,101,102
  Hezekiah 59,102
  John 60
BALDRIDGE, James 79
BALDWIN, John 72
BALES, Thomas 11
BALEY, John 52
BALLARD, Joseph 74
BALLEY, Wallis 96
BALLINGER, James 66
  Moses 91
BANKS, Thomas 40
BARBY, John 152
BARCLAY, George 20
BARKER, Thomas 154
BARKLEY, George 36
BARKSDALE, Charles 13
BARNARD, John 132
BARNATT, John 44
BARNETT, William 100
BARNS, John 150
BARREN, William 19
BARRITT, John 99
BARRON, James 35
  John 26,195
  Joseph 35
BARRONS, Joseph, Sr. 19
BARROTT, Thomas, Jr. 154
BARROW...29
  Betsy 183
  Henry 183
  James 20,34,183
  John 122
  Matthew 183
  Sherrard 183

BARTAIN, Andrew 171
BARTON, Samuel 104,122,181,182,184,185,192,195
  Thomas 55
BASHINE, John 15
BAXTON, William 141
BAY, Andrew 182
BAYLES, David 22
  Hezekiah 22
  John 32,33
  Reuben 21
  Samuel 20,28
BAYLEY, Benjamin 139
  Carr 54
  Jacob 93
  Thomas 75
BEACOTE, Peater 139
BEAK, Robert 106
BEALE, George 40
BEALER, Jacob 34
  John 38
  Joseph 52
  Willery 40
BEAN, Jesse 4,81
  Joseph 136
  Robert 96
  William 4,35
  William, Sr. 36
BEARD, Andrew 32
  Hugh 24,89
  John 62,70
  John Lewis 145
BEARDE, John 89
BEARDON, Thomas 76
BEASLEY, William 14
BECHEN (see BEHEN)
BECK, William 142,146,176
BEDDY, Thomas 29
BEELEY, Christopher 131
BEEN, Jesse 20
  John 21,33
  Robert 10
BELAR, Jacob 54
  John 52
BELL, James 20
  John 34
  Robert 178,181
  William 11,34
BENNET...33
BENNETT, John 88
  Stephen 47
BENTON...4
  Jesse 131
BEORE, William 77
BERMON...27
BERRY, Frances 51
  Thomas 156,159
  William 4,11,15,16,18
BEWLEY, Anthony 23
BIFFLE, Adam 38
BIDDLE, Thomas 29,34
BIGGES, Robert 72
BIGGS, Robert 86
BIGHAM, John 107
  William 16,68,74
BILLINGSBEE, Samuel 50,51
BILLIPS, John 158
BIRD, Amos 8,63
  Jonathan 14,21,26
  Joseph 73,89
BIZZELL, David 143
BLACK, William 48,55,60,63
BLACKAMORE, John 134
BLACKBURN, Archibald 68
  John 64

BLACKBURN, cont'd:
    Robert 9,14,64
    Thomas 84
BLACKEMORE, John 128,135
BLACKFORD, Joseph 136
BLACKLEDGE, Richard 112
BLACKLEDYS, Richard 109
BLACKLEY...16
    Robert 17,19,34
BLAIR, Alexander 69,91,94
    James 53,66,67,85,91
    John 16,27,68,78,150,
      151,182
    Thomas 172
BLANTON...40
    John 47,54
BLEAR, John 17
BLEDSOE, Anthony 49,50,53,
    137,194
    Isaac 136,137,162,174,
      187,193,194
BLEVENS, William 49
BLEVINS, William 52
BLITHE, James 29
BLOUNT...89,149
    Frederick 157
    Jacob 119
    John 138
    John Gray 113,114,115,
      116,117,118,120,138,152,
      178,180,182,184,185
    Reading 138,151,152,160,
      168,169,173
    Thomas 113,114,115,116,
      117,118,120,186
    William 71,138,180
BLYTH, James 43
BLYTHE, James 20,23,25
    Joseph 140
BOEZ, Edmund 71
BOGLE, Joseph 62
BOHANNON, Alexander 129
    Archibald 135
    John, Jr. 122
BOILES, Barnabas 171
BOILSTONE, Jesse 130
BOND, George 37
BONNER, James 154,157,158
    John 154,157,158
BONNERS, James 184
    John 184
BONUN, Nathaniel 51
BORDEN, Michael 72
BOREM, William 194
BOSLEY, James 138,188
BOSTON, Jacob 173
BOWEN, Charles 135
    John 194
    Kezia 90
    William 134,195
BOWERS, John 156
BOWMAN, Cornelius 14
    Sparling 89
    William 145,162,163,164
BOWNON, Franklen 90
BOX, Edward 27
    Michael 78
    Robert 18
BOYD, Adam 111,143
    Andrew 174
    John 124,149,174,175,
      186
    Robert 70,87
BOYLSTON, William 88
BRADCUTT, Richard 27
BRADLEY...99
    Abraham 5
    Edward 131
    George 157
    James 70,122,140,152,
      153,160
    Robert 142
BRADSHAW, James 101
    John 72,88,89

BRADSHAW, cont'd:
    William 123
BRAGG, David 38
    Joseph 44
    Thomas 54
BRAIDON, Charles 179
BRALEY, Walter 104
BRANCH, Christopher 19
    John 85
    William 85
BRANDON, James 104
    Thomas 17
BRANK, Christopher 19
BRANKS, Robert 193
BRANNON, Thomas 17,19
BRANTLEY...1
    Charles 73,134
BREAKEY, Andrew 147
BREHEN/BREHON (also BECHEN)
    James Glosler 168,169,
      170,176,178,180,182
BREVARD, Alexander 146
    Joseph 146
BRICKELL, James 144
BRIGHAM, James 38,41,42,52,
    92,194
BRIGHT, Simon 170
BRISTON, James 178
BRITAIN, Abraham 55
BRITTON, Daniel 89
BROCK, George 64,90
    Joseph 162,165,166,189
    Moses 11
BROCKE, Christopher William 141
BROILS, Matthias 19,27
BROOKS...26
    George 45
    Stephen 167,168
    Thomas 95,141
BROSHARE, Robert Samuel 50
BROWN...3
    Alexander 65
    Charles 134
    David 78
    Hugh 72,86
    Hugh, Jr. 89
    Jacob 30
    James 101,136,142,179,
      180
    John 111,119,122,175,
      180,181
    Joseph 4,24,25,33,84,86
    Joseph, Sr. 30
    Peter 29,30
    Seivis 143
    Thomas 8,13,21,24,69,
      119,184
    William 30
BROWNFIELD, Robert 139
BROYLES...30
    Nicholas 32
    Syras 26
BRUMLEY, Augustin 81
    Augustine 90
    Austin 65
    John 90
    Thomas 72
BRUMMECK, Thomas 20
BRUMMETT, Thomas 30
BRUNK, Christian 21
BRYAN, Bryant 67
    Ebenezer 69
    James 83
    Morgan 162
    William 26,90
BRYANT, Barrah 132
    James 152
    Morgan 191
    William 75
BRYSON, Hugh 74
BUCHANNON, Ezekiel 30
    John 150,169,171,176,
      177,186,189,191,196

BUCHANNON, cont'd:
    Samuel 149,195
BUCKANNON, John 142,185
BUCKNER, William 55
BUDD, Samuel 138,159,160
BUDDLE, James 66
BULLAR, Isaac 9
BULLAR/BULLER, John 11,31
BULLAR, Joseph 4,5,8,32
BULLARD, Isaac 71,84,87
    Joseph 61,62,63,64,76,
      84,93,94
BULLEN, Michael 142
BULLOCK, Richard 26
BUNCH, James 79
BUNCOMB, Thomas 152
BUNDY, Simon 7
BUNN, John 94
BUNTON, Andrew 18
BURDWELL, George 42,48
    Robert 55
BURGESS, Absalom 141
    Philip 141
    Thomas 135
    William 135
BURLESON, Aaron 2,11,21
    Aaron, Jr. 16
BURLIEO...54
BURTON, Robert 148
BUSH, John 156
BUSHE, William 139
BUSHELL, Eusebius 158,159,
    166
BUTLER, Elisha 29
    Isaac 146
    John 143
BUTTEN, Joseph 26
BUTTS, Archibald 146
BUXTON, William 149
BYRD, Amos 59
    John 80
    Richard 81
BYRNS, James 194
BYRUM, Ebenezer 12,98

CABBAFEETY, Moses 45
CAEN, Jesse 190
CAFFERY, Barnard 32
CAFFREY, John 124
CAIN, James 40
CALAHAN, John 22
CALDWELL...36
    James 94
    Robert 74
    Thomas 41,46,47,73,93,
      99,100
CALDWELLS, John 69
CALER, Frederick 50
CALINGHAM, Cornelius 186
CALLAHAN...31
CALLENDER, Thomas 139
CALLIHAN...21
    Robert 157
CALLISON, James 87
CALLOM, John 59
CALLOWAY, John 137
CALSS, Robert 156
CALVETT, Moses 55
CALVITT, Frederick 39
    William 39
CAMERON, James 80
CAMPBELL...(see PHILLIPS &
    CAMPBELL) 20,177,178,
    179,180,182,183
CAMPBELL, Alexander 3,23
    Arthur 52
    Charles 37,46,125
    David 5,17,18,56,67,98
    Dempsy 153
    James 25,33,47
    John 68,141
    Robert 4,8,47,51,190
    Thomas 153
    William 13,31,86,94,123

CAMPEN, James 158
CANNON, Lewis 176
  Minor 173
CANTRELL, Stephen 154,194
CANTWELL, Stephen 169
CAPER, Robert 180
CARDER, Godfrey 2
CARIGER, Godfrey 81
CARLISLE, George 130
  James 50
CARMACK, Cornelius 92
CARNAHAN, Andrew 160
CARNEY, John 48
  Thomas 31
CAROTHERS, John 43
CARR, Jane 48
  Joseph 160
  Kesiah 26
  Patrick 15
CARREY, Thomas 31
CARRUTHERS...7
CARRYGIN, Godfrey 31
CARSON...29
  Moses 26,30,65,70
  Robert 26,31
CARTER, Abram 67
  Benjamin 90,140
  Caleb 73
  Daniel 65
  Emanuel 5
  Giles 146
  Jacob 66
  John 5,25,26,36,65,111
  John, Jr. 67
  Joseph 73
  Landon 30,36,37,90,92,
    107,119,120
  Levi 74
CARTERIGHT, Robert 166
CARTRIGHT, Robert 127
CARTWRIGHT, Joseph 155
CARVIN, Edward 130
CARY, James 193
CASADY...21
CASEY, James 84
CASH, James 30,33
CASHITTS, Michael 132
CASSALMAN, Jacob 180
CASSELMAN, Benjamin 179
CASSON, William 34
CASTEEL, John 65
CASTLEMAIN, Jacob 157
CASUN, Charles 26
CASWELL...28,33
  Alexander 98
  Martin 37,56
  Richard 1,37,57,60
  Richard William 158
  William 1,37,41
CATE, Philip 142
CATHEY, George 111
  George, Sr. 105,106
  Richard 171
  William 105,171
CATRON, Pater 128
  Philip 128
CAVATT...25
  Moses 38,50
CAVELL, Alexander 42
CAVENAUGH, Hugh 68,72
CAVILL, Moses 12
CAYSWOOD, John 126
CAYWOOD, Berry 128
CHAMBERLAIN, Andrew 57
  Jacob 21,28
  Jeremiah 59,61
  John 59
  Nehemiah 24
  Ninean/Nenian 26,59
CHAMBERLIN, Jacob 5
CHAMBERS...42
  Alexander 20
  Daniel 123,128

CHAMBERS, cont'd:
  Mark/Marke 42,100
CHAPMAN, Abner 61,71,84
  Thomas 28,82
CHARTER, James 11
CHASTAIN, John 41
CHASTIAN, James 44
CHEAT, Jesse 71
CHEFSOM, Abraham 129
CHESAM, Elijah 49
CHESOLONY, John 11
CHILD, Francis 140
CHISOLM, John 24,34
CHOATE, Christopher 25
CHOLE, Aulston 6
  Benjamin 27
  Christopher 27
CHOOK, Christopher 20
CHOOTE, Christopher 23
CHOTE, Auston 29
  Christopher 29,30,38
  Nancy 54
CHRISHAM, Elijah 46
CHRISTIAN, Gilbert 37,107
  Lewis 85
  Thomas 71
CLARK, Dennis 127
  Henry 55
  John 24,29,32,50
  Lardner 141,143,146,155,
    165,178,181,188,189,190,
    191,194
  Nathaniel 43
  Robert 85
  Thomas 191
  William 26,68
CLARKE...102,109,110
  Downham 111
  Henry 111
  Lardner 157,159,180
  Thomas 139,157
  William 159,172
CLAYTON, Isham 133
CLENDENNING, James 128,195
  John 162,169
CLERER, John 175
CLIKE, Peter 55
CLOUD, Jason 51,53,70
  Joseph 41
  Peter 143
  William 69,71
COBB...15,17,35
  Ben 21
  Benjamin 32
  Pharoah 19,30,31,32
  Stephen 84
  William 19,21
COCK, Michael 64,72
COCKE, Peter 46,47
  William 65,71,78,79,81,
    105,129
COCKEN, John 50
COCHRAN, John 40,49
COCHRAM, William 176,177
COCKRAN...39
COCKRELL, John 128
COCKRILL, John 130
COCKS, Richard 12
COFFMAN, Andrew 65
  David 64
COILE, Robert 65,70,72,73,
  92,95
COLBREATH, Alexander 69
COLE, Joseph 41,53
  Joseph, Sr. 53
  Solomon 38,54
  William 152
COLEMAN, John 85
  Spilly 135
  William 78
COLLER, Levi 156
COLLIAR, William 78
COLLIER, William 137

COLLINGSWORTH, William 127,
  189,194
COLLINS, John 157
COLPOH, Henry 47
COLSON, Isaac 156
COLSTON, James 146
COLYER, William 33,34,36
CONDRAY, James 35
-CONDRY, Dennis 122
  John 125
  Richard 25
CONLY, John 28
CONN, Samuel 134
CONNER, James 62,75,77
CONRAD, Nicholas 131
  Philip 131
CONWAY, Henry 59,78,107
  Joseph 85,86
  William 60,86
COOK, George 43
  James 132
  Jesse 161
COONROD, Nicholas 154
COOPER, James 45,47,49,51,
  107
  John 48,107
  Patience 24
  William 121
COOR, James 110,111
COOTES, John 102
COPELAND...59
  David 69,71,72
  James 46,48
  Joseph 87
COPENHAFER, Thomas 43
COPLAN, William 51
COPOH, Henry 40
COPTON, David 81
CORBETT, John 59
CORBIT, John 64
CORDERY, John 163
CORVAN, Robert 40
COSSWAY, Joseph 172
COTTEN, Thomas 146
COTTER, John 38,94,132
COULTER, John 90
COWAN, John 125
  Robert 22,28
COWARD, James 2
  Zachariah 25
COX, Abraham 50
  Benjamin 74
  Edward 47,110,136,194
  Ephraim 73
  Jacob 48
  James 35,88,90
  John 50,54,189
  John, Jr. 39
  Phenix 186
  Richard 135
  Samuel 72,86
  Thomas 97,194,195
  William 26,161
COXE, William 19
COYLE, Robert 46
COYLES, Robert 95
COZBY, James 74
CRADDOCK, John 173
CRAFFORD, Hugh 39
CRAFT, Michael 43,48
CRAGON, Patrick 47
CRAIG, David 60,135
  John 42,134
  William 134
CRANE, Lewis 131
CRAWFORD, David 120
  John 18,38,46,96,100
  Samuel 25
CRESSWELL, James 76,91
CRINER, John 93
CROAT, Alexander 3
CROCKETT, Andrew 100,135,
  189

CROCKETT, cont'd:
  James 128,136
  John 43,60,137
  Joseph 54
  Robert 46
  Zophar 171
CROSBY, James 63
CROSS, Henry 18,90
  Richard 110
CROUCH, Joseph 36
CROUTCHER, Anthony 157,165,
  179,190
CROUTHERS, Anthony 152
CROW, Benjamin 72
  John 57,59,124
CROWSON, William 81
CRUMPSTOCK/CRUMSTOCK,
  Thomas 188,189
CRUTCHFIELD, James 125
CULBERSON, Samuel 8,11
CUMMENS, John 171
CUNNINGHAM, Charles 14
  Christopher 6,9,24,30
  James 129
  John 81
  Paul 21
  William 20,21
CURRY, Samuel 7,55
CURTIS, Nathaniel 70

DAGY, Gasor 78
DAKE, Pleasant 66
DALE, William 11
DALLAM, Richard 106
DAMRON, William 11
DANIEL, James 44,87
  William 95
DANTHEN, Elijah 96
DARDEN, John 187
DARMOND, John 77
DAUGE, Richard 151
DAUGHERTY, George 64,65,67,
  68,73,82,83,84,103,108,
  109,110,111,113,123,138,
  142
  Joseph 124
  Robert 125
DAUGHTERTY, George 109
  Henry 136
DAVIDSON, Ephraim 110,112
  George 106,112,139
  James 112
  Jane 109
  Joseph 22
  Mary 111
  Thomas 109
  William 88,110
DAVIES, David 96
DAVIS, Edmund 41
  Elisha 141
  Isaac 69,85
  James 21
  John 30,31,157
  Jones 21
  Joshua 152,154,155,160
  Nathan 3,27
  Nathaniel 2,34,48,69,70
  Nicholas 74
  Robert 18
  Thomas 72,124,143
  William 143
DAVISON, Lewis 124
DEAKINS, Richard 28
DEAN, Charles 139
  Francis 83
  James 185
DEESON, John 131
  Samuel 125
DELANEY, James 2,65
  John 19,70
  William 42,43,45
DELANY, James 6
DELAY, George 46
DEMOTT, Robert 94,99

DEMUNROE, Timothy 158
DENETH, Charles 137
DENTON...25
  James 5
  Joseph 7,22,29,30
  Samuel 27,28
  Thomas 135
DENNY, Abraham 156
  David 158
DEVER, James 111
  John 48,180
DEVERS, John 185
DEYAMOND, John 22
DICKSON, John 176
  Joseph 102
  William 18
DICKY, Thomas 146
DIDWELL, Martin 9,12
DILLINGHAM...38
  Vachel 43
  Vauch 4
DILLON, William 186
DINSMORE, Adam 45
DISHE, Robert 123
DIX, William 175
DIXON, Charles 169
  James 73,100
  John 191
  Joseph 162
  Nathaniel 140
  Tilghman 138
  Tilman 169
DOAK, Samuel 37
  William 61,62
DOBBINS, William 106,158,
  159,162,166
DODGE, Richard 122
DODSON, Elisha 45
  Jesse 88
  Rawleigh 54
DOHERTY, George 27
DONAHOE, Bartholomew 93
  William 130
DONELSON, John 75,98,125,
  129,142,170,172,177
  John, Sr. 126
  Spencer 156
  Stokeley 37,38,47,62,63,
  74,75,76,77,89,91,92,93,
  95,96,97,98,99,100,103,
  106,113,169,170
  William 61
DONNELLY, James 149
DONOHOE, Thomas 140
  William 162
DOSSETT...38
DOTSON, Elisha 77
  Lazarus 54
  William 33,35
DOUGE, James 152
DOUGLAS, Edward 184
DOUGLASS, Benjamin 79
  David 183
  Edward 155,166,173
  Elmore 133,135,195
  Ezekiel 131
  James 173,190
  John 84
  Jonathan 39,48,49,81
  Reubin 154
  Robert 141
DRAKE, Benjamin 123,129,
  173,194
  Benjamin, Jr. 121
  Cornelius 184
  Ephraim 127
  Isaac 122,190
  John 125,128,141,176,
  188
  Jonathan 110,123,128,144,
  170,171,172,193
DUDLEY, Thomas 139
DUFF, William 49
DUGAN, John 109

DUGAN, cont'd:
  Thomas 101
DUGEN, Thomas 104
DUGGAN, Daniel 49
DUGGARD, Mary 30
DUGIN, James 112
DUKE, Pleasant 67
  (also DAKE)
DUNCAN, Charles 7,20,29
  John 55,88
  Joseph 2,9,19,25,27,33,
  35
DUNCENS, Jeremiah 22
  Thomas 21
DUNGIN, Jeremiah 28
DUNHAM...20
  Daniel 2,127
  Henry 74
  John 15,124
  Joseph 58
DUNKAN, John 134
DUNKHAM, Daniel 121
DUNLAP, Abraham 35
  Ephraim 83
DUNN, Daniel 26
DUNNOCK, Peter 143
DUNWOODY, Samuel 57,75
DUPREAST, Randall 25
DUVALL, Jacob 55
DYKE, William 47

EAGEN, Edward 22
EAGLETON, David 64
EARLEY, Thomas 18
EARNEST, Henry 8,26
EASLEY, Stephen 12,38,39,
  43
EATEN, Joseph 61
EATON, John 173,176,185
EATTON, Joseph 64
EBENEZER, John 96
EBORNE, John 158
EDEN, James 31
EDMISTON, William 194
EDMUND...25
EDMUNDSON, Thomas 178
EDMUNSON, Thomas 123
EDWARDS,...70
  David 141,142,144
  Frederick 131
  Nicholas 45
ELIOT, William 84
ELLER, Jacob 54
ELLIOTT, Faulkner 193
ELLIOT, John 169,179,180,
  193,195
ELLIOTT, William 53
ELLIS, Christopher 89
  William 128
ELLISON, Joseph 163
  Robert 8
  William 12
EMERY...24
EMMETT, James 145
EMMOUT, George 34
ENGLES, Thomas 76
ENGLISH...20
  Andrew 2,3,8,9,11,72
  James 2,3,4,10,26,29
  John 15,16
  Joseph 34,71
  William 73
ENMAN, Abednego 12
ENMON, Abednego 3
ENTREE, Thomas 34
ERVIN, David 40
  Robert 191
ERWIN, Thomas 25
ESHMEAL, Thomas 74
ESPEY, James 121
ESPY, George 124
  James 195
  Robert 121
ESTES, John 120,121

ESTIS, John 132
EVANS, Andrew 87
   Evan 87,88,126
   John 76,77,96,123,125
   Jonathan 62,73
   Nathaniel 65
   Thomas 19,153,154,183
EVERETT, John 29
EWING, Alexander 167
   Andrew 130
   George 58
   William 90

FACON, William 140
FAIN...6
   David 133
   Nicholas 5
   Samuel 16,28
   William 27
FAINE, John 14
FAITTE, William 149
FANNER, Richard 154
FARMER, Thomas 162
FARNSWORTH...73
   Henry 58,64
FARRIS, James 126
FAULKNER, Abraham 64
   Frances 178
FENN, John 70
FENNER, Richard 110,147,
   148,162,165,166,175,179
   Robert 103
FERGUS, James 140
FIEN, John 90
FINE, Peter 74
FIONEY...195
FISHBACK, Jacob 74
FISHER, Archibald 48
   Frederick 186
FITRELL, Isaac 45
FITSWORTH, Isaac 41
FITZGERALD, Garret (also
   Garret, Garratt, Garott,
   Garrott) 44,45,48,50,
   51,55,57,58,59,82,84,85
   John King 78
FLANAKEN, Samuel 3
FLANERY, Daniel 192
FLEMING, Joseph 150
FLETCHER, John 137
   Simon 99
   Thomas 12,144
   William 129,156
FLIPPEN, Thomas 61
FLOOD, Alexander 161
   Benjamin 143
FLOREN, Lazaras 138
   Richard 138
FLOWERS, David 119
FORBES, Joseph 155
FORD, Elias 169
   John 25,36,157,166,167,
   169
   Lloyd/Loyd 43,55
   Mordecai 53
FORK(FORD?), Loyd 44
FORGES, Andrew 39
FORNES, Thomas 155
FORT, Elias (also Ford),
   179,181
FOSTER, Anthony 185
   James 126
FOWLER...9
   Joseph 3,59
FOX, Andrew 89
FRAME, William 131
FRANCISCO, John 74
FRANKLIN, James 126
FRANKS, John 185
   William 10
FRASER, William 193
FRAZIER, Daniel 132
   George 173

FREELAND, George 137,195
   James 126,133
FRENCH, Henry 31
FULCHART, James 59
FULKERSON, Abraham 65, 69,
   73,80
   John 89
FULKINSON, John 129
FULLER, John, Sr. 26
FUNKHOUSER, Christopher
   130
FUTON, William 167

GABBARD, George 33
GAILY, William 98
GAINER, Samuel 185
GAINS, Richard 169
GALBREATH, Arthur 93
   James 67,70
GALLIHER, Thomas 76
GALLOWAY, John 127
   William 129
GAMBELL, Bradley 16,178
GAMBILL, Bradley 10,179,
   182
   David 46
   Moses 36
GAMMON, Richard 43,53
GARDNER, Jacob 47
GARLAND, Samuel 31
GARRETT, Daniel 127
   William 69
GARROLD, John 154
GASS, John 67,69
GATES, Charles 43,46
   James 47
   John 45
   Joseph 48
GAVIN, Anthony 141
GENTEREY, Charles 89
GENTREY, John 55
GENTRY/GENTREY, Charles
   9,11,48,88
   Nicholas 55,122
   Robert 21,66
GEORGE, Edward 77
   Silas 56
GERRARD, Charles 139,181
GIBBONS, Thomas 46,92,93
   William 195
GIBSON, Hymphrey 13
   James 27,70
   John 85,132
   Jordan 137
GILBERT, James 65
   John 50
   William 105
GILBREATH, Arthur 52
   John 85
   Thomas 65
   William 71,101,103
GILGORE(KILGORE), Charles
   74
GILKEY, John 133
GILL, Thomas 104
GILLAHAN, John 21
GILLASPIE, George 36,57,59
   James 67
   John 65,87,90
   Thomas 26,28,30,31,36,
   56,57,58,76,77,104,127
   William 123
GILLELAND, John 36
GILLESPIE, George 5,11,12,
   56
   Thomas 5
GILLIHAM, Devirres 95
GILLIHAN, John 48
GILLILAND, John 3,18,79,81,
   82
GILMORE, Charles 154,155,
   156,158,162,173
GIST, Benjamin 5

GIST, cont'd:
   Joseph 71
   Joshua 58,59,91
GIVANS, Robert 130
GIVEN, Thomas Jones 126
GIVENS, James 136
GIVIN, David 123
   James 32
GLASCOW, James 37,92,94,
   147,153,156,161,168,
   190,196
GLAZE, Lawrence 88,90
GLOOTER, Thomas 171
GLOSTER, Thomas 178,181
GOACHER, Henry 3
GOFORTH, William 67,90
GOIN, Thomas 29,71
GOOD, John 41
   William 52,53
GOODEN, Drury 7
GOODIN, Benjamin 65,66,70,
   78,81,82
   James 71
   Thomas 60
GOODLO, Robert 110
GOODLOR, Robert 111
GOODMAN, Chloe 180
   Joseph 29
   Tobias 161
GOODWIN, Joseph 13
GOSSNEY, William 131
GOWAN, David 130
   William 122
GOWER, Abel 126
   Elijah 126
GRAGG, Nathan 5
   Samuel 83
GRAHAM, James 23,61
   John 103
   Richard 104
   Thomas 73
GRAIG, John 49
   Samuel 72
GRAMMER, John 189
GRANBERRY, John 181
GRANT, Alexander 49
   Daniel 38
   James 107
GRAVES, Perry 137
GRAY, George 8,13
   James 176
   Joseph 176
   Robert 38,39,41,43
GREATE, David 30
GREEN, Elizabeth 79
   Francis 87
   Furnifold 80
   George 133
   James 78,80,127
   James West 155
   John 80
   John, Jr. 79
   Jonathan 128
   Joseph 78,79,80
   Joseph, Jr. 79
   Joshua 20
   Nathaniel 138
   Phillemon 80
   Richard 51
   William 122,176
   Zachariah 126
GREENAWAY, John 194
GREENBY...21
GREENE, William 80
GREER, Andrew 29,30
   Joseph 31,119,121
   Robert 66,171
GREERS, Alexander 102
   Thomas 102
GREGORY, William 27
GRICE, Christopher 189
GRIEL, Christopher 191
GRIFFIN, William 2,35,123

GRIGG, Henry 86
GRIGGS, Charlie 155
GRIMES, David 47
  James 3,4,10
  Willard 126
GRISHAM, William 27
CROSS, Jacob 54
  Richard 125
GROVES, John 93
  John, Sr. 92
  William Barry 118
GRUB, Abraham 40
  Jacob 51
GRUBBS...39
  Abraham 44
GUBBINS, William 149,158
GUDGER, William 19
GUESS, Jonathan 155
GUEST, Benjamin 64
  Joseph 17
  Joshua 92
GUICE, Christopher 141
GUIN, Christopher 191
GUNN, Adam 32
GUTHRIE, Robert 22
GWINN, John 89

HABBARD, Samuel 130
HACKER, Julius 46
HACKETT, John 60,61,62,75,
  76,77,83,88,90
  Thomas 60
HADLEY, Joshua 140,152,167,
  177
HAGGARD, Henry 66
HAIL, Abednego 34
  John 42
  Meshech 27
  Nicholas 29
HAILE, Nicholas 12
HAINEY, Thomas 133
HALE, Mesheck 8
  Nicholas 30
  Phillip 86
  Shadrach 27,28
  Shadraih 24
  William 27
HALEY, David 66,71,94
HALFACRE, Michael 66
HALL, Clement 139
  James 109
  John 50
  Philip 79
  Thomas 83
  William 50,51
HALMARK, George 66
HAMBLEN, David 94
HAMBLETON, Josiah 8
  Robert 49
  William 88
HAMEY, Selly 139
HAMILTON, Isaiah 28
  Jacob 28
  James 29,51,141
  John 16,122,126,186,187
  Thomas 126,154,155
HAMMELTON, Thomas 179
HAMMER, Isaac 71
  John 34
HAMMILL, Robert 89
HAMMOND, John B. 169
HAMPTON, Adam 193
  Andrew 69,162
  Robert 27
HANDLEY, Samuel 15,188
HANKINS, William 97
HANNAH...24
  John 20
  Joseph 132
  William 85,86
HANNAWS, Henry 152
HARBERSON, Daniel 70
HARDEMAN, Thomas 4,10

HARDEN, Henry 135
  John 61,62,156
  Joseph 6,14,58,62,64
  Martin 135
HARDIN, John 101
  Joseph 10,57
  William 102
HARGESS, Shadrach 112
HARGETT, Frederick 139,183
HARGISS, Abraham 145
HARGROVE, William 138
HARKLEROAD, Honey 52
HARP, Thomas 182
HARPER, Jesse 98
  Robert Goodlo 78
HARR, George 23
  Walter 23
HARRIL, John 169
HARRINGTON, Charles 11
HARRIS, Edward 107,108,120
  James 11,39,41,130
  James W. 6
  John 193
  Samuel 1,9,32,108
HARRISON, Daniel 15,16
  Jesse 154
  Thomas 41,45
HARROLD, John 49
HART, Anthony 152,157,160,
  161,165,166,167,172,173,
  174,181
  David 118,164
  Nathaniel 134
HARVEY, Augustus 109
HARWOOD, James 126
HATLER, Michael 84
  Philip 80
  Sebastian 30
HAUGHLETT, William 120
HAW, Julius 51
HAWKENS, Philemon 120
HAWKINS, Elias 2
  James 65
  William 111
HAWORTH, Abraham 91
HAY, Joseph 125
HAYES, Charles 14,21
  James 59
  Nicholas 73
  Robert 159,163
HAYLAND, James 93
HAYS, Charles 2,69
  Hugh 126
  James 136
  John 180,182
  Nathaniel 126
  Robert 104,105
  Samuel 125
HAYWOOD, John 107,175
  Mordecai 46
HAYWORLD, Absalom 24
HAYWORTH, George 66
HAZARD, Moses 152
HEAD, William 194
HEADRICK, Jacob 25
HEATHERICK/HEATHRICK,
  Jacob 35
HEATHERLY, Evans 13,14
HEATON, Amos 121
  Robert 194,196
HEDRACK, Jacob 37
HEDRICKS, Jacob 31
HELL, Bennett 182
HENDERSON...78,79
  Andrew 56
  Archibald 141
  Daniel 3
  James 68
  John 49,124,194
  Joseph 123
  Nathaniel 132
  Pleasant 132
  Richard 137

HENDERSON, cont'd:
  Thomas 69,74
HENDRICKS, John 135
  Joseph 161
HENLEY, Jesse 56
HENRY...14
  David 124,170
  Hugh 130
  Hugh, Sr. 124
  Isaac 132
  James 75
  Samuel 5,7,11
  William 128
HEPLEY, Samuel 163
HERD, John 134
HERITAGE, John 56
HERKLEROAD, Henry 54
HESTON, Abraham 29
HETHERLY, Hains 35
HIBBARD, Samuel 74
HICK, John 142
HICKERSON, James 2
HICKMAN, Edwin 155,156
  Thomas 163
HICKS, Jonathan 65
  Shadrach 39
HICKWOOD, John 47
HICORY, Henry 131
HIGGISON, John 128
HIGHDER, Michael 4
HIGHLAND, Henry 129
HILL, Green 143,144,145
  James 59,60
  John 23,61
HIMBERLIN, Jacob 127
  Michael 127
HINDS, Joseph 98,104
  Levy 98
HINES, George 51
HINSON, William 133
HITCHCOCK, John 69
HIRD, William 95
HIRKLEROAD, Henry 53
HIXON, Joseph 57
HOBBART, James 64
HOBBLES, Joel 132
HOBSON, John 130
HODGE, Francis 32,123
HODGES, Benjamin 145
  Charles 56
  Drury 68
  Welcome 73,94
HOGAN, Edward 126
  Humphrey 144
  Richard 137
  Samuel 140
HOGG, Thomas 161,179,181
HOGGES, Ambrose 3
HOGGETT/HOGGOTT, James
  154,189,190,191
HOGON, Daniel 121
HOLBROOK, John 4
HOLDERNESS, William 144,
  161
HOLLAND, Benjamin 23,30
  James 103
  Joseph 185
HOLLAWAY, William 32
HOLLEY, Frank 9
  John 9,12
  Jonathan 6
  Nathaniel 193
HOLLICE, James 130
HOLLIDAY, John 124
HOLLIS, James 17,38,39,40,
  48,129,144
HOLLOWAY, Archilles 128
  John 51
  William, Jr. 32
HOLMES, Hardy 145
HOLT, Francis 44
  John 136
HOMER, Charles 185

HONEYCUTT, Alston 14
  John 5,6,14,42
HOOD, Robert 56,62
  William 128
HOOPER, Absalom 189
HOOVER, William 78
HOPKINS, George 88
  Joseph 182
HORDE, William 96
HORNBACK, John 62,63,95
HORNBECK, John 88
HORNER...25
  William 20,22
HORNS, Philip 36
HORTON...21
  Joseph 103
HOSKENS, John 6
HOSKINGS, John 2
HOSKINS, Jesse 10
HOUDISHALL, Henry 127
HOUGH, John 78
  Joseph 73
HOUGHTON, John, Jr. 12
  Joshua 5,8,16
  Thomas 3
HOUSER, George 109
HOUSTON, James 58
HOUZER, John 52
  Nicholas 52
HOWARD, John 3,22,70
  Joseph 162
  Joshua 142
HOWSAR, John 20
HUBBARD, James 24,56,57,
  59,62,76,78
HUBBART, James 60,90
  Zebulon 156
HUD...21
HUDDEN, Anna 22
HUES, David 13
  Francis 15
  Henry 37
  John 7
  William 6,13,20
HUETHERLY, Evans 12
HUFF, Peter 86
HUFFMAN, David 21,28
  Peter 54
HUGGINS, James 106
HUGHES, David 8,49
  Francis 27
  Henry 47
  John 131
  Thomas 33,45
HUGHLET/HUGHLETT, William
  68,108,111,152,156,168
HUGHS, Francis 11
  Henry 153
  James 49
  Nathaniel 141
HUMBER, Samuel 89
HUMPHREY, John 28
  Richard 4
  Ruben 11
HUNT, Elisha 142
  John 93
  Memicum 142
  Uriah 2,4
HUNTER, Caleb 8,17
  James 172,177
  John 25,31
  John, Sr. 30
  Robert 68
  Theophilas 103
HUSE, Henry 38,39
HUTCHESON, James 85
HUTCHINS/HUTCHINGS, Thomas
  75,97
HUTCHINS, Smith 66
HUTCHISON...86
  William 87
HUTTON, William 17
HYDE, Michael 6
HYLAND, James 50,93

INGLES, John 152
  Thomas 91
INGRAM, Edwin 22
INMAN, Abednego 4,56,58,61
  Shadrach 61
IRELAND, Joseph 99
IRESON, James 191
IRVEN, Robert 183
IRVIN, Robert 106
IRVINE, Robert 9,13
IRVING, Alexander 160
IRWIN, George 73
  Robert 5,107
ISBELL, Jason 81
  Thomas 59,154,162
ISHABELL, Thomas 57
IVEY, Curtis 139

JACK, Jeremiah 7,23,58
  Joseph 50
JACKS, John 21
JACKSON, Jacob 73
  John 47,105
  Joseph 136
  Thomas 92,96,100
  William 159
JAMES, Daniel 167
JAMESON, Benjamin 63
JAMISON, James 141
JARNAGIN, Thomas 57,59
JARROT...2
JARROTT...13,47,48
JAUNT, Thomas 142
JEFFRYS, Thomas 182
JENKINS, Dempsey 145,196
  Roland 33
  William 158
JENNINGS, Edmund 132
  John 142
  Jonathan 129
  Thomas 144
  William 43
JIMMERSON, William 157
JISTE, John 35
JOB, William 80
JOBE, David 5
  Samuel 12,47
JOBES, Samuel 8
JOHN, Jennitt 131
JOHNSON, James 88
  Thomas 20
JOHNSTON...84
  Amelia 118
  Crafford 181
  Daniel 123
  David 86,88
  Enos 86
  Henry 145
  Hugh 94
  Isaac 15,16,121,122,194
  Jacob 74
  James 74
  John 51,66,89
  Joseph 48
  Kince 61
  Robert 160
  Seth 97
  Thomas 24,86,178
  Walter 45
  William 63,123,144
  Zophar 85
JOHNSTONE, David 87
  Thomas 9
JONAKEN/JONAKIN/JONIKEN,
  Thomas 8,12,57
JONES, Abraham 127,185
  Ambrose 164,167
  Benjamin 158
  Daniel 164,181
  David 162,177
  Hardy 145
  Harwood 60
  Henry 78
  Jacob 122

JONES, cont'd:
  John 85,90,166
  Nathaniel 104,140
  Philip 171
  Samuel 138
  Seburn 178,181
  Thomas 129,190
  Tignall 106
  William 85
JONSTON, David 89
  Hugh 99
JORDAN, Lewis 36
  Robert 146
JUSTICE, Moses 100

KANADY, Daniel 14,16,18
KANNADY, Abraham 169
  David 153
  George 132
KANNON, Samuel 178
KEE, William 55
KEEF, Thomas 29
KEENER, Hawson 92
KEENYS, John 80
KEILLER, Frederick 52
KEITH, Daniel 7,10
  Solomon 118
KELLUM, John 77
KELLY, Alexander 58
  John 78
  Joshua 21
KELSEY, Hugh 75,87
  Samuel 23
KENAR, Francis 46
KENNADY, John 130
  Daniel 17
  Jacob 94
  John 17
  Moses 26,27
  Samuel 17
KERCHEN, Godfrey 23
KERCHENDALE, Joseph 18
KERE...21
KERR...87
  Andrew 59
  David 26,60
  George 26
  James 104
  Joseph 102,104,170
  Robert 56,89,161,188
  Samuel 104
KETRONE, Lawrence 53
KETT, Solomon 148
KILGORE, Thomas 129,136,194
KILLO, Andrew 122
KILPATRICK, Joseph 103
KINCADE, Joseph 46
KINCAID, Andrew 72
  David 98
KINCANNON, Andrew 43,130
  Matthew 152,161
KINEY, John 68
KING...25,49
  Edward 7
  James 83,96
  John 7,40,44,130
  Martin 127
  Peter 86
  Robert 55,68,70,75,77,
    91,95,101,103,141
  Thomas 47,51,52,55,75,
    83,95,101,103
  William 50,53
KINGSBURY, John 140
KINKAID, Joseph 39
KIRCHEN, Godfrey 24
KIRK, "Widow"46
KIRKPATRICK, Alexander 175
  Hugh 86
  Robert 86
KISSINGER, John 128
KITTRELL, Isaac 133
KOIL, Robert 53
KOIN, John 152

KOON, Phillip 33
KOONS, Philip 35,36
KROUSE, Goolleb 176
KUYKENDALE, Abram 7,9
  John 9
  Peter 24
KYLER, Joseph 81
KYLES, Robert 94

LACKEY, James 62
  James Woods 63,76
LAIN...36
  Aquilla 50,61
  Dutton 2,4
  Lambeth 50
  Richard 50
  Thomas 95
LAINE, Joel 106
  John 8,12
LAMB, Abner 143
  Gideon 147
  James 156
  Robert 85
LAMSDEN, John 132
LANCASTER, John 179
LANCER, James 156
LANDERS, Julius 126
  Samuel 127
LANE...76
  Aquilla 58
  Corbin 71
  John 28
  William 46
LANG, Joseph 62
LANGDON, Jonathan 84,89
LANCHAM, Elias 107
LANHAN, Abel 70
LANAIR/LANIER, James 148,
  150,151,160,161,162,163,
  171,190
  William 105
LARGAN, William 84
LARKIN, John 156
LASH, Christian 172
LATHAM, William 49,50
LAUGHLIN, Alexander 41,94
  James 41
  John 44
LAUNDERS, James 144
LAURENCE, Adam 178,180
LAURENS, Nathaniel 141
LAWLESS, James 136
LAYMAN, John 22
LAYMOND, John 28
LEA, James 100
  William 93
LEACH...29
LEATH, Josiah 84
LEATHERDALE, John 69
LEE, James 56,164,183
  John 74,184
  Nicholas 69
  Thomas 71,74,80
LEEPER, Andrew 40
  George 130
  Gigan 51
  Hugh 104,132
  James 133
  John 46
LEFEAVER, Isaac 133
LEIGHTON, William 124
LEIPER, Mary 37
LENOIR, William 77
LENTON, William 138
LEPER, Andrew 63
LESTON, W. 7
LEWIS, Aaron 11,19,20
  Andrew 84
  Hugh 191
  Joel 78,81,146
  Micajah G. 105
  Micajah Greene 110
  Nathan 30

LEWIS, cont'd:
  Nathaniel 50,51
  Samuel 89,190
  Valentine 162
  William T. 64,77,103,
  104
  William Terrell (Wm.)/
  Terrill/Tyrell, 56,67,
  79,92,93,105,106,110,
  113,120,158
LIGHT, Jacob 29
LIME, Bartlett 47
LINCOLN, Isaac 30
LINDSAY, David 70,71
  Isaac 122
LINDSEY, Isaac 194
  William 48
LISBEY, Aaron 48
  William 48
LISLER, John 71
LITSWORTH, Isaac 44
LITTLE, Andrew 39
  George 37,40
  Jonas 28
  Jones 4
  Matthias 30,39,52
  Valentine 39
LLOYD, John 61
LOCK, Matthew 102
LOCKE, James 162,169
  Matthew 170
  Richard 102
LOCKETT, Pleasant 178
LOCKHART, Samuel 103,154
LOCKSLEY, Robert 54
LOGAN, Benjamin 121
  Hugh 136
  Humphrey 20
  William 87
LOGGAN, William 136
LOGGINS, William 122
LOGUE, John 169
LOMAS, William 143
LONG, John 42,84,96
  Nehemiah 139
  Nicholas 106
LOOMAS, Jonathan 140
LOONEY, Benjamin 38,43
  David 42,46,52,54,127,
  131,164
  John 40,94
  Moses 43,51,52
  Peter 127,131
  Robert 137,195
LOVE, David 122
  Josiah 174,175
  Robert 28
  Thomas 62,87,161
LOVELADY, Marshall 69
LOVELELLY, Joseph 87
LOVELL, Henry 133
  Thomas 182
LOYD, John 90
LUCAS...195
  Benjamin 89
  Isaac 126
  Robert 130
  William 30,137
LUDSPEAK, Christopher 80
LUFSEY, Josiah 27
LUSK, Joseph 58,59
  Robert 7,24
  Thomas 73
LUTZ, Henry 81
LYLE, Henry 11
  John 12
  Samuel 14
LYLES...14
  David 89
LYNE, Edmund 51
LYNN, Adam 192
  Stephen 143
LYON, John 34
  Nathaniel 37,99

LYONS, John 65
LYTLE, Archibald 138,151,
  184,186
  William 150

MC ABOY, Murthy 135
MC ADAMS, James 14
  John 61
MC ADON, Arthur 124
  James 124
  John 6,68
MC ADOO, John 18
MC AFEE, Robert 31
MC AMISH, James 70
MC BEE, James 19
  William 23
MC BRIDE...16
  William 8
MC BROOM, John 46,93
  Thomas 53
  William 66,68
MC CAIN, James 183
MC CALL, Peter 45
  Thomas 31
MC CALLEB, Archibald 71
MC CALLEY, Peter 46
MC CAMEY, Samuel 85
MC CANN, Ephraim 193
MC CANN, Nathaniel 155
MC CARMICK, Robert 101
MC CARNING, James 42
MC CARRELL, John 6
MC CARTHY, Jacob 172
MC CARTNEY...8,21,24
  Charles 124
  James 71,91
MC CAWLEY, Matthew 138
MC CLAMMY, Joseph 166
MC CLEARY, Abraham 90
  Patrick 67
MC CLENNON, Abraham 39
MC CLUNG, Hugh 58
MC CLURE, Nathaniel 193
  William 152
MC CONNELL, Jacob 74
MC CONNON, Charles 101
MC CORD, David 6,12,16
  James 13,15,18
MC CORMACK, William 45,54,
  130
MC COSKEY, John 81
MC COY, Ananias/Annanias
  57,59,75,76,84
  David 50
  Snior(?) 110
  Spencer 49,50
  Spruce 98
MC CRAID, Samuel 160
MC CRAY...25
  Daniel 31
  Robert 192
MC CRORY, Thomas 151,161,
  162
MC CROSKEY, John 81
MC CUESTION, James 146
MC CULLAK, Joseph 70,94
MC CULLOCH, Benjamin 110
  Joseph 62,99
MC CULLOCK, Alexander 109
  Joseph 100
MC CULLOK, Robert 172
MC CUTCHEN, John 169
  Patrick 124
MC CUTCHEON, Samuel 192
MC DANIEL, James 51
  Thomas 177
MC DONALD, James 67,85
  John 63
  Joseph 173
  Josiah 142
  Magnessa 129
MC DOWALD, Joseph 139
MC DOWELL, Joseph 173

MC EADON, William 161
MC ENNIS, James 83
MC EWEN, David 186
MC FADDEN, James 194
MC FARLAN, John 45
   Joseph 67
MC FARLAND, John 173
   Robert 84
MC FARLIN, Alexander 10,57
MC FARLON, Morgan 184
MC FARRON...38
MC FERRON, Andrew 72
MC FEETERS, Samuel 14,47
MC FETTORS, Samuel 46
MC GARICK, William 195
MC GARY, Hugh 123
MC GAUGHEY, William 59
MC GAVOCK...137
   James 135,193
MC GEE, John 119
MC GILL, James 62
   William 72
MC GIRT, John 77
MC GOUCH, William 134
MC GOWAN, Samuel 190
MC INTIRE, John 83
MC INTOSH, Benjamin 192
   Thomas 192
MC KAEN, James 190
MC KEAN, James 127
MC KEE, Alexander 110
   Matthew 96
MC KEER...84
MC KENNIE...35
MC KESSECK, James 105
MC KINLEY, Samuel 43
MC KISE, Alexander 24
MC LAUCHLIN, Henry 19
   John 17
   Thomas 92
MC LEAN, Ephraim 106,112,
   122
   George 109
   William 106
MC LEARY, Abraham 85
MC MACKIN, John 19
MC MAHAN, Daniel 144
   John 3,8,15,17
   John B. 3,6
   John Blair 7
   William 27
MC MERRY, William 126
MC MILLAN, Alexander 63
MC MILLEN, Alexander 56
MC MIN, John 92
MC MULLEN, William 54
MC MULLIN, Alexander 90
MC MURRAY, John 41
   Samuel 38
MC MURREY, Samuel 184
MC MURRY, John 194
   Samuel 125,193
   William 131
MC MURTREE, Joseph 67,85
MC MURTREY...20,128
MC MURTRY, John 136
MC NABB, Baptist 4,7,14
   John 18,74
   William 5
MC NAMEE, Peter 5
MC NARE, James 87
MC NEAL, Archibald 125
MC NEES, John 142,164,179,
   180
MC NEILY, William 154
MC NITT, Anthony 36
MC NUTT, George 86
   Robert 18,62
MC PHEARN, Andrew 67
MC PHERRON, William 71
MC PHERSON, John 155
MC QUESTON, James 106
MC QUIN, Alexander 20

MC QUISTION, James 172
MC RANDELS, Joseph 62
MC REA, David 180
MC RORY, John 160
MC ROY, James 139
MC SPADDEN, Archibald 77
   John 77
MC VEY, John 125
MC WHERTER, James 51
   William 136
MC WHITER, James 45

MABANE, James 183
MABERRY, Frances 98
   Francis 96,100
MABRY, Frances 96
MACON, John 140
   Samuel 158
MADDISON, Rowland 123,130
MADO, William 5
MAEDEN, Benjamin 75
MAHAM, Samuel 106
MAHAN, James 67
   John 63
MAHAU, David 38
MALDING, James 135
MALLETT, Daniel 118
MALLOY, Thomas 180,189,192
MANDFIELD, Thomas 25
MANEFIELD, John 41
MANESCO, James 100
MANIER, Gasper 193
MANIFEE, Jarrott 134
   John 50,51
MANIFIELD, John 45
MANN, Ebenezer 137
MANPHALL, Thomas 137
MANSKER, Gasper 133
MARDERY, William 146
MARLEN, Archibald 153
MARLEY, Robert 149
MARR, John 102
MARSH...34
MARSHALL, Dixon 140
   Henry 95
   John 153,156,157,172,
   174,175
   William 194
MARSOM, Samuel 167
MASSEY, Thomas 183
MARTAIN, Andrew 8
   James 2,29,34
MARTEN, Joseph 43
MARTIN, Alexander 138
   Andrew 26,90
   George 33,35,101
   James 109,111,146
   Joe 27,29
   Joseph 10,24,44,77,180
   Josiah/Josih 23,24
   Richard 68,101
   Robert 110
MASSENGALE, Michael 2
MASSENGILL, Henry 15,17
MASSINGALE, Henry 20,35
MASON, Philips 126
   Robert 35
MATTHEWS, Alexander 23
   Jacob 142
   Missendon 152
MATTOCK, David 20
   Morse 30
   Moses (Moore?) 54
MAXEY, Jesse 133,193
MAXFIELD, David 126
   Jesse 126
MAXELL, George 38,45,192
MAXWELL, Jesse 38,106,195
   Nathaniel 50
   Thomas 47
MAYFIELD, James 122
   Sutherland 141,146
MEAGLEN, Robert 27

MEANS, William, Jr. 24
MEARS, James 194
MEBANE, Alexander 177
   James 182
   William 138
MEDLOCK, William 196
MEEK, Adam 60
   Adam, Jr. 60
   Jeremiah 71
   William 20,34
MEEKES, Moses 23
MELONE, John 40
   William 41
MENEES, James 195
MENNETT, Stephen 156
MENON, William 73
MENTFLORENCE, James Cole
   140 (also see Montflor-
   ence)
MERRITT, Benjamin 38
MERTAIN, Joseph 13
MESSER, Richard 55
METCALFE, Charles 125
MICHAEL, Mark 27
MIER...21
MIGGERSON, Thomas 136
MILHERRIN, James 168
MILHORN, George 32
MILKERRIN, James 169
MILLER, Abraham 189
   Adam 186
   Daniel 38,52
   David 21,24
   Frederick 113
   James 69
   Jasper 89
   John 45,54,132
   Thomas 34
MILLHORN...35
MILLIGAN, Joseph 127
MILLIKEN, James 67
MILLS, Andrew 122
   James 140
MILNER, John 123
MINER, John 40
MIRES, Elias 133
   Jacob 3
   John 89
MITCHELL, Andrew 61,67
   David, Jr. 127
   James 19,20
   Joab 42
   Joseph 144
   Mark 42,80
   Richard 96
   Thomas 6,20
   William 136,155
MOCK, Henry 48
MOLDEN, Martin 125
MOLLOY, Thomas 193
MONEY, Benjamin 53
MONTCRIEFE, Thomas 154
MONTFLORENCE (also Ment-
   florence/MonFlorence),
   James Cole 147,148,162,
   166,172,175,178,180
MONTFORD, Henry 104
MONTGOMERY, Alexander 95
   James 90
   John 121
   Michael 163
   Robert 138
   William 136
MOONEY...50
   George 100
MOOR, William 127
MOORE, Alexander 71,85
   Anne 28,33
   Anthony 57
   Elijah 139
   Isaac 157
   James 5,9,21,61,63,94,
   125

MOORE, cont'd:
  John 31,71
  Joseph 47
  Moses 19
  Samuel 21,24
  Shadrach 20
  William 4,70,73,75,118,
    136,188
MOORFIELD, John 41
MORGAN, Charles 51
  John 134
  Richard 88
  Thomas 90
MORRILL, John 49
MORRIS...76
  Chedd 17
  Drury 2,5,23,33
  Gideon 6,22,71,94,99
  John 65
  Shadrach/Shadrick 9,10,
    13
  William 129
MORRISON, James 55
  Meshack 44
  Michael 94
  Patrick 33,48
  Peter 44
  Thomas 55,183
MORROW, Alexander 12
  Samuel 126
  William 70
MOSELEY, Joseph 138
MOSELY, John 7
MOTHERELL, John 178
  Samuel 184
MOYERS, Jacob 189
MULHERRIN, James 135,187
  John 130,189
MULKERRIN, James 168,171
MULLEN, Melone 152
MULLETT, Theodore 176
MULLINS, John 39,48
MULLOY, Thomas 138,172
MULSBEY, John 96
MUNAFEE, Jonas 121
MUNCHER, George 130
MUNFORD, Robinson 119
MUNGLE, Daniel 134
MUNTFORD, Joseph 140
MURFREE, Hardy 139,140,146,
    154
MURFRO, Hardy 101
MURPHEE, William Hardy 106
MURPHREE, Hardy 141,142,
    143,145
MURPHY, Archibald 112,120,
    158
  John 51,58
  Levi/Levy 44,47
  Solomon 25
  William 2,6,7,8,12,88
MURRAY...25
  Shadrach 31
  Thomas 33,193
  William 188
MURREY, Morgan 34
  Thomas 35
MURRILL, Thomas 50
MURRY, Titus 132
  William 189
MUSSICK, Jacob 155
MYERS, Christopher 85
  Martin 54

NANCE, David 13
NASH, Abner 112,113
  Sarah 161
  William 162,168
NATION, Joseph 88
NAUTER, Philemon 37
NAWLEN, Bryant Ward 44
NAWLIN, Bryant Ward 42
NEALE, Peter 9

NEALEY, George 127
NEALY, William 125
NEALLY, Andrew 33
  John 33
NEAVE, Titer 9
NEDEAVER, Jacob 52
NEELY, Isaac 128
  Matthew 135
  Robert 129
NELSON, Alexander 139
  Hugh 86
  John 103,105,146
  Robert 146,150,151,159
    167,176,188,191,193
  William 13,24,57,90
NELLSON, William 56
NEVILL, George 143,193
NEWELL, George 128
  Samuel 137
NEWING, William 135
NEWLAND, Eli 149
NEWMAN, John 63,64
NICHOLAS, James 66
NICHOLLS, Hancock 142
  John 141,142,150,151,
    152,161,162,169,171,
    172,178,185
NICHOLS, Joshua 104
NILSON, John 142
NOBLE, Mark 189,195
NODDY, William 26
NOEDING, William 21
NORRIS, Robert 165
  Thomas 158
NORTH, John 36
NOWLIN, John 1
NUMAN, Anthony 105

O'BRIAN/O'BRIEN, Laurence
    180,181
O'BRYAN, Sara 180
ODAM, James 45
ODELL, William 2
ODENEAL, Bartholomew 25
ODLE, Caleb 25
  Isaac 16
OFFIELD, James 41
OFILON, James 38
OHARA, Henry 133
OLLIPHAN, John 68
ONEAL, Cornelius 29
  Robert 27
ORR, Robert 66,68
ORTH, Adam 43,44
OSBORNE, Morgan 131
OSBURN, Edward 89
OUTLAW, Alexander 56,57,67
OVERALL, William 123,127
OVERTON, John 184
OWEN, John 137
OWENS, Christopher 141
  Elijah 20,25
  James 32
  John 37
  Owen 21,25
  William 67

PABLE, John 21
PAIN, Matthew 134
PAINE, George 134
PALATE, Ann 51
PARESS, Robert 73
PARKER, Benjamin 128
  William 91,135
PARKINS...36
PARKISON, Rebecca 139
PARKS, William 18
PARR, William 142
PARRAMORE, Ezekiel 23
  Matthew 16,18
PARRESS, Robert 68
PARRETT, John 65
PARRON, Joseph 31

PARSONS, Harrison 182
PASHIRE, Thomas 154
PASSMORE, David 172
PATE, Matthew 68
PATTEN, Elijah 100,108
  Samuel 103
  Samuel, Jr. 101
PATTENS, Samuel, Jr. 102
PATTERSON, James 10,38,49,
    94,108,120
  John 13,64,66,68,69,70,
    73,87
  Robert 40
  William 2,40,73
PATTON, Robert 109
PATRE, Adam 37
PARTON, John 100
PAUL, James 84,86
PAUSE, Robert 67
PAYNE, Charles 53,100
  Henry 101
  Joziah 182
  Thomas 24,35
  William 27,38,53,54
PAYNOR, Peter 143
PAYTON, Ephraim 134
PEARCE, James 13,67
  Thomas 89
PERCIFIELD, Samuel 29
PEARCY, Nehemiah 161
PEARRY, John 74
PEAT, Matthew 65
  Matthias 68
PEEK, Adam 100
PEEL, James 142
PEIRCE, James 90
PEIRPOINT, Larkin 54
PEMBERTON, John 8,47
  William 39
PENNINGTON, Isaac 146
  Jacob 193
PENSON...14,21,36
  Joseph 13
PEOPLES, John 34
PERKENS, Isaac 33
PERKINS...33
  Constantine 78
  Daniel 84
  George 35
PERRIMORE, Matthew 14
PERRIN, Joseph 83
PERRY, David 12,23,55
PERRYMAN, Benon 84
PERSAMES, William 23
PETER, Michael Smith 5
PETERS...37
  Coonrod 41
  Ebenezer 193
PETERSON, Isaac 193
PETTIT, Nehemiah 90
PETTITT, Benjamin 134,195
PEVESHOUSE, John 33
PEYTON, Ephraim 186
PHACK, John 126
PHARRIS, Thomas 128
PHARRUS, Moses 132
PHELPS, Solomon 133
PHIFER, Caleb 105,146
  Martin 102,105
  Martin, Jr. 140
PHILLIPS (see also PHILLIPS
  & CAMPBELL) ..177,178,
  179,180,182,183
  (Also under CAMPBELL)
PHILLIPS, Abraham 119
  David 157
  James 34
  John 131,137
  Joseph 107
  Mann 158,160,179,181
  Phillip 173,179
  Richard 145
PICKENS, James 17,18

PICKENS, cont'd:
  John 6,16,19
PIERCE, James 87,88
  Jeremiah 195
  John 144
PIERCEFIELD, Samuel 28
PINNICK, Joshua 128
PLEMON, Peter 6
POE, John 133
POGE, Robert 39
POLK, Charles, Jr. 103
  Ezekiel 101,104,144
  Ezekiel, Jr. 103
  James 102
  Thomas 101,102,103,104,
    105,106,109
  William 106,107,109,141
PONDER, William 144
POOLE, Alexander 47
POOR, David 169
  Moses 97
PORTERFIELD, James 118
  John 107
POTTER, John 13,157
POWELL, Demsey 101
  Thomas 144
  William 25
PRATHER, John 22
PRATT, Ephraim 131
PREWITT...25
  David 68
PRICE, Abraham 135
  Mordecai 32
  Samuel 126
  Will 130
PROVINES, John 40
PRYOR, Joseph 90
PURDIE, James 143
PURNELL, William 125,131
PURTLE, George 123
PURVEYANCE, James 108
PUSHON, Philip 124
PYBURN, Benjamin 2

QUIGBY, Patrick 127
QUNAN, Robert 85

RAINEY, Joseph 89
  William 58,70,102
RAINS, John 121
  Meredith 126
RAMSAY, Francis Alexander
    56
  John 85
  Josiah 40
RAMSEY, Francis Alex/Alex-
    ander 57,58,60
  Jonah 195
  Henry 121,195
  John 178
  Thomas 39
  William 176,179
RANDELS, William 7
RANDOLPH, James 18,66
  Thomas 15
RANDOLS, James 93
RANKEN, Thomas 88
RANKIN, David 62,85
  Richard 89
RAWLINGS, Aron 17
  Asahel 15,18,22,24
  Daniel 15,34
  Ezekiel 32
  John 17
  Michael 17,32
  Nathaniel 17,18
RAY, Benjamin 73
  James 10,123,137
  Joseph 68
  Thomas 64
  William 137,172,180
REARDON, Dennis 158
  Elizabeth 143

REARDON, cont'd:
  Nancy 143
REASON, William 161
REAVES, George 22
RECTOR, Benjamin 89
REDDEN, John 24,30
REDDICK, John 93
REDDY, James 7
REED, Alexander 108,175,
    191
  Andrew 10,15,16
  Benjamin 142
  Daniel 15,88,90
  David 67
  Jesse 152,174,175
  John 168
  Joseph 126
  Michael 65
  Samuel 80
  Solomon 59
  William 57,66,67
REEIVES, John 87
REELAND, Lewis 137
REES, John 88
REESE, David 1
  John 148
REEVES...21
  William 28
REID, Jesse 156,157
REILEY, John 31
REILLY, John 53
RENFRO, Stephen 37
RENFROE, William 125
RENTFRO, James 129
  Moses 123
  Stephen 37
RENTFROE, Isaac 124
  Joseph 130
  Peter 124
  Stephen 48
  William 124
RESTON, Abraham 147,148
REYNOLDS, Henry 20
RHEA, John 41,52,91,98
  Stephen 134
RHEM, Peter 172
RHODES, Christian 45
RHYMES, Jesse 176
RICE, Daniel 84
  Elisha 147,148
  Henry 48,72
  John (also John Rice
    & Compy?) 5,14,80,94,
    95,110,118,119,120,147,
    148,160,163,167,179,181,
    182,185,190,191,192,193,
    195
  Spencer 78
RICHARDS, John 95
  Stephen 91,95
RICHARDSON...29
  James 78
  John 68,143
  William 49,50
RICHERSON, James 2
RICHEY...28,33
  Gideon 59
  John 6,9,14
  William 2,13,16,17,18,
    23,34
RICHMAN, Mark 155
RIDDLE, Cornelius 124
RIDER, John 29
RIDLEY, George 39,41,43,45,
    47,92
  George, Sr. 75
RIGGES, Edward 70
RIGGS, Edward 72,78
  Jesse 65,94
RIGHT, Isaac 171
RIGHTS, John 109
RIGLAND, Reuben 28
RING, John 85

RIPE, Abraham 172
RITCHEY, William 15
ROACH, Jordan 21
ROAD, Christian 50
ROBENSON, John 13
  Mark 133
ROBERSON...12,26
  Charles 8,25
  John 49
ROBERTS, Edmund 13,72
  George 47,55
  James 51,77,157
  Jesse 159
  Obed 188
  William 52
ROBERTSON...25,28
  Alexander 101
  Charles 51,78
  Daniel 87
  Elijah 42,101,104,105,
    120,154,157,164,165,173,
    185
  Elisha 195
  Felix 105
  James 31,77,102,104,110,
    125,144,145,157,182,185,
    188,192,193,194,195
  John 6,53,125
  Mark 193
  Michael 102,185
  Peter 165
  William 60
ROBESON, Charles 161
  David 15
  James 23
  Lewis 72
ROBINSON, Charles 35,134
  Elijah 135,136
  Jacob 181
  James 76,85,130,132,137,
    144
  John 22
  Mark 103,128
  Moses 55
  Roesdon 26
  Thomas 28
  William 93
ROBISON, David 18
ROCK, Jordan 80
RODDY, James 7,58,60
RODDYE, James 58
RODESAND, Christopher 41
RODGERS, Joseph 52
  Robert 13
  William 38
ROGERS, Abraham 183
  Benjamin 171
  James 25
  John 40
  Joseph 45,99
  Thomas 24
  William 46,49
ROLLS, Horatio 137
ROLSTON, David 182
RONE, Hosea 25
ROSE, Hosea 6,27,34
ROSEBERRY, Robert 136
  William 62,67,93,100
ROSS, David 51,92
  Henry 180
  James 142
  Joseph 172,173
  Samuel 183
  William 146,148,149
ROTCHELL, Job 145
ROUNSIVALE, David 121
ROUTLEDGE, Sarah 158
  Thomas 107
  William 44
ROWAN, Francis 88
  Henry 84,86
  William 184
ROWLAND, James 170

ROWLER, Martan 41
RULE, Andrew 128
  Henry 134
RUNNELS, William 2
RUSSELL, Brewer 40
  Brice 55
  George 8,9,10,16,27,43,
    48,63,64
  James 189,191
  John 20,25
  Robert 129,179
  William 10,48,125
RUTHERFORD, Griffith 101,
  109,110,146,170,172
  Henry 106,108,111,188
  John 105
RYAN, John 33

SAMPLE, George 71
  Samuel 63,64
SAMPLES, Thomas 14
SAMS, Thomas 168
SANDERS, James 189
  William 140,174
SAPPINGTON, James 148
SARREYMORE, Edward 128
SARRICK, Michael 129
SAUNDERS, James 145,148,
  154,163,170,171,173,
  190
  William 149,153,156,164
SAVAGE, Ransom 143
SAWYER, John 130,193
  Miller 152
  Thomas 146
SAWYERS, Sampson 135
SAYMON, John 35
SAYMOND, John 28
SCATES, Joseph 89
SCOTT...20,35
  Burwell 96
  John 15,17,21,41,42,43
  Marmaduke 142,156
  Samuel 123
  William 43,44
SCULL, John Gambier 145
SCURLOCK, James 168
SCUYDON, Thomas 153
SEARSEY, Bartelet 124
  John 125
SEATH?(see LEATH)
  Josiah 56
SEATTEN (PEATTEN?), Henry
  88
SEDUSKY, Emanuel 27
SEETON, James 89
SELLARS, Robert 46
SELLERS, Sebert 86
SEMMONS, William 15
SENTON, Hezekiah 156
  Silas 144
SEROGS, Ebenezer 23
SEVIER, John 19,57,60,101,
  103
  Robert 9,34
  Valentine 28
  Valentine, Sr. 22
SEVILL, John 132
SEXTON, William 143
SEYPEART, Robert 67
SHACKLER, Philip 178,181,
  186,187
SHAFFER, Richard 174
SHANE, Maurice 130
SHANKLIN, James 136
SHANKS, Moses 71
SHANNON, David 128
  Samuel 167,190
SHARER, Michael 123
SHARP, John 54
  Thomas 48,193,195
  William 1,28
SHARPE...49
  Abner 108

SHARPE, cont'd:
  Anthony 54,101,103,104,
    110,139,194
  Edward 109
  John 38,42,48
  Thomas 103,106,133
  Thomas Rice 108,109
  William 5,23,108
SHAW, Benjamin 29
  James 133,146,189,195
  William 171
SHEETS, John 50
SHELBY, David 45,47,48
  Evan 12,155,182,194
  Isaac 131,194
  John 10,38,45,53,192
  Moses 158,194
SHELL...52
  Arnold 39,41
SHELLEY, David 179
SHELLY, Phillip 6
SHELTON, David 112,135,152,
  179
  Lewis 39,41
  Ralph 94
  Samuel 126
  Stephen 25
SHEPHERD, Martha 107
  William 107
SHEPPARD, Benjamin 149,150,
  151,155,160
  Martin Gardner 163
  Nancy 160,161
  William 154,170
SHERRATT, Isaclore 166
SHERRER (SHERRIL), Adam 73
SHERRER (SHERRILL), Ac-
  quilla 73
SHERRETT, Isedore 167
SHERRIL, Martha 7
  Samuel 7
SHERRILL, Adam 4
SHERRIN, William 102
SHIELD, John 85
SHIELDS, John 26,32
SHIPLEY, Richard 52
SHIRE, William 25
SHOAT, Augustine 1
SHOCKLEY, John 136
SHORES, John 65
  William 79
SHORRES, John 76
SHORT, Peter 106
SHOTE...20
SHOULDS, Patrick 41
SHULTES, David 99
SHUTE, Jesse 152
  John 46
SHUTTS, Martin 51
SIMASTER, Abraham 131
SIMMS, Job 81
  Rice 25
  Richard 125
SIMPSON, Andrew 72
  Henry 46,55
  Hugh 127
  William 129
SINCOLM...27
SINGLETON, John 85
SISK, James 185
SITGREAVES, John 108,164
  Joseph 113
SKITMORE, John 95
SLADE, William 171
SLOAN...22
  Archibald 25,36
SMENCER, Jacob 76
SMITH, Alexander 95
  Anderson 38
  Benjamin 108,110,112,
    113,145
  Brittain 66,67
  Bryant 145

SMITH, cont'd:
  Daniel 133,156,163,172,
    190,194
  Edward 22,29
  Jacob 4
  James 46,137
  Jeremiah 172
  John 16,25,59,184
  John, Sr. 73
  Joseph 38,39,41,43
  Michael 143
  Nicholas 68
  Peter 39
  Samuel 40,41,53,96
  Sol 52
  Solomon 45
  Thomas 22,35,156
  Tilghman 86
  William 47,51,94,95
  William Briley 23
SMYTH, John 15
SNELL, James 154
SNODDY, William 129
SNODGRASS...50
  John 38,46
  William 55
SOUTHERN, James 21
SPAR, Henry 50
SPARKS, Samuel 27
SPEER, Henry 79
SPENCER, Thomas 137,144
SPURGEON, John 68
SPURGEN/SPURGIN, William 53
SPYERS, Abraham 144
STAMP, Frederick 188
STANDFIELD, Thomas 72
STANDLEY, John 155
STEED, Jesse 113,140
STEEL, Andrew 129
  Jacob 127
  Nicholas 56
  Robert 28
STEELE, James 55
  Robert 27,40
  William 26
STEPHENS, Lawrence 129
STEPHENSON, Robert 13
STERN, William 125
STEVENS, Edmund 35
  Jacob 129
  William 80
STEVENSON, Hugh 21
  John 78
STEWART, David 3
  James 21,22,24
  John 2,194,195
  Robert 22
  Thomas 4
  William 131,134,163,183
STINSON, James 9,15,84
STOCKTON, Thomas 58,72
  William 9
STOKES, John 109
STOLOP, William 155
STONE, William 24
STONES, Michael 129
STORIES(STORY?), John Trim-
  ble 2
STOUT, Hosea 69
STOUTH, Hosea 74
STUART, David 29,56,57,60,
  61,62,64,78,80,81
  James 5,12,28,32,63
  John 13
  Joseph 72
  Robert 32
  Thomas 5
STUBBLEFIELD, Robert Lox-
  ley 29
  Weight 45
  William 54
STUMP, Frederick 121
  Jacob 121
SUDUSKY, Emanuel 24

SUGG (also SCUGG), Acquilla 167,170 (Scugg) 168
  George A. 168,170,186
  George Augustus 167
SUMMERS, James 144
  William 128
SUMNER, John 101
SUTHERLAND, David 96
SWAGGERTY, Abraham 57,58, 76,77
  Frederick 58
SWANSON, Edward 131
SWEARONE, John 24
SWETAIN, Edward 7
SWIGG, Daniel 157
SWITAIN, Edward 2

TADLOCK, Joshua 68
  Thomas 36
TALBOT, Matthias 25
  Matthew 7,8,9
  Thomas 2,26
TALBOTT, Matthias 28
  Thomas 23
TALEENA, Howell 165
TALIGHAM, James 12
TALLY, John 46,48
TARIS, Nathan 128
TARRISS, Elijah 132
TATE, Caleb 107
  James 140
  John 35
  Samuel 4,22,23,27,34, 35,36
  William 86,155,163
TATOM, James 141,159
TATUM, Absalom 196
  Barnard 156
  Howell 173,178,180,181, 182,184,196
TAUNT, Jesse 169
TAYLOR, Andrew 6,8
  Archibald 137
  Benjamin 81
  Christopher 9,34
  David 59
  George 9
  Isaac 30,56,57,58,60, 63,64,76,77,87,91,95
  James 19,162
  John 154
  Joseph 90
  Leroy 16,23
  Permanas/Permenas 68,87
  Thomas 52,142,160,174, 186
  William 128
TEENAN, James 100
TEMPLE, Major 58
TEMPLETON, James 112
  Thomas 106
TENNER, Richard 163
  Robert 138,141
TERRIBLE, Joseph 139
  William 140
TERRILL, John 64
  Timothy 132
TETUS, Ebenezer 122
THACKSTONE, James 139
THOMAS, Andrew 127
  Benjamin 158
  Isaac 76,173
  Jesse 195
  John 31,123,189
  Micajah 161,171
  Philemon 163
  Richard 142
  William 17,45
THOMPSON, Absalom 131
  Alexander 127
  Andrew 16
  Charles 132
  Daniel 157

THOMPSON, cont'd:
  Henry 81
  James 48,53,136,145
  Jason/Jasen 145,165,172, 173,177,191
  John 52,149,173
  Robert 144,171,173,179, 188,189
  Samuel 61,102
  Thomas 102,129,160,162
  William 152
THORNTON, William 20
TIERNEY, Henry 122
TINNEY, Thomas 139
TIPTON, ,,,29
  Jacob 31,70
  John 21,30
  Jonathan 2,9
  Joseph 17,28,68
TIREY, John 10
TITSWORTH, Thomas 43,48
TITUS, Ebenezer 136,194
TODD, James 134,168
  Low 81
TOLBERT, Thomas 10
TOLBOTT, Thomas 101,111
TOLBUTT, Matthew 10
TOLER, James 135
TOMLINSON, Edward 129
TOMMAS, Isaac 6
TOOL, John 66
TOOLE, John 59,75
TOPP, Robert 49
  Rodger/Roger 39,51,124, 128,134,135
TORBETT, John 31
  Samuel 22
TORBITT, John 10,13
TOWER, Thomas 66
TOWLE, James 127
TRACY, Nathaniel 15
TRAMMELL, Nicholas 126
  Phillip 125
TRAMMY, Phillip 160
TREDWAY, William 45,51
TRIMBLE, John 58,59
  William 12
TROTTER, John 29
  Richard 105
  Samuel 16,18
TROUSDALE, John 179
TULLY, Michael 35
TURNBALL...152
  William 159
TURNBULL, William 160
TURNEN, James 81
TURNER, Daniel 127
  Jacob 146
  John 127
TURNEY, Henry 43
  Peter 96,195
TURPIN, James 135
  Nathan 128
  Solomon 130
TUTON, Oliver 149
  William 149,160,166,170
TYE...20
TYLER, Owen 176
TYNER, Arthur 155

UTTER, Abraham 62
UNDERWOOD, Elizabeth 141
UZZELL, John 73

VALEK, Adrian 119
VANCE...50,190
  David 102,104
  John 157
  Samuel 58
VANTERS, Jesse 42
VANUNT, George 27
VANZANT, Isaac 87
VARNER, Samuel 193

VAWTER, Philemon 38
VENCENT, Thomas 50
VENUS, Margaret 54
VINCENT, George 81
VINCINT, George 46
VINSENT (VAN SANDT), Isaiah 86
VINZANT, Garret 7

WADDLE, John 6,7,10,61
WADE, David 39
  Edward 45
WAGGONER, David 33,36
  Henry 45
WAGONER, George 67
  John 65
WALDERON, James 27
WALDROP, James 39
WALDRUPE, John 13
WALKER, David 77,89,100
  Felix 28,54
  James 56
  John 59,71,146,191
  Phelix 54
  Robert 105
  Samuel 123
  William 66,68,158
WALL, Frethias 74
  James 102
WALLACE, John 1
  Matthew 66
  Thomas 48
  William 40,171
WALLACS, Joseph 38
WALLEN, Elisha 49
  Joseph 50
WALLING, Elisha 95
WALTON, Jesse 5
  William 146
WARD, Benjamin 31,32
  Edward 47
  Ennis 152
  John 81,86
  William 4,22,28,96
WARREN, William 54
WARRICK, Martin 52
WASHINGTON, William 144
WATERS, William 155
WATKINS, Henry 128
WATSON, John 70
  William 7,29,30
WEAKLEY, Robert 103,105, 108,149,171,175,176, 192
WEAR, John 26
WEAVER...21
  Christian 45,53
  Creesly 43
  Michael 49
  Samuel 20,24
WEBB, Benjamin 40
  David 40
  George 44
  John 6,19,41,56,104
  Martin 4,13,19
  Moses 132
  Richard 70
WEBSTER, Reuben 73
WEER, John 65
WEKOFF...189 (see WYKOFF)
WELCH, John 169
WELLABA, Matthew 94
WELLS, George 158
  Haden 122
  John 144
  William 28
WEST, Eli 168
  Elijah 59
  Thomas 25,64
WHATLOOK, John 32
WHEALER, James 51
  John 7
WHEALOCK, John 34

WHEELER, cont'd:
    Mourning 141
WHETFIELD, William 79
WHITE, Burgess 134
    Ezekiel 144
    Isaac 58
    James 61,67,74,75,76,
       77,97,171
    John 132,143,184
    Joseph 87
    Richard 11,33,35
    Solomon 189
    Thomas 78
    William 7,135,144
    Zachariah 122
WHITFIELD, Needham 79
    William 66,79,80
WHITLOCK, William 67
WHITTMILL, Blount 158
WHITNEE, Lewis 52
WHITSELL, John 169
WHITSON, William 81
WHITTENBARGER, Frederick
    81
WHITTERDES, William 16
WHOLE, Solomon 125
WICKOFF, William 184
WIDENER, Lewis 48
WIER, Hugh 80
    Samuel 21
WIKOFF...102,109,110,157,
    159
WIKOFF & CLARKE..166,179,
    191
WIKOFF, William 192
WILDER, Jaob 27
WILHIGHT, Adam 32
WILHITE, Matthias 79
WILICKSON, William 57
WILKINSON, Thomas 89
WILKISON, Moses 193,194
WILLABA, Matthew 99 (see
    WELLABA)
WILLIAMS, Curtice 189
    Curtis 17,181
    Daniel 121
    Edmond/Edmund 4,5,9,10,
       27,31
    Jarvis 170
    John 14,141,145
    Mason 142
    Nathaniel 139
    Robert 50
    Sampson 167,172,173
    Samson 186
    Samuel 5,6
    Tedzik 144
    Thomas 14,17
    Turner 192
    Willoughby 147,152,154,
       155,157,168,177,179,187
WILLIAMSON, John 155
WILLIS, James 66
    John 25
WILLOUGHBY, Andrew 42
WILLS...28
    Hayden 160
    William 14
WILLSON, Adam 56
    Augustine 47
    James 6,15
    Robert 15
WILSON, Adam 6,13,18,27
    Adam, Jr. 10,17
    Alexander 86
    Augustey 98
    David 104,177
    Isaac 11
    James 16,18
    James, Jr. 19
    Jesse 27
    Jo 24
    John 87,106,129,130,152,
       156,160

WILSON, cont'd:
    Joseph 14,16,18,65
    Ralph 137
    Robert 3,8,11,17
    Sampson 134
    Samuel 31,52,81,82,87,
       92,93,122
WIN, George 163
    James 163
WINBORNE, Henry 144
WINCHESTER, George 183
    James 183
WINDSOR, John 118
WINNEGAR, Andrew 51
WINNINGHAM, Jarrot 93
WINTERS, Moses 126
WISDOM, Larkin 33
WITHERS, John 128
WITT, Caleb 60
    Elijah 23,57
    Joseph 57
WOLSEY, John 69
WOMACK, Jacob 10
WOOLHIGHT(WILHOIT), Con 19
WOOD, Belford 95
    John 57
    Samuel 19
WOODARD, Noah 157
    Simon 131
    Thomas 131
WOODS...26
    Bartholomew 9
    Bartholomew, Sr. 17
    Batt 3
    John 91
    Michael 25,63
    Richard 59
    Samuel 21
WOODARD, Thomas 156
WRAY, James 8
WRIGHT, Edward 65
    Isaac 87
    John 18
WYATT, William 73
WYKOFF...14(also KIKOFF)
WYKOFF & CLARKE...162,164,
    165,181
WYKOFF, William 155

YOUNG, Abraham 184
    Charles 34,36
    Elizabeth 41,95
    John 22,55
    Joseph 10,13,15,22,36,
       40,41,45,46,84,95
    Robert, Sr. 20
    William 1

_____, George 154
_____EY, Emannuel 17

#

www.ingramcontent.com/pod-product-compliance
Lightning Source LLC
Chambersburg PA
CBHW020649300426
44112CB00007B/302